THE
GREY SEAS
UNDER

Farley Mowat

BALLANTINE BOOKS • NEW YORK

For the stanch little ships and
the great-hearted men who struggle
with the Western Ocean so that
other ships and other men may live.

Copyright © 1958 by Farley Mowat

All rights reserved.

Library of Congress Catalog Card Number: 58-11440

SBN 345-23784-6-125

This edition published by arrangement with
Atlantic-Little, Brown

First U.S. Printing: May, 1964
Second U.S. Printing: February, 1974

First Canadian Printing: May, 1964
Second Canadian Printing: May, 1966

Cover art by Chris Mayger

Printed in the United States of America

BALLANTINE BOOKS, INC.
201 East 50th Street, New York, N.Y. 10022

CONTENTS

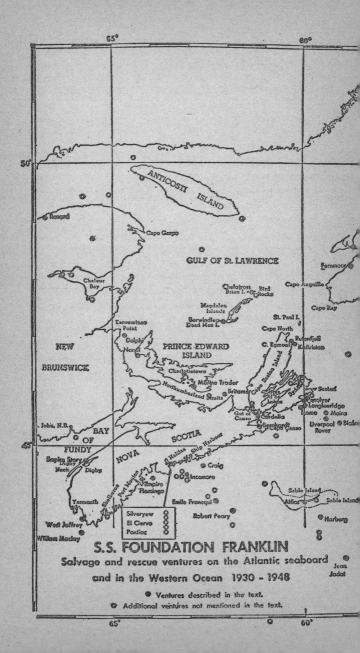

S.S. FOUNDATION FRANKLIN

Salvage and rescue ventures on the Atlantic seaboard

and in the Western Ocean 1930 - 1948

● Ventures described in the text.
⊘ Additional ventures not mentioned in the text.

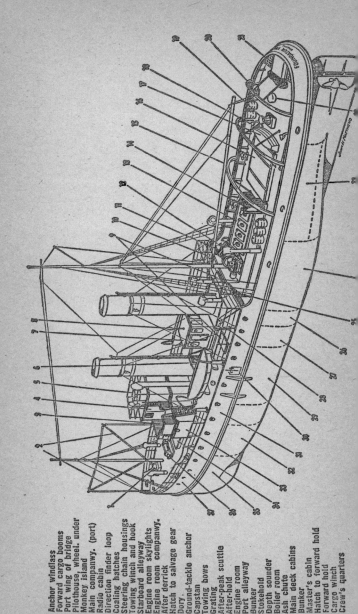

1 Anchor windlass
2 Forward cargo booms
3 Port wing of bridge
4 Pilothouse, wheel. under
5 Monkey island
6 Main companwy. (port)
7 Radio cabin
8 Direction finder loop
9 Coaling hatches
10 Steering chain housings
11 Towing winch and hook
12 Starboard alleyway
13 Engine room skylights
14 Engine room companwy.
15 After derrick
16 Hatch to salvage gear
17 Dory.
18 Ground-tackle anchor
19 Capstan
20 Towing bows
21 Grating
22 After-peak scuttle
23 After-hold
24 Engine room
25 Port alleyway
26 Bunker
27 Stokehold
28 Depth sounder
29 Boiler room
30 Ash chute
31 Main deck cabins
32 Bunker
33 Master's cabin
34 Hatch to forward hold
35 Forward hold
36 Cargo winch
37 Crew's quarters

🔷 A WORD OF THANKS

THIS BOOK is the outcome of two of the happiest of all my years. During that time I was given the friendship of the most admirable of men. I have been to sea with some of them, and I have come to have a consequent respect for the Western Ocean which is only equaled by my regard for those men and vessels who spend their lives thwarting the hunger of the sea.

Because I have told their story in the restricted context of one ship it is inevitable that many of these people, and their ships, have been left out. I salute them now: such men as Captains Sid Chapman and Wally Myalls, and such vessels as *Foundation Frances* and *Foundation Josephine II*. While this is not their tale in terms of absolute facts, it is nevertheless their story in all the real essentials.

It must be understood that the opinions and attitudes which have delineated in this book are essentially those of the men who actually manned the salvage vessels, rather than those of the vessels' owners. That these do not necessarily represent the attitudes and opinions of the owners or their representatives should be obvious.

In adhering to my ambition to see through the seaman's eyes I have accepted the sailor's tendency to give a semi-mythical status to the commanding figures who governed the salvage vessels as distinct from the distant realms of land-locked officers. Furthermore, wherever there has been a choice between a sailor's interpretation of the nature of the larger historical event, and the unadorned facts as set down in official documents, I have usually given preference to the seaman's version.

If, in hewing to my line, I have done less than justice to those individuals, without whose distinguished direction *Foundation Franklin* and her sisters would not have sailed at all, I can but plead that this is, first and foremost, the study of one ship and of those men who were a living part of her.

The book would not have been possible without the magnificent co-operation of the shore poeple, who suffered a "green hand" with inexhaustible patience and understanding.

7

Richard Chadwick, Arthur Sullivan, Minnie Millsom, Frances Thomson, High Milroy and Maurice Evans bore the brunt of my importunities.

Finally there is Lionel McGowan, and the Foundation Company of Canada, who made the whole thing possible.

I thank them all—not simply for their assistance—but for giving me one of the most memorable and vital experiences that I have even known.

FARLEY MOWAT

Palgrave, Ontario.
April, 1958

1 🐚 A SHIP IS FOUND

IN THE GREAT ship basin of Hamburg harbor, along the endless miles of docks and across the greasy waters, the atmosphere was one of desolation, accentuated by the dark winter skies and the biting North Sea winds.

In that January of 1930 the harbor was a graveyard, made more terrible by the nature of its dead. They lay in interminable rows—the liners and the freighters that had once spanned the world's oceans carrying men and cargoes to four continents; and in their shadows lay rows of lesser ships, the coasters, the trawlers and the tugs—and all were lifeless. One single living vessel, red with rust and streaked with salt, making her way reluctantly up the empty harbor, seemed only to emphasize the nature of this morgue—for she too was doomed to join the deserted hulks whose bankrupt owners had abandoned them.

There was not much of the fabled romance of the sea about that scene; nor was there much of it in the appearance of a man who stood on the end of a stone quay and stamped his feet to bring some warmth to them. He might have passed, quite unremarked, as only another dockside worker, except for the ill-defined awkwardness of posture which marks a seaman on the land.

Captain James Sutherland would wait no longer for the ship broker whom he had been told would meet him on this wharf. With a quick glance along the sad ranks of silent ships, he turned his back on them and began to descend a corroded iron ladder set in the quay face.

At the bottom rung he swung about with a ponderous agility and paused a moment to look closely at the vessel waiting for him there.

No one but a man of intuition and of rare perceptions would have given her a second glance. She was a little ship and she was dwarfed into insignificance by three moribund liners lying just scross the basin. The ravages of prolonged disuse lay on her. Even her name, *Gustavo Ipland*, had almost been effaced from her bluff bows. Her twin stacks, that stood ramrod straight with never an inch of rake to ease their uncompromising lines, were red with running sores of rust. Her iron decks were scaling like a scrofulous dog's back. Some of her ports were broken and the stench that lifted out of them was laden with a tale of long neglect. Nevertheless she possessed a quality which set her apart from the scores of lifeless vessels that encrusted the nearby wharves. Those other ships had about them only the dull resignation of inert iron, but she was different. As Sutherland let go the ladder and leaped aboard, he felt her move a little; a barely perceptible motion; but enough. She was not dead at all, she only slept.

He made his way through her starboard alleyway to the forward well-deck, where his shoulder brushed against a brass bell, gone green with verdigris. He rubbed his hand across it until the inscription came clear, and then he read this legend:

H.M.S. FRISKY
Dundee—1918

"I knew no squareheads ever built you, girl," he said softly. "You're too much ship for that . . . *Goo*stavo Ipland!" And he grunted with disdain.

Sutherland was still aboard her when the early winter dusk came down. By then he knew her well. He had explored the engine room and had wondered at her massive triple-expansion engine which was big enough to have powered a frieghter of five thousand tons. He had been through her primitive accommodations and had recognized in them the hard-lying which is the traditional lot of British naval ratings. He had been down into her belly and had crawled on hands and knees into the most secret recesses of her body. His knuckles throbbed where he had pounded them, hard-fisted, against iron plates to test their soundness. Subconsciously he had absorbed her lines, so that he already knew, without thinking much about it, how she would behave in a seaway.

Now he emerged through the companion on her boat-deck, climbed the ladder to her bridge and tugged at the swollen door of the wheelhouse. It resisted him momentarily, and then swung outward, creaking, and he stepped inside. He laid his hands upon the big teakwood wheel and looked out through the dirt-streaked glass. The graveyard seemed to vanish from his sight and in its place was the hard, clean sky of the Western Ocean and the long pulse of the greatest of all seas. The little vessel stirred once more beneath his feet, and Sutherland's body quickened to her with the age-old affection that only a good sailor can feel for a good ship.

The Hamburg ship broker, a harried and overeager little fellow, arrived belatedly upon the scene as Sutherland was scaling the iron ladder on the quay. His guttural apologies stuttered into momentary silence as he beheld the look upon the seaman's face. The broker was an astute little man—he rubbed his hands and beamed.

"She iss good ship? *Ja Herr Kapitan?*" he asked.

Sutherland grunted noncommittally. "Take me to a cable office, Mister," he demanded.

Early the following morning a man named Richard Chadwick sat at his desk five thousand miles away in an office in Montreal and read these words pasted to a sheet of yellow flimsy:

ARRIVED HAMBURG LAST NIGHT TO INSPECT EX ADMIRALTY SEA-GOING SALVAGE AND RESCUE TUG FRISKY STOP 156 FEET OVERALL X 653 GROSS TONS 1200 HORSEPOWER RANGE 20 DAYS UNDER FULL POWER STOP HEAVY DUTY TOWING WINCH STOP CARGO HOLDS FOR SALVAGE GEAR AND ACCOMMODATION FOR 26 MEN STOP VESSEL BUILT 1918 BUT HARDLY USED SINCE THEN ONLY REQUIRES DOCKING FOR INSPECTION AND SOME REFITTING OTHERWISE IN EXCELLENT CONDITION . . .

and so on for an additional hundred and fifty enthusiastic but very expensive words to this conclusion:

. . . PRICE VERY LOW CONSIDERING VESSELS VALUE STOP SHE LOOKS LIKE A MAGNIFICENT SEABOAT AND WOULD BE WONDERFUL ON GULF AND ATLANTIC COAST STOP CAPABLE OF TOWING EMPRESS OF CANADA IF NECESSARY STOP SUGGEST YOU CONFIRM PURCHASE SOON AS POSSIBLE
SUTHERLAND

Chadwick put the cable down and absently began stroking out the superfluous words with a blue pencil; but that was purely a reflex action, and his mind was not on it. His imagination had been seduced away from the concrete realities of his work by certain words that kept reappearing, again and again, before his inner eye:

"Seagoing . . . seaboat . . . salvage and rescue tug . . ."

In that office, which was devoted to the direction of the men and machines of a construction company, these were strange words. But they were not strange to Chadwick, for long ago this quizzical-visaged, indomitable engineer-cum-businessman had been infected by a romantic passion for the sea and ships.

He had concealed it well, since in the business world romanticism is synonymous with weakness. He had hidden it so successfully that its presence was unsuspected by his associates, or even by the directors of the Foundation Company of Canada—of which he was the president.

True, he had occasionally displayed some overt symptoms of the disease, but these had always been well masked by business logic. In 1926, for instance, he had accepted a series of contracts for the construction of wharves and other marine structures along the St. Lawrence River and the Gulf, and he had thereby been *obliged* to charter ships to carry equipment to the distant sites. In addition, the relative success of these ventures eventually provided him with sufficient justification to build a derrick boat, which he called *Foundation Jupiter*.

The *Jupiter* turned out to be a prime example of the conflict in Chadwick's nature. He envisaged her with the brain of an engineer—but she was conceived out of the spirit of a romantic. The result was half construction engine—and half ship.

She suffered from a split personality. During her first passage she also displayed an uncanny affliction, for she would not go where she was looking. Instead, she made her way down the narrow St. Lawrence ship channel in a series of majestic spirals which resembled the slowly marching circles a child draws when it is being taught to write. Other vessels on the river quickly learned to recognize her at a distance, and to flee outside the dredged channel as she approached. Once arrived at her destination, she proved to be an effective piece of construction plant, but while she was en route she was a hoodoo, and one that frequently required the services of hired tugs to get her out of trouble.

Nevertheless she was less troublesome than her predecessor—an ancient schooner hulk, with no motive power, which had been roughly refitted as a derrick barge.

It was this ancient vessel which gave Chadwick his first sharp understanding of the meaning of the word "salvage." In 1928, while she was lumbering across the Gulf in charge of a chartered tug, she ran into a heavy gale. The tow-line soon parted, and the tug promptly scurried for the nearest port, leaving Foundation's pride to go drifting off into the storm scud by herself.

The hulk's master did what he could to save her. He ordered both anchors hove overside—but the rusty chains immediately parted. He then turned to a novel alternative. The heavy Shipmate galley stove was manhandled up on deck, made fast to one end of a Manila line, and heaved over in its turn.

The old vessel was still dragging the remnants of the stove along the bottom of the Gulf the next day when a Norwegian freighter hove in sight, passed a line to the derelict, and took her in tow for Gaspé harbor.

Chadwick was most grateful to the rescuers—until the salvage arbitrators in London announced the size of the cash award due to the Norwegian. It was in five figures; and it shocked Foundation's president into a painful awareness of the fact that there were more ways of making money from the sea than he had realized.

That costly experience with a chartered tug, combined with the unpredictable antics of the *Jupiter*, led inevitably to the next step.

One December day in 1929 Chadwick called the *Jupiter's* master, James Sutherland, into his office.

"Captain," he said, "I think we need a tug."

Sutherland fervently agreed.

"There's one advertised for sale at Hull in England," Chadwick continued. "Powerful enough to tow our floating gear, but small enough to be handy on construction jobs. You go and look her over and see if she will do."

Two weeks later Sutherland was in Hull examining the tug. He found her to be hopelessly infirm, and he was on the point of booking his passage home when he encountered an old shipmate in a dockside pub. Sutherland recounted the story of his mission, and of its failure.

"If it's a tug you're lookin' for then, b'y," the shipmate said, "I know where you can lay hands on the finest one in all the western sea. She's up in Hamburg now, I seen her there when we was to the Elbe with grain last month. And she's a wonder-boat. Laid up, and lookin' pretty tough—but all the same, a wonder-boat."

Because Sutherland was a master mariner and accustomed to decision, he caught the boat-train for Dover without bothering to consult with Montreal. The first intimation of what he had done was contained in the yellow cable lying limp on Chadwick's desk.

That cablegram had reason to be limp. It had been so thoroughly ravaged by the blue pencil that a wartime censor might have envied the result. But still those words remained.

"Seagoing," Chadwick muttered to himself. "Salvage and rescue tug . . ."

That was his secret self speaking. His conscious mind was busy pointing out to him that Foundation Company required a ninety-ton, three-hundred-horsepower workboat; that there was a depression on; that deep-sea salvage was as far removed from construction work as the moon was from the earth.

"Magnificent seaboat," whispered Chadwick's inner self—and he reached for a message pad.

The reply that Sutherland received that night was a masterpiece of brevity,

PURCHASE CONFIRMED was what it said.

And the next day, in Montreal, Chadwick fixed his incredulous directors with a gimlet stare.

"No other choice!" he barked. "If we hadn't bought her, Sutherland's cables would have bankrupt us."

2 ❦ CHADWICK'S NAVY

CHADWICK HAD BOUGHT a ship, but she still lay more than five thousand miles away from her intended home. She had no crew, and she was in a deplorable condition. Sutherland began to set things right. Shipwrights and mechanics swarmed about like starving flies, and whatever else one may think about the Germans, they are thorough workers. Under Sutherland's suspicious eye they slaved. The thick layers of rust upon the decks came up beneath the ear-splitting rattle of scaling hammers. The bowels of the ship rumbled and rang as if they had been gripped by devils. Men crawled about the upper-works and scaled, sanded, painted and refurbished until the rare February sun one day found its rays being thrown back from a now shining ship which had been cloaked in sullen dirt for too many years.

Sutherland left the scene briefly to visit England and find a crew. He brought them back to Hamburg early in March, and on the eleventh of that month they signed the articles.

The following day *Frisky* made steam. She lay alongside the wharf with her stacks pouring black smoke into a grey sky. Sutherland took the bridge and cupped his hands around his mouth:

"Let go the springs . . . *the springs, you damn squareheads* . . . Let go forward! . . . Now let go aft!"

He reached for the whistle cord and *Frisky* cleared her throat with a long, sonorous blast. The steel sides of the dead hulks flung back the echoing sound until it rang over the whole anchorage.

She backed out into the stream, with the dirty waters

thumping and foaming under her counter; then slowly her engine went ahead.

As she began the fifty-mile run down the River Elbe, she seemed as sedate and cautious as an elderly lady picking her way along a village street; but when she dropped the pilot at the river mouth and swung out into the North Sea, *Frisky* decided that she could also drop her pose. With Sutherland's hands to steady her she met the ocean swell and—her people swear to this—she frolicked.

A man of small imagination might have said that her frivolity was due only to badly trimmed bunkers, and to a cross-sea. He might have been partly right, but he would also have been a fool. Sutherland was no fool. He held her hard. "Come now, old girl," he said. "Just steady down a bit." He knew the way she felt.

The chief engineer worked her up to three-quarter speed; he did not dare give her her head, for her engines needed their Scottish makers' touch to put them into shape. But at eight knots she went along like a proper ship, her skittishness forgotten. There was a nasty slop running in the Channel, but she took it easily and without dramatics. Her straight stem neither clove the seas nor buffeted them aside. She just went through them with a minimum of fuss.

Before they raised Selsey Bill, Sutherland had taken her measure, and he was well satisfied.

She came into Southampton Water and immediately went into dock. Men from the shipyards climbed aboard. Among them was a superintendent who had watched her under construction in 1918 in Glasgow, and who had followed the course of her career since then.

"We built her for the Admiralty," he recalled. "Her class was to be something new in tugs—big boats, and powerful, intended mainly for the open sea in southern waters. A seaboat first, you understand, and *then* a tug. She was a Navy ship, and her main job was to have been assisting naval vessels. We built her so she could handle a battleship if she had to; and so she could live through a typhoon and still do her work. We built her of iron so she would last. And strong? Man, she had the strength of ten!

"The Navy commissioned her in the spring of '19, but by then the need for her was past. They kept her for a while, towing old warships to Scapa Flow, but after that she was laid up. In 1924 they sold her foreign, and for about two years she was on the Rhine and in the Baltic doing a little towing work, but mainly lying idle at her dock. Then a big German outfit bought her to tow a fleet of barges across the South Atlantic to the Argentine; but before they were ready with the first barge the whole thing fell through. So

14

she was laid up again. It was a damned shame the way that she was treated. She never had a chance to show the kind of stuff that we put into her."

She spent two weeks at Southampton undergoing repairs and inspection and, at the end of it, submitting to a new baptism. Word had come from Montreal that the name *Frisky* would not do. Reregistered under the British flag, she took a new name and bore it handsomely along her bows and on her stern the day she cleared Southampton for her passage of the western sea.

Foundation Franklin
Montreal

the legend read.

When she was two days out from the Lizard, the North Atlantic undertook to squash this new addition to the herds of marine lice that infest its surface. The wind blew out of the north and blew steadily and with mounting power for three days, then having built the seas into thundering giants it switched to the west and blew a dead muzzler. The consequent cross-sea, breaking into a ferocious turmoil, revealed a certain tendency on *Franklin's* part to roll.

She rolled all right. She lay over on her side with her gunwales almost under, then she shook herself and rolled all the way back again. She was not slow about it. There was none of the sickening hesitation which, in some ships, makes you wonder if they will ever right themselves again. *Franklin* rolled jauntily. She did it as if she enjoyed it. Her crew did not.

Even less did they enjoy her desire to be a clean and well-bathed lady. With barely five feet of freeboard forward, she did not even attempt to throw away the seas that broke over her bow. She welcomed them aboard, and they were nothing loath. They marched up over her foredeck until the wheelhouse and the uninhabitable open bridge became a little island in a seething flood.

The wheelhouse was a separate structure, in that it had no covered communication with the main-deck accommodation. To get to it from inside the vessel required that a man emerge on the boat-deck just abaft the forward funnel, run the gamut of the seas until he reached the wheelhouse, and then scramble through a door which also gave the North Atlantic full access to the interior. Sutherland soon concluded that this was an inadequate arrangement—all right for beasts crossbred from monkey fathers and duck mothers, maybe; but not for men.

The crew made their discoveries too. Once the storm broke it became necessary to seal up all openings, much as if *Franklin* had been a submarine about to dive. There was no ventilation in the living quarters and the interior of the little ship soon came to resemble the black hole of Calcutta.

Entombed in *Franklin's* crowded belly, her people might well have cursed her to a fare-thee-well. But they did nothing of the sort. They were too mightily impressed by her performance as the days went by and the seas rolled higher still.

Not far to the north two liners radioed that they had been forced to heave-to. *Franklin* reduced her speed, but held her course.

The seas were noted in the log as running thirty to forty feet in height—and those *are* seas that qualify for the weary adjective of mountainous. *Franklin* met them head on, took enough of them aboard to titillate herself, and then jauntily lifted her bows and climbed to the towering crests. Sliding down again she reached the bottoms of the troughs and not once did she attempt to dig a hole and dive down into it; she came up with the resiliency of a rubber ball. There was about her, in this performance, an attitude neither of bravado nor of disdain for her adversary. She looked and felt exactly what she was: alert and careful, able and resolute.

Oh, she was resolute!

And the stokers in their pit, the sailors in the dog-kennel aft, cursed the roll, and cursed the sea, and cursed their gods—but did not curse their ship.

Franklin steamed into Horta, in the Azores, for bunkers on April 6. She had then been twelve days at sea, and that is a long passage from Southampton. But it had been a good deal longer for some larger ships that had also been making for Horta. A four-thousand-ton fruit boat foundered while still a hundred miles out of that port. Others made the harbor, but they showed by their smashed lifeboats and their buckled rails what they had suffered.

Franklin showed nothing at all amiss, save that to the tops of her funnels she glistened brilliantly with salt.

Her master was so proud of her that he became a little insufferable. Nevertheless he made his vow that *Franklin* should one day have a proper foredeck and a proper pilothouse. "Otherwise," he told his unsympathetic chief engineer, "somebody's going to drown hisself on that damn bridge."

The voyage continued and on April fifteenth this entry appeared in the maritime columns of a Halifax newspaper.

One of the largest and most up-to-date salvage vessels

in North America arrived here yesterday after a difficult trip from Hamburg. The vessel is the *Foundation Franklin*, the owners being the Foundation Maritime Ltd., a new subsidiary of the Foundation Company of Canada. The *Franklin* will be stationed during the summer season at Rimouski on the Gulf and will be available for salvage work in the St. Lawrence and on the Atlantic. A fully equipped salvage base is being established by her owners at Rimouski.

Thus the birth of Foundation Maritime Limited, Towing and Salvage Contractors, was announced in the early spring of 1930. But as one of those concerned in it remembers the event: "It was a breech presentment, you might say. Backside foremost. Nobody figured it would live six months."

The odds were certainly against survival. In 1930 new companies were not being born; on the contrary, long-established concerns were dying in myriads. The business world had totally reverted to the law of tooth and claw. The carnage was tremendous and, in their struggles to exist, the strongest companies in every field destroyed their weaker rivals without a qualm.

Foundation Maritime, Salvage Division, was born into the world between two particularly powerful competitors. One of these, Quebec Salvage and Wrecking Company with its headquarters in Quebec, was the child of that giant shipping enterprise. Canadian Pacific Steamship Lines. The other, Halifax Shipyard, was the protégé of an equally gigantic industrial and mining complex called Dominion Steel and Coal. Supported by a government subsidy, Quebec Salvage's two vessels, the *Lord Strathcona* and the *Traverse,* had a strangle hold on the St. Lawrence River and on the Gulf; while the salvage ship *Reindeer I,* belonging to the Halifax Shipyard, was virtually in control of salvage along the whole of the eastern Canadian seaboard.

Quite apart from the competitive situation, Foundation Maritime displayed a formidable list of inherent defects at birth. Despite the optimistic newspaper release, it possessed no salvage gear worthy of the name, except for a few ancient steam pumps (bought at a fire sale) that later proved to be quite useless. It had no harbor as a base of operations, since the only suitable ones were already occupied by the rival firms. It did not have a single man on its staff with any knowledge of the complicated technical aspects of salvage; and the one man who had the seamanship to make him a reasonably effective master of a salvage tug was soon to be driven away with a fecklessness that is hard to comprehend.

That man was Sutherland. It had been his understanding that he would not only command the ship which he had found, but that he would also be made salvage master for the new company. But on his arrival at Halifax he found that he was to be relegated to the supernumerary position of sailing master, which meant that while *Franklin* would still rely on his knowledge and experience for her safe navigation, she would not be his ship, but would belong to another captain and to one, moreover, who did not even have his deep-sea ticket. This was more than Sutherland could stomach and so he quitted both the company and the little ship which had roused such an admiration in his heart.

Consequently Foundation Maritime began life with only two real assets. It had the *Franklin*—and it had the implacable desire of Richard Chadwick that it should succeed.

Chadwick soon began to gain some insight into the magnitude and complexity of the new business in which he was now involved. In an attempt to ease the competitive situation a little, he endeavored to persuade the Canadian Pacific Steamship Company to reach a working agreement with Foundation Maritime so that the two organizations would supplement rather than compete with each other. This offer was met by the counter-suggestion that Chadwick get out of the salvage business before he was pushed out; and immediately thereafter the dean of North American salvage firms, Merritt, Chapman and Scott of New York, was invited to take over active management of Quebec Salvage.

Chadwick thereupon sailed for London in the hope that he might persuade the London Salvage Association to espouse his cause. But that all-powerful arbiter of the world's salvage organizations told him, in effect, that he had no business trespassing on ground hallowed by Merritt, Chapman and Scott; and that his company had not a snowball's hope of surviving.

Nevertheless the journey to England had not been wasted, for Chadwick had taken the opportunity to inquire searchingly into the nature of salvage work, and he had learned a good deal about its intricacies.

He had discovered that the number of ships which get into trouble and which require assistance is staggeringly large. Although not many marine accidents make the world's headlines, an average of about six thousand ships a year get into difficulties from which they can be extricated only by highly trained and competent salvage teams.

Chadwick found that the variety of troubles which beset ships is almost legion. A random list of the commonest causes of disablement includes the loss of a propeller while at sea; the breakdown of the propelling machinery; damaged lost rudders; fires and explosions; leaking; structural failure; shortages of fuel, of supplies, of water and—in at least one well-authenticated case—of rum; strandings (on dry land as opposed to) groundings (on underwater shoals and reefs); collisions with other ships, drifting wrecks, whales, icebergs, buoys and anything else afloat; being caught in ice-packs; enemy action in times of war, and afterwards through loose mines drifting about the seas; the effects of winds and storms in general; and failure of the crews due to illness, inexperience, exhaustion, injury and mutiny.

Chadwick also discovered that a salvage company must be able to give assistance by conducting sea searches; by escorting partially disabled vessels safely into port; by steering rudderless ships by means of lines taken from their sterns; by towing every type of disabled vessel, ranging from ships broken in half, through the smallest trawlers, up to the largest liners; by fighting fire; by saving life under a formidable variety of circumstances; by supplying materials to stricken ships (such things as food, water, fuel and repair materials); by supplying special services, including transportation, man power, electric and steam power; by keeping sinking ships afloat with pumps and other gear; by raising and emptying ships that have already sunk; by releasing vessels trapped in ice; by releasing grounded and stranded ships, using ground tackle, pumping, pulling, dredging, jettisoning, and a score of other methods; by repairing damaged ships and making them temporarily seaworthy; by cargo salvage from wrecked or sunken ships; and by breaking up vessels that have become total losses, but whose bones form an obstacle to the safe navigation of other ships.

As if all this was not enough to occupy his mind, Chadwick was also made aware of the peculiar and singular difficulties of salvage work in the area where his company would have to operate.

The North Atlantic is a hungry ocean, hungry for men and ships, and it knows how to satisfy its appetites. From September through to June a sequence of almost perpetual gales march eastward down the great ditch of the St. Lawrence valley and out to the waiting sea. They are abetted by the hurricanes which spawn in the Caribbean and which drive north-eastward up the coasts as far as Labrador. Only in summer are there periods of relative calm on the eastern approaches to the continent, and even in summer, fierce storms are common.

Gales, and the high seas that accompany them are, of

course, the weapons of all oceans; but this unquiet seaboard has two special weapons of its own.

First of all it has the ice—continental masses of it that come sweeping down with the Greenland current to form a great, amoebalike bulge extending from the coasts of Nova Scotia eastward as much as a thousand miles, and southward five hundred miles from Flemish Cap. The bulge swells and shrinks and throws out new pseudopods from month to month, but there is no season of the year when it or its accompanying icebergs withdraw completely from the shipping lanes.

The second weapon is in many ways the most formidable of all. It is the fog. There is no fog anywhere to compare with the palpable grey shroud which lies almost perpetually across the northern sea approaches, and which often flows far over the land itself. There are not a score of days during any given year when between Labrador and the Gulf of Maine the fog vanishes completely. Even in the rare fine days of summer it remains in wait, a dozen or so miles off shore, ready at any moment to roll in and obliterate the world. It has presence, continuity, and a vitality that verges on the animate. In conjunction with its ready ally, the rock girt coasts, it is a great killer of men and ships.

The coasts themselves are brutally hard. Newfoundland, Labrador, Nova Scotia, and the Gulf shores appear to have been created for the special purpose of destroying vessels. They are of malignant grey rock that has flung its fragments into the sea with an insane abandon until, in many places, these form an impenetrable *chevaux-de-frise* to which the Newfoundland seamen, out of a perilous familiarity, have given the prophetic name of "sunkers."

The coasts are of tremendous length. Newfoundland alone exposes nearly six thousand miles of rock to the breaking seas. Everywhere the shores are indented with false harbors that offer hope to storm-driven ships and which then repulse them with a multitude of reefs. The names upon those coasts betray their nature. Cape aux Morts, Cape Diable, Rocks of Massacre, Dead Sailor's Rock, Bay of Despair, Malignant Cove, Baie Mauvais, Misery Point, Mistaken Point, False Hope, Confusion Bay, Salvage Point, and a plethora of Wreck Bays, Points and Islands.

Yet by the very nature of their animosity towards seafaring men these coasts have brought out of themselves the matter of their own defeat. Men in these parts have always had to take their living from the sea, or starve; and those who survived the merciless winnowing became a race apart. There are no finer seamen in the world. The best of them come from the outports of Newfoundland and Nova Scotia.

nd from the islands of Cape Breton and the Magdalens.
he best of them are men to ponder over, for they can hold
heir own no matter how the seas and the fog and ice and
ocks may strive against them.

And yet it is also true that these men do not properly
elong in our times, for they follow an outmoded creed with
ndeviating certainty. They believe that man must not at-
empt to overmaster the primordial and elemental forces
nd break them to his hand. They believe that he who would
urvive must learn to be a part of wind and water, rock
nd soil, nor ever stand in braggarts' opposition to these
ings.

"Ah, me son," as one old Newfoundland skipper phrases
, "we don't be *takin'* nothin' from the sea. We has to sneak
p on what we wants, and wiggle it away."

That would make an excellent creed for any salvage firm;
ut in 1930 Foundation Maritime would have paid it scant
eed. Despite the fact that after Chadwick's return from
ondon the company began to have some idea of how
eavily the odds were stacked against it, most of the potential
ifficulties still remained as abstract quantities. Secure in the
elief that such familiar obstacles as human competitors and
urely engineering problems could be dealt with, there was
o one in the new company who comprehended the true
ature of the real antagonist—the sea itself.

❧ THE INNOCENTS

OUNDATION MARITIME's first act was to send the *Franklin*
n a personal-appearance tour.

When she arrived at Quebec the crews of the rival tugs,
ord Strathcona and *Traverse,* displayed no perturbation.
Very glad to see her," one of their people was heard to
ay. "We've wondered for quite a while how to get shed
f the pulpwood boats and fishing schooners. She can take
are of them."

Nor was the reaction of the various ship's agents, and of
he steamship lines, much more encouraging. They called
er Chadwick's Folly, and traded jokes about her as she
eamed away upriver toward her next port-of-call.

One of the most unkind remarks was made by the master
f a local tug as he watched her pass. Pointing with the
em of his pipe to the jaunty new house-flag streaming
om *Franklin's* truck, he said to his mate: "Well, there goes
hadwick's navy—showing the flag. Now that'll put us natives
a our place!"

At Montreal *Franklin* was on public display, and visitor
were cordially invited to come aboard. She drew a consider
able audience, for the publicity releases concerning her wer
of good quality—but she drew few of the seafaring frater
nity, and most of these were content to gaze at her from a
distance. As one of them put it many years later: "She wa
a dandy-looking ship, no doubt of that; and anyone coul
see. that she was able. But with the gang of green hands sh
had to run her, she might as well have been a ferryboat."

Foundation Maritime was sublimely unaware of the deroga
tory reaction *Franklin* was stimulating, until a representativ
of the London Salvage Association passed semi-officia
judgment on her.

Although nominally a free agency, this association receive
its support from the world's shipowners and insuranc
underwriters. It maintains representatives in every majo
port and the primary duty of these men is to protect th
owners' and the underwriters' interests in any ship which get
itself in difficulties. Thus, when a marine accident occurs
the nearest association man hurries to the scene where h
becomes an adviser to the master of the distressed ship i
all matters concerning the vessel's salvage. He also become
the unofficial, and often unwelcome, supervisor of th
work of rescue. He watches the salvors like a suspiciou
hawk, and if there is any sign of inefficiency, bad planning
or poor workmanship, he stoops on them. His talons ar
honed by the insurance companies, for they are the peopl
who will ultimately pay, or refuse to pay, the salvage claim
Although he is without overt power to issue orders, he ca
make suggestions, and his suggestions have a regal rin
about them.

The Montreal representatives of the association examine
Franklin with meticulous care. Their verdict was devastatin
She is a good basic salvage ship, they said in effect, but sh
is almost completely unequipped for that work, and she ha
nobody to show her what to do, or how to do it.

Even Chadwick, with his unfortunate experience in Lor
don still fresh in his mind, had not expected the opinio
of the Association men to be so utterly damning. But th
would-be salvors were resilient. They reacted by borrowin
every scrap of equipment from the parent construction con
pany which might conceivably be used in salvage work
Then they rented an office next door to that of the Salvag
Association, in the apparent hope that propinquity migh
bring about a change in attitude.

At the same time work was going forward feverishly t
establish a salvage base, and a home port for the *Franklir*
at Rimouski.

Rimouski lies on the neck of the leonine head of granite which is the Gaspé Peninsula. In 1930 its port could accommodate the local bateaux and, if circumstances were just right, a few of the tiny gulf steamers; but there was so little water over the bar at low tide that even fishing boats sometimes took the ground. *Franklin,* drawing fourteen feet, could only enter or leave during a period of about three hours in each tide.

However this was a difficulty that Chadwick knew how to overcome. Someone persuaded the Dominion Government to spend a great deal of money dredging the entrance channel and deepening the port itself; and it was a remarkable fact that Foundation Maritime obtained a contract for much of this work.

By the last week in May most of the preparations had been completed and Foundation Maritime, Salvage and Towing Contractors, had taken possession of its new base. The company was ready to show what it could do.

The first call on its services was received almost immediately. In midafternoon of May 29 a telegram arrived from the tiny port of Mechins, seventy miles to the north-west along the Gaspé coast, to the effect that a vessel called the *A. Renard* required assistance. There were no further details, but no more were needed to inspire *Franklin's* people to an instant and overwhelming enthusiasm. As her whistle sounded and resounded, echoing back from the Gaspé hills with a kind of hoarse abandon, *Franklin* put out from Rimouski with both stacks growing high black plumes, while her master and the salvage superintendent stood on her bridge resplendent in immaculate new uniforms. This was their moment. Somewhat grim-visaged, as befitted the occasion, they stood to their work: steadfast and dedicated men.

Franklin came abreast of Mechins at midnight. There was a full moon and an almost cloudless sky and her people could see the surf breaking hard into the little port. The officers trained their eyes for a sight of the distressed vessel but, to their perplexity, they could see nothing of her. The ghastly thought occurred to them that she might already have gone down. The spectacle of white seas breaking on the moonlit coast was unnerving enough to give rise to all sorts of sailor's nightmares, and *Franklin's* officers could not bring themselves to take their ship closer than half a mile from shore. Even at half a mile they should have been able to make out the superstructure of a stranded steamer or, if she had sunk, they should have seen her spars at least. They saw nothing but the ominous breakers.

Completely nonplused, the superintendent ordered the

whistle to be blown as a signal to the land, and then had *Franklin* stand off that dangerous-looking coast.

They stood off until dawn, uncertain what to do. The initial mood of exultation had changed to one of peevish bewilderment that became outright disgust when daylight revealed no sign of any vessel in Mechins. Instead it revealed a little motorboat putting out with casual disdain through that formidable-appearing surf. A figure standing in the stern sheets was beckoning peremptorily for the salvage ship to come in closer to the land.

Franklin edged in cautiously and the motorboat came alongside. A salty gentleman swung aboard the tug and introduced himself as "the owner of that sunk ship in there." At which he pointed toward the tiny wooden wharf. Again *Franklin's* officers strained their vision; this time with success. They could see her now . . . the stubby foremast and the minuscule deck-house of a typical St. Lawrence *goélette*—one of the little wooden power-schooners that carry pulpwood from the outport hamlets.

"She's sunk level to her decks," her owner explained cheerfully to the glum salvage experts. "But she can't sink any further. She's full of wood. Just you go alongside and put your pumps aboard, and in a half an hour she'll be pretty near as good as new." He chuckled amiably, but there was no answering echo from the salvors as they considered how their hopes for a good-sized steamer had shrunk to the dimensions of this miserable little hulk.

As for going alongside the wreck—it was clearly out of the question. As any good merchant navy captain would have done, *Franklin's* master resolutely refused to risk his vessel on that lee shore. The salvage superintendent did not attempt to persuade him otherwise. It probably did not occur to either of them that a salvor's business is to risk his ship.

In any event, the curious citizens of Mechins were treated to a rare spectacle that sunny morning. Lining the wharf they watched the little motorboat come back to harbor, turn about, *and tow the sodden* A. Renard *out to the waiting salvage vessel.*

In due course the entire seventy-four tons of the *Renard* was wallowing alongside *Franklin*. The superintendent decided to make short work of her, and instead of putting a small pump aboard the wreck, he ordered his men to break out a huge ten-inch centrifugal which, with its gasoline engine, weighed upwards of five tons. *Renard's* deck was already awash, and the weight of the big pump forced her down another foot. With ponderous agility she demonstrated

24

her resentment by rolling her bulwarks under and soaking the pump engine so thoroughly that it would not run at all.

"Now then, me lads," she seemed to say, "what'll you try on next?"

The salvors were now thoroughly exasperated, and their mood was not eased by the impatience of *Renard's* owner, who seemed quite unable to understand why the job was being attempted in mid-Gulf while a comfortable harbor lay so near at hand. In the end they were so stung by his pointed remarks that they made a stern decision. With *Renard* gallumphing heavily alongside, *Franklin* headed bravely in toward the Mechins wharf.

The terrors of the surf proved quite ephemeral. Within an hour *Franklin* and her charge were tied up at the dock, and the work had begun anew.

The pump engine was dried out and started. In twenty minutes it had pumped *Renard* down to the bottom of the suction line; but before anyone quite realized what was happening, it began to suck air and lost its prime. While the sweating salvors tried to restore it to action, *Renard* quietly filled herself up and sank again.

This was disheartening. It proved more so when it was discovered that *Renard* possessed no pumps of her own capable of holding the water down once the salvage pump had done its job. The situation became positively sickening when, during the second pumping, a pulp log charged against the pump's engine and smashed an oil line. The engine promptly became overheated and seized-up.

The climax was reached when the owner, after considering this latest setback, grew philosophic. "Well, boys," he said, "you might as well quit. There isn't enough money in the old hulk to pay for the time you've spent on her already. Best call it off."

There was nothing else to do, for the tyro salvors had not obtained an agreement from the *Renard's* owner in advance. Had they made use of the legendary salvage contract known as Lloyd's Open Form, they could have completed the salvage despite the owner's wishes, and they would probably have been reasonably well rewarded for their work, if only on the basis of the pulpwood cargo, which they could have easily recovered. But the Open Form was something still beyond their ken.

The Open Form is an innocuous-looking document written in the most obscure legal jargon. It was devised by Lloyd's Committee in London some sixty years ago as an extension of the gambling element which is implicit in all insurance business, and for the specific purpose of standardizing salvage agreements and contracts. Despite its formidable legalese it is headed, surprisingly, by the simple phrase:

NO CURE—NO PAY

The essence of its meaning lies in those four words. Essentially it is a contract between the master of a distressed ship and the people who are prepared to render aid. Under its terms a would-be salvor agrees that he will not claim so much as a penny if he fails to save the endangered ship; while the ship's master, owners, and underwriters agree that —should the ship be saved—they will be liable to pay a salvage award commensurate with the value of the vessel and her cargo.

The L.O.F., as it is called in the trade, is not the only basis for a salvage agreement. Some salvage companies, particularly in the United States, prefer to work on a fixed daily rate of hire or for an agreed lump sum. But it is axiomatic that preference for the L.O.F. is the best indication of the worth of a salvage outfit. Obviously no salvor who consistently worked under the L.O.F. contract could long survive bankruptcy unless he had the ability to cheat the sea.

However, the signing of an L.O.F. is only the first step in a prolonged legal game that may take six months to a year to bring to a conclusion. The game is played like this:

When a casualty, as distressed ships are called in salvage language, is safely delivered to port under the L.O.F., the salvors cable Lloyd's in London requesting that the ship's owners, or their underwriters, post a security bond roughly equal to the sum the salvors hope to receive as an award. The owners have two weeks within which to comply. Should they fail to do so, the salvors may nail a sheriff's writ to the casualty's mast, and thereby place her under arrest pending the outcome of the affair.

Since an idle ship is a costly ship, the security is almost invariably posted. The casualty is then free to go about her business. The salvors, meanwhile, have been hard at work preparing an extraordinary document known as a salvage brief. It describes the operation in the most meticulous detail. A really good brief can make you hear the thunder of breakers and yearn for the reassuring feel of a life-belt around your waist. Nevertheless it must be subtly done since it will be dissected by cold legal minds, and ultimately it will reach the hands of an impartial arbitrator whose knowledge of the sea is unsurpassed. The preparation of the brief is a highly skilled exercise in creative writing. Not fiction, mind you, but subjective fact.

On completion it is sent to the salvage company's legal advisors in London, who thereupon ask Lloyd's Committee to appoint an arbitrator and set a date for a hearing.

Meanwhile the owners of the rescued vessel have also been busy preparing a counterbrief of their own, with the declared purpose of proving that the whole salvage operation was somewhat easier than rolling off a log and that, in any case, the casualty did not really need the salvor's help at all.

And then a perfectly extraordinary thing happens . . . something that could only occur in English jurisprudence. Both the opposing sides *trade briefs* before these are presented to the arbitrator. It is a procedure equivalent to unmasking all your guns before a war begins.

Eventually the date set for the hearing arrives and the arbitrator gets the briefs—both of them pretty well thumbed by this time—and after listening to the arguments of lawyers on both sides, he decides what the salvage award should be. But the game is not yet over. His award is not final and may be appealed by either side. It then goes to another hearing by an appeal arbitrator whose verdict is irrevocable.

The whole procedure may seem to be an unnecessarily cumbersome and long-drawn-out way of getting paid for doing a job of work; but a quick look at the size of the salvage awards which result from it will readily explain its popularity amongst salvage men who know their business.

There was a certain ship that lost her rudder not far off the American coast a few years ago. She radioed an SOS and a tug promptly came out to her from New York. The casualty's master offered to sign the Lloyd's Form, but he was told that this particular salvage company preferred to operate on a hire basis at the rate of fifteen hundred dollars a day. The master accepted these terms with ill-concealed delight. Four days later his ship was delivered to a safe port and, though the tow could probably have been completed in three days, he was not disposed to complain. The rescue cost his underwriters six thousand dollars.

Time passed, and two years later the same vessel broke her propeller shaft while fifty miles off the Canadian coast. This time the tug which steamed to her assistance demanded, and got, the L.O.F. Two days later the casualty was safe in port, and eight months later the owners of the tug received an award of eighty-seven thousand dollars.

It may be wondered why the underwriters tolerate, let alone sponsor, an agreement which can cost them such formidable sums. The answer is that the L.O.F. breeds salvors, and it is salvors who save ships. On the other hand the daily hire arrangement breeds tow-boat men. Consequently the underwriters would rather pay a great deal for risks well taken

27

by trained salvage crews, than to pay considerably more to ship's owners for vessels which sank because of the absence of a proper salvage service.

The obverse of the coin, from the salvor's point of view, is that the L.O.F. often results in extreme risks that endanger the salvor's major investment, as well as his men—for no return at all. But there is no salvor worth his salt who would have it otherwise.

4 ⚓ INTO THE ICE

THE SUMMER AND AUTUMN PASSED and there was very little work for Foundation Maritime, although the two rival companies seemed to keep busy enough. Then, in mid-December *Franklin* was ordered to Halifax for her annual inspection and for the long-overdue alterations which would better suit her to the North Atlantic.

She stayed on the slip for three months. The shipwrights began her transformation by extending the boat-deck forward to her stem, thus adding six feet of freeboard forward. The new below-deck space resulting from this change was turned into quarters for the crew, and the black hole aft, which had been theirs, was converted into a hold for stowing pumps and other salvage gear. The after mast was strengthened and fitted with an eight-ton boom to handle the big pumps and the ground-tackle anchors. The bridge structure lost its gay, excursion-boat appearance and was completely housed-in, leaving only monkey's island, atop the pilothouse, for would-be promenaders.

The work was well executed. When she again took the waters of Halifax harbor *Franklin* had lost all suggestion of friskiness, and had acquired a singularly resolute, if somewhat strait-laced appearance that was more in keeping with her new name. She looked to be quite capable of seeking out a north-west passage through the arctic ice and, as things turned out, she was soon to be put to a test that bore some similiarities to the experiences of Sir John Franklin's doomed but indomitable little ships, the *Erebus* and *Terror*.

Looking extremely fit in her new black paint, her green-and-white funnel markings, and her varnished upperworks, *Franklin* put out from Halifax in the last days of February to take up station at St. John's, Newfoundland, for the balance of the winter. She made a good passage over, despite very heavy weather, and arrived at her new port on March 3, to be received by what amounted to a civic welcome.

Newfoundland was then in dire economic straits. Poverty was the common lot, except amongst the semifeudal merchant class which, for a century and more, had held most of the people in a form of slavery by virtue of the debt system. St. John's one major industry—shipbuilding—was nearly moribund. There was no new ship construction in those years, and so the yards were dependent on repair work to keep them going.

The people of St. John's had good reason to welcome *Franklin*, for they thought she might assist them by bringing crippled vessels to their shipyard. They streamed down to visit her with this thought in mind—but since Newfoundlanders were, and are, the finest seamen in the world, they stayed to stare because of something else.

They came to see her: old dory-men who had given their years to the Grand Banks; the young fishermen who took their little schooners laden with salt cod to Portugal and Spain each winter; the men of middle years who sailed the coasts of Labrador in search of cod, and who braved the ice for seals. They came and stood silent—for that is their way—and took her in. And out of the depths of a living knowledge of the sea and ships, they sensed her quality.

They gave her their unrestrained admiration then—and through the years which were to stretch ahead, they were to give her service that was as dedicated as only man's understanding love for a good ship can be.

But in the beginning she served them.

For generations the island's sealing vessels had put out from St. John's and from a score of lesser ports each spring, to seek the immense herds of seals that drift southward with the ice and bear their pups—the whitecoats—on the shifting floes. For generations the annual seal hunt had brought the only notable cash income that many Newfoundlanders ever saw. In 1931, the year of black adversity, a successful hunt had become vital to the actual survival of many families.

Consequently the early spring of that hungry year saw every sizable vessel which could be kept afloat sail out to meet the ice. Many of those ships were so old and rotten that they would not have made safe coal-barges in a sheltered harbor. They were crowded to the gunwales, for in Newfoundland they still believe in sharing what they have, be it no more than an opportunity. Some of those ancient vessels carried more than two hundred people, in hulls of less than five hundred tons burthen. No man was left ashore who wished to come, and not many boys were left there either.

Early in March, when *Franklin* was making her way into St. John's, the sealing fleet was already far to the north; part of it bucking the ice in Belle Isle Strait, and the rest cruising the edge of the ice barrier off the great eastern bight that enfolds Notre Dame and White Bays. The seals were there—but well inside the ice—and they could only be reached by entering the pack. Desperation drove the searching ships into the ice, with the full knowledge that some of them might not emerge again.

On March 14 the sealer *Viking*, six hundred tons, with "about" two hundred and thirty men and boys aboard, found herself far in the vanguard of the fleet and trapped in thick pack ice a few miles off the island of St. Barbe.

Viking was the patriarch of the fleet. Built in Norway in 1881, she was a wooden ship designed for sail, but fitted with a primitive low-powered steam auxiliary engine. She had lived her whole life in the north, and it had been a hard and unremitting struggle that had aged her more than the years should have done. Half a century of arctic ice had weakened her, and the rot was deep in all her timbers.

Her skipper, Captain Abraham Kean, was well aware of her disabilities. As the ice shoved and heaved about his ship he could feel her deck beams begin to buckle. She had insufficient engine power with which to extricate herself, but there was one remaining weapon her people could use against the ice. In a small hold aft, under the officers' accommodations and alongside the engine room, was enough blasting powder to force a path to freedom. As the early winter dusk came down on March 15 Captain Kean ordered the bosun to break out the powder.

The bosun and four men made their way to where the powder was stored, carrying a number of small tin canisters which were to be filled, then fitted with fuses. Through the night they labored and towards dawn they had almost completed a sufficient supply of bombs with which to begin their task.

Ashore, on the bleak rocks of St. Barbe—or Horse Island, as it is known locally—the young man who operated the antiquated spark-gap radio which was the island's only communication with the outer world was working his set. His shanty, with its single tiny window facing west, was one of a dozen that clustered on the treeless rock, and that made up the whole of human settlement upon the island. Otis Bartlet seldom glanced through the clouded glass of his window, for there was nothing to be seen from it except the crumbling waste of ice that stretched twenty miles to the mainland shore.

It was dark enough so that his oil lamp was still in use when the interior of the shanty was suddenly and brilliantly illuminated from outside. Bartlet jumped to his feet and thrust his face against the windowpane, frightened and awestruck by the intensity of the light which had come flooding in upon him. The light was gone almost immediately and he was still staring into darkness when the rock beneath his feet shook with a heavy tremor, and a great and terrifying sound came thundering across the ice.

At 9 A.M. the radio operator at Twillingate, some sixty miles away, heard the faint squeal of a carrier wave in his earphones, and then the stutter of Morse.

HORSE ISLAND TO TWILLINGATE HORSE ISLAND TO TWILLINGATE TERRIBLE EXPLOSION IN THE ICE THIS MORNING WRECKAGE OF BURNING STEAMER VISIBLE EIGHT MILES WEST PARTY FROM HERE TRYING TO GET ON THE ICE SURVIVORS SEEN TRYING TO WORK TO SHORE. . . .

That first message from Horse Island was relayed immediately to St. John's, the capital, and a few hours later was further amplified by Bartlet's key.

ICE IN BAD CONDITION HEAVY SEA AND WIND BLOWING OFF SHORE FIRST CROWD OF SURVIVORS MAY REACH ISLAND OTHERS HAVE LITTLE CHANCE SHIP BELIEVED TO BE VIKING OUT OF ST. JOHNS

As the tragic day drew down to darkness, there was one further message:

HAVE SOME SURVIVORS MORE THAN ONE HUNDRED MISSING AND TWENTY-FIVE KNOWN KILLED WE HAVE NO SUPPLIES FOOD OR MEDICAL NO CHANCE OF REACHING MAINLAND HELP MUST COME BY SEA

Help for the *Viking's* people was already on its way. At 2 P.M. that day *Foundation Franklin*, under emergency charter to the Newfoundland Government had put out from St. John's carrying three doctors, five nurses, and a full cargo of food, blankets, and medical supplies. Two hours later she was followed by the government steamer *Sagona*, and by noon of the following day both ships were entering the slob ice outside the pack.

Nor were they alone. From Belle Isle Strait the sealers *Beothic, Ungava, Eagle, Neptune,* and *Sir William,* all of whom had found seal and had just begun to make their harvest, gave up their work, rounded Cape Bauld and began trying to enter the pack from the northward.

No one aboard any of these vessels knew more than the bare fact that there had been a frightful explosion near Horse Island. But they were familiar with disaster in the pack, for through the years more than two score sealing ships and close to a thousand men had been destroyed by the consuming ice. They guessed the truth: that in the early hours of dawn on March 16 something had touched off the powder in *Viking's* hold. And they knew with certainty that those who had survived the blast and the flames which followed would die quickly on the ice unless help came.

From the south and from the north the rescuers drove into the pack—but the barrier might as well have been composed of adamantine rock. Onshore gales had rafted it so heavily that not even an ice-breaker could have broken past its outer ramparts. The sealers tried. They drove their greenheart-sheathed vessels against those ramparts until wood shrieked and splintered and steel plates buckled. The measure of how hard they tried is to be found in the fate of the *Sir William*, a wooden schooner of two hundred tons out of Port Union who, in this hour, took the ice with as little hesitation as if she had been sheathed in steel. She found a little lead, drove into it, and two hours later was a crushed and sinking wreck, Her men escaped to safety aboard the *Eagle*, but the *Sir William* died.

Nor could *Franklin* make any better progress. She was not built for ice and could not risk the bruising which *Sagona* later dared—though not even *Sagona* could get through. The two steamers lay six miles off the island, and through the ice "blink" on the horizon they could see a dark encrustation on the floes, and knew it for the burned bones of a ship, and the bodies of men.

On March 18 they were joined by the sealing vessels, which had worked right down the seaward boundary of the pack, unsuccessfully seeking a lead. There were now seven ships lying off the island, but unable to approach.

The news from Bartlet grew steadily worse. Dazed by the blast, and many of them badly burned, a hundred of *Viking's* people had straggled to the island after enduring an agonizing passage of the ice and endless hours of subzero gales. Most were in urgent need of medical attention—all were in need of warmth and food and clothing. The meager resources of the islanders had been exhausted in a single day. There was nothing left to give.

The men aboard the rescue vessels knew the frustrations of the damned; until they found their own solution. They put their dories on the ice, ran hauling lines out from them, and took to the pack like seals themselves. Plunging through slush-covered cracks, staggering in freezing clothes, they half-swam, half-crawled across the floes, dragging their boats, which were laden with supplies and with the doctors and the nurses.

It took six hours for each dory to make the passage in and no man can tell how it was done at all. The sealers rested for an hour or two ashore, and then—in darkness—began the return journey to the ships, hauling the most seriously injured men behind them in the boats.

Franklin stood by the ice edge to receive them, while *Sagona* cruised the pack to the south-west in search of survivors who might have gone adrift on the moving floes. She found three living men and seven corpses, and these were the last of the *Viking's* people who were ever found.

The moving bridge across the ice from the island to the ships was maintained until March 20 and by then a hundred and twenty-seven men had been brought out to *Franklin* and *Sagona*. There were no more to come. There was no more to do. The sealers went aboard their ships, and those frail vessels turned northward to seek the seals once more. Dead men were dead; but ashore in every port in Newfoundland were hungry people who were still alive. The sealers went back north, back to the bitter ice.

Franklin steamed south, and from the hour that she landed her cargo of survivors at St. John's she ceased to be a foreign vessel—now she belonged to the islanders—and they to her.

5 ❦ EBB TIDE

THE *Viking* EPISODE brought good will to *Franklin*, but little money, and no change in her luck. If anything, her luck grew worse.

As spring passed to summer, and summer into fall, it became depressingly apparent that the few jobs of the preceding year had come her way largely through fortuitous circumstances. In 1931 there were no jobs at all.

The effect of that year of inactivity upon the morale of *Franklin's* people was incalculable. When, in December of 1931, she again sailed for her winter station in St. John's, her people were in a mood of abject depression. They felt that their ship was living on borrowed time—and so were they. And if they lost their jobs, they knew they would have no place to turn except to the Relief Offices; for there were already fifty seamen on the beach for every birth available at sea.

December passed without a job, and January of 1932 as well. There were gales at sea and vessels in trouble, but no work for *Franklin*. American tugs out of Boston and the *Reindeer* out of Halifax took everything that came; for they were hard-driven ships that went to sea at the first faint rumor of a vessel in distress. But the people who intimately directed *Franklin's* destinies seemed unwilling to follow suit.

They proved unable to support Chadwick's larger gamble by taking the necessary risks at their own level.

February came, and it was as hard a month on the Canadian seaboard as any that survive in memory. The seas writhed in prolonged agony under the lash of the incessant gales. The coasts shone with encrusted ice that made and made anew as the great waves broke and the flung spray froze. The pack ice drove south past Newfoundland and then swung west until it held the sea to within fifteen miles of Halifax itself. Louisburg and the other Cape Breton ports were blockaded. There were few ships at sea, and those that dared the storms were brutally assaulted.

On February 24 the Danish freighter *Aggersund* was caught in a full hurricane while three hundred miles east of Newfoundland, and shortly afterwards she began to transmit an SOS. Her call was weak and laboriously sent, for her mate was serving the radio in place of the operator, who had been seriously injured.

With so few ships about it was a near-miracle that the distress call was heard at all; but heard it was by a little British freighter, the *Vardulia*, which, with great audacity, had put out of the Irish Sea eight days earlier and was now lying hove-to some two hundred miles south-west of the *Aggersund*. *Vardulia* relayed the message to the Canadian shore, and the powerful land stations sent it back to sea. It was received in the Azores, in St. John's, and by the motor vessel *Blankaholm* two hundred miles to the south-east.

Vardulia reported that the stricken ship had been clean swept, had lost all her boats and her funnel as well, was without power, heat or light, and had a forty-five-degree list to port. The little Britisher risked her own life to swing out of the wind and try to lay a course for *Aggersund*.

Then a new signal came on the air. It was a reply to *Vardulia's* call from the British salvage tug *Humber*, at Oporto in the Azores, eleven hundred miles distant from the casualty. *Humber* announced that she was under way; but there was faint hope that she could arrive in time to be of help..

Neither *Reindeer* at Halifax nor the New York or Boston tugs could have reached the scene ahead of *Humber*, and therefore none of them went out. In St. John's, a scant three hundred miles from *Aggersund*, lay one of the finest ocean rescue vessels in the Western Ocean; but *Franklin* remained at her dock while Foundation Maritime waited for further information which would give a certainty of some return for any effort she might make.

They dallied for six vital hours until a further message from *Vardulia* assured them that *Aggersund* was lost unless a tug could reach her soon.

Franklin cleared the harbor then and stood southward down the coast, but she had not gone twenty miles when she found herself amongst drifting ice. Her speed was reduced from twelve knots to three. She was making progress, but the conditions of ice and wind were enough to daunt any man who had not been bred to them. The question of whether she could have broken through to freedom and to the *Aggersund* must remain an academic one. The fact remains that she did not. After thirty hours she was still within sight of Newfoundland, and on the morning of February 26 she re-entered St. John's harbor and tied up to her wharf.

Meanwhile the struggle at sea had reached its final stages. *Vardulia's* master radioed another relayed SOS from *Aggersund* to the effect that the stricken ship would have to be abandoned soon unless assistance came. *Humber* was still six hundred miles away.

As for the *Franklin*, she was no longer even in the area. At noon on the twenty-sixth she had sailed from St. John's for Halifax on business of her own. She was well to the west of Cape Race when her radio operator picked up *Vardulia's* final call for help, and though she turned about, it was only for an hour or two before she resumed her course for Halifax.

Later her officers contended that they had no choice, that they could not have penetrated the floes, and that in order to have circumvented the ice they would have had to steam a thousand miles in a great arc to the south and east.

Whatever the truth of that may have been, there was no doubt about the fact that *Franklin*—a ship designed to work under conditions which would frustrate the efforts of ordinary vessels—had run away. It was the *Vardulia,* a little freighter hardly larger than *Franklin* herself, and with less than a third her power, who eventually reached the dying *Aggersund* at dawn on February 27.

The sea was so immense that *Vardulia* could not launch a boat until several hours later when the tanker *Blankaholm* came surging on the scene like a whale awash, and pumped out oil to tame the seas a little. Then, in a truly heroic effort, *Vardulia's* boats took off every man of *Aggersund's* crew. Having no salvage gear, the rescue ships could do nothing for *Aggersund* herself, and so she drifted off and vanished in the spume.

Humber arrived the following day, but though she searched for twenty-seven hours, she did not find any trace of the abandoned ship. The search was hopeless from the start. With no man's hand upon her wireless key to send out direction signals, *Aggersund* was swallowed up forever in the snow-smoke of the northern gale.

Franklin continued her voyage to Halifax, arriving in that port on February 28. She came into harbor almost unnoticed, and it may have been that she was glad enough of that, for the *Aggersund* affair had not been one in which any man aboard, nor the ship herself, could have taken pride.

The failure—for such it indubitably was—did not go unremarked. Seafaring men along the coast were outspokenly critical about it, but what was perhaps even harder to bear was the reaction of the London Salvage Association. The small portion of good will which Foundation Maritime had been able to build up was now largely forfeited, and *Franklin* was marked with a stigma which would take some time to wipe away.

Rightly or wrongly, *Franklin's* officers were made to pay for the fiasco and two days after she docked in Halifax she had a new skipper, Captain Lewis, and a new first officer, John Pynn.

Pynn's coming was an omen (though it was not then recognized as such), for he was the first of the many Newfoundlanders who would serve the *Franklin* in the years ahead.

Pynn fitted into his new surroundings so completely that he almost vanished in them. But Captain Lewis was another type of man. Dapper, and with an air of elegant assurance which came from years of associating with first-class passengers, Lewis was a conspicuous anomaly aboard a salvage tug. He held a foreign-going ticket, and had been first officer and sometimes master of many well-known mail ships in the trans-Atlantic run. According to the hierarchy of command at sea, his acceptance of the *Franklin* represented a long step down the ladder; while in the diverse field of maritime activity, the new command was something almost totally outside Lewis's experience. Nevertheless, world shipping conditions had become so desperate by 1932 that captains of far greater seniority were unable to find commands at all. Even a lowly salvage tug, possessed of a dubious reputation, was better than the beach.

When Lewis assumed command he found the vessel herself to be in good condition; but he found the crew reduced to such a low level of morale that they were almost hopeless. He set himself to improve things, using the methods which he knew; the methods of the crack mail ships and of the Navy. He had the vessel scrubbed and holystoned, scraped and varnished, chipped and painted, until within a week she shone like a private yacht. He insisted that all the officers must purchase neat blue uniforms and wear them while on duty. Discipline, till then the casual relationship which char-

36

acterizes coastwise vessels, was remodeled on quasi-naval lines.

Each man acts out of his own experience, and Lewis was acting out of his. But there was all too little time for him to fully institute his new regime before *Franklin* was called to sea.

6 🐚 THE HUNGRY SEA

As MARCH SUCCEEDED FEBRUARY OF 1932, it brought no relief from the gales which had doomed the *Aggersund*. If anything, the weather worsened. During the first week of the new month, conditions were so appalling on the eastern approaches of the continent that the number of ships at sea fell off to less than a quarter of the normal total. The ice fields, under the malignant influence of the roaring winds, swirled in a great frozen maelstrom off the Nova Scotian coasts, and hid their terrors under a shroud of driven snow. Sable Island, that infamous sickle of the sea, concealed itself beneath the driven scud of a perpetual surf, while the waiting reefs of the mainland coasts broke from the containing water in a paroxysm of grey foam.

Nevertheless, some ships still sailed. On February 23 the Hamburg-America freighter *Harburg* put out from Bremen bound for St. John, New Brunswick, carrying a two-million-dollar cargo of manufactured goods, and bearing fifteen passengers. *Harburg* was a relatively new vessel of five thousand tons gross register, with a reputation as a fine sea boat.

Before she left the English Channel she was embattled, and through the succeeding sixteen days she struggled westward with a stubbornness that was almost, but not quite, a match for the animosity of the sea.

During those sixteen days she was swept three times. Her superstructure was battered, and all her starboard boats were smashed. On her best day she made good a hundred and twelve miles. On her worst, she was carried back sixteen.

At dawn on March 9 she had so far overcome the gales that a radio bearing on Sable Island showed her to be only fifty miles south-west of its reaching bars. That was too close for comfort, for the storm was driving from the west and might at any moment swing into the south. *Harburg's* master ordered a change of course. The wheelsman put the helm down; there was a moment of resistance, and then the wheel spun loosely in his hands.

The sea, giving up its gaming, had struck to maim. It had snapped *Harburg's* rudder stock, so that she fell off the wind into the canyoned troughs and lay there helpless, to be savaged at the sea's own time.

Harburg's SOS went out into an ice-laden gale that was blowing force 9* as it left the land and that gained strength as it drove out to Sable, and beyond, into the wind's own void. At Chebucto Head the government radio picked up the call and immediately cleared the air of traffic. The other shore stations fell silent. The few ships scuttling for shelter along the coast were still. In a score of earphones there was no sound save the crackle of the storm as the tense listening-watch commanded by an SOS began.

When the contents of the SOS message was telephoned to Foundation's salvage superintendent at 9 A.M. that morning, *Franklin* was still in Halifax and, what was more important, her chief competitor, the *Reindeer,* was fully occupied in raising the sunken dredge *Fundy* in Bedford Basin. But even with this assurance that no competitor would interfere, Foundation Maritime once more decided to play safe. Instead of dispatching *Franklin* immediately, she was held in harbor while the company contacted *Harburg's* agents to negotiate a salvage contract.

Franklin was not ordered out until 5 o'clock that afternoon. She felt the first fruits of that eight-hour delay as she cleared Sambro lightship. The gale, now at hurricane force, had swung into the north shortly after noon so that it was now taking *Franklin* on the beam, instead of from astern. The cross-sea built up by the change in wind became more vicious for every mile that *Franklin* made to seaward. She was soon yawing and pitching like a demented thing in the indescribable turmoil generated by two sets of thirty-foot waves, running almost at right angles to each other. Her speed dropped off to eight knots, then six, then two. She seemed to shrink in stature as she drew farther from the land.

The waves were in such conflict that they crushed the water of their substance beyond endurance and sent it pillaring wildly skyward. Franklin was half-drowned. Every door and hatch was dogged down as tight as human strength

* BEAUFORT'S WIND SCALE

Force 4	Moderate Breeze	13-18
Force 5	Fresh Breeze	19-24
Force 6	Strong Breeze	25-31
Force 7	Moderate Gale	32-38
Force 8	Fresh Gale	39-46
Force 9	Strong Gale	47-54
Force 10	Whole Gale	55-63
Force 11	Storm	64-75
Force 12	Hurricane	Above 75

could make it, but still the freezing sea came in. Seas broke above her and poured down her funnels until the stokers worked in water to their knees. Water sluiced ankle-deep along the alleyways on the main deck and sent up stinking gouts of acrid steam from the hot ashes piled beside the chutes. In the stokehold the temperature rose to one hundred and twenty-five degrees, while in the wild world outside the salt spray was freezing to the steel.

And she rolled! She had been built lively—but now she surpassed herself.

Wedged in a corner of the pilot-house Lewis watched as she tried to lay her belly to the wind, and the knuckles of his hands grew white. Nothing that he had ever experienced in big ships had prepared him for this unholy dance, and he did not understand how *Franklin* could survive. Even the helmsman, staring at the mad gyrations of the compass card, thought longingly of ancient joys handlining for cod on the Grand Banks from a safe little dory, with only half a gale to make it interesting. John Pynn, soaking wet and nearly frozen, fought his way along the exposed sweep of the boat-deck to the bridge and struggled through the door. Lewis turned, wordlessly, to look at him.

"By golly, sorr," said Pynn. "I reckon she be coming on to blow."

Lindsay McManus—"Sparkie"—isolated and besieged in the radio shack between the funnels, unable even to open his door let alone attempt to reach either the bridge or the accommodations, stuck to his wireless. From time to time he was in touch with *Harburg;* and the news she had to give was bad. She was beginning to list as her cargo shifted, and she was taking more damage to her upperworks with every sea that broke across her. But there was worse news in the air that bitter night.

Two hundred and fifty miles west-south-west of *Harburg* the four-thousand-ton Dutch collier *De Bardeleban* was calling frantically for aid. She too had lost her rudder, and the seas had smashed in half her hatches so that she was filling rapidly. Two United States Coast Guard vessels, *Conyngham* and *Ossipe,* had gone out to give her aid, but by midnight the *Conyngham* had suffered such severe damage—including the loss of her afterhouse—that she had been forced to put back. The *Ossipe* had lost her boats, but was still plunging on, while the New York salvage tug *Willet* was bucking her way outward from Cape Cod.

Throughout that night the snow-charged and frigid gale roared out of the north at eighty miles an hour, until at dawn it suddenly fell back into the nor'west and moderated to a mere mile a minute. It was now full on *Franklin's* stern but, rather than helping her, it brought on a new danger. Despite her steam steering engine, two men were now required at the wheel, for she yawed so wildly that a single pair of hands could not control her. There was the gravest danger that she might broach-to.

At dawn Sparkie called through the speaking tube into the bridge.

"Cap . . . ," he shouted over the wind's roar, "*Bardeleban* has gone down," and *Harburg's* sending a general SOS to any ship that can get out to her."

There was nothing much that Lewis could do about it. If he had been allowed to put to sea eight hours earlier, "on spec," he would probably have been up to *Harburg* by dark on March 10. As things now stood he knew he would be lucky if he found her in the next forty hours, for she was drifting off to the south-east at four knots, while *Franklin* in pursuit could barely manage five.

At 7 A.M. Sparkie shouted a new message down the pipe. "*Willet* just called *Harburg*. He's coming on. We've got ourselves a race."

This report also had little effect on Lewis. He knew that *Franklin* led the rival tug by at least a hundred miles and, in any case, he was less concerned at the moment with the *Harburg* than he was with the question of whether *Franklin* could be kept afloat. Staring down at her fore-deck, which was buried to the stanchions in white water, or glancing astern at the gargantuan combers rolling after him, he was not overoptimistic.

All that day, and through the succeeding night, the battle between the little ship and the grey seas went on. No one rested, for there was no place aboard where a man could rest. Down in the engine room Chief John Sommers and his second, Reginald Poirier, dared not leave the throttle for an instant, for as *Franklin* plunged and climbed, her screw alternately was deep below the sea then racing wildly in the air. The galley fires were out, but in any case there was a thick and nauseous fug throughout the ship that robbed men of desire for food. It was a time when every normal appetite and human desire was sublimated to one requirement alone —the need to endure the unendurable.

As dawn broke dark and ugly on the morning of the eleventh, Lewis's dead-reckoning put *Franklin* about thirty miles from the original position given by *Harburg*. However, *Harburg's* position had changed drastically and, without a glimpse of sun or stars to provide a fix, the navigators could only estimate where she was now. Sparks worked doggedly to get a radio bearing on her and at 9:30 A.M. he was successful. He passed the information to Lewis. *Harburg* now bore forty degrees off the starboard bow.

Lewis gave the order to alter course; and at that instant the hoary primeval ancestor of all great seas rose up astern. It came down on *Franklin* like a mountain on a mouse and caught her just as her head began to swing to starboard. It struck her with a solid blow that sent a shudder through every plate and frame and that buried her stern under a hundred tons of water.

The two helmsmen clung frantically to the wheel to prevent her broaching-to . . . then one of them cried out:

"She won't answer—she won't come!"

Lewis and Pynn jumped for the wheel, and it spun easily beneath their combined weight, but *Franklin* still fell off. Within a minute she was lying broadside in the trough.

The steering impulses from *Franklin's* wheelhouse were carried aft by means of two very heavy chains. In normal use these chains would tend to slacken-off, and periodically they would be brought up again by tightening the turn-buckles which were part of the linkage. Keeping the chain taut was part of the routine of harbor maintenance, but during the long idle months of the preceding year no one had checked the chains. Under the tremendous strain of the past few days, the slack had become progressively worse, and now the resulting play and chuck had snapped the port turnbuckle, fracturing a two-inch steel rod as easily as if it had been a clay pipestem.

Franklin was helpless and the seas drew themselves up and walked over her in triumph.

Lewis took one appalled look aft, where the open deck was inundated and the water was already pouring in through a broken skylight, and made up his mind that his ship was doomed. A minute later Sparkie was flashing a new SOS out of the storm's heart.

Meanwhile the struggle for *Harburg* was being intently watched by *Reindeer's* owners, the Halifax Shipyard. The yard had its own interests to serve, for times were hard and most of the slips and berths lay empty. The owners knew that the battered *Harburg* could keep the idle shipwrights busy for weeks—if she was brought to Halifax. They also knew that if *Willet* won the race, *Harburg* might well be taken to a New England port. Consequently *Reindeer* had been ordered to stand by for sea, even before disaster struck the *Franklin*.

Now *Reindeer* was designed as an onshore salvage ship, rather than a deep-sea tug. This fact, combined with her age—she was built in 1894—made her a most uncertain risk to send to sea on such a night. But the essence of salvage work is risk. Shortly after *Franklin's* SOS was heard, *Rein-*

deer put to sea. Her primary objective was the *Harburg*, but her master had also been instructed to take off *Franklin's* crew in the event that the tug had to be abandoned.

Reindeer put out in a sorry state of unreadiness. Most of her special gear—including her all-important salvage pumps —had been left aboard the *Fundy*. Her compasses were off, and while her officers were attempting to swing them in a hurry at the harbor mouth, she struck on Meagher's Bar and was aground for half an hour.

Once clear of Chebucto Head, she found herself faced by a sea which was more formidable than any she had previously encountered. Although her master, Captain Reginald Featherstone, now realized that he had only a slim chance of reaching *Harburg*, he was of the adamantine breed which cannot accept the prospect of failure in advance. *Reindeer* drove on, but as she worried her way seaward she was pounding like a pile driver.

Willet was having better luck than either of her rivals. Her course was roughly east-north-east, shouldering into the worst seas, so that she was having an easier passage— though it was only easier by comparison. More important, *Harburg* was drifting down upon her at almost as good a speed as *Willet* could make herself. By midnight on the eleventh *Willet* was only fifty miles away from the battered prize.

Meanwhile the daylight hours of the eleventh had seen the playing out of an almost incredible drama aboard *Foundation Franklin*. Her master's certainty that she was doomed had faded under the slow realization that not only was his vessel an extraordinary ship, but that she was manned by no ordinary men. Minutes after the SOS had been dispatched the crew had risen spontaneously to the challenge. Poirier and two seamen had made a dash from the port alleyway and had managed to get themselves firmly wedged into the angle of the after deck where the steering chain ran down from the boat-deck. Then, while the seamen held him, Poirier set himself to shorten the chain by sawing out three links.

At every second breath he and his two companions were buried under the freezing waters of the breaking seas, for *Franklin* was rolling so badly by then that she was putting her gunwales under. Her people were being flung about so mercilessly that they hardly dared to free one hand from the job of hanging on. The pumps were working at capacity —not to counter leaks, for the ship was sound, but simply to hold in check the water that forced its way in through the skylights, down the funnels, and under the hatches.

Poirier stuck to his work for three and a half hours, and at the end of that time he had removed three links and had closed up the chain. By then he was so nearly frozen that he could not unbend his body, and he had to be hauled back into shelter on the end of a line.

Meanwhile Sommers had *built* a new turnbuckle, working under conditions that made any sort of work below patently impossible. Pynn's deck-hands installed the buckle, and then turned to the major task.

When the old turnbuckle broke, the slack chain had fallen off the toothed semicircle of the rudder quadrant, which was located in the extreme stern of the ship under a low wooden grating on the after deck. This chain had now to be replaced. In order to replace it two men had to make their way aft across the swept and flooded deck, crawl into a space fourteen inches high by four feet wide, and lever the heavy chain back into position while the full weight of the Atlantic beat down through the open grille above them. To accomplish this in harbor, while at a steady mooring, required the maximum effort of two men. To attempt the same thing under the circumstances then prevailing seemed to verge on the suicidal.

Nevertheless two seamen volunteered. With life-lines tied about them they inched their way aft. Sometimes they were on their knees—more often on their bellies. Their progress was a series of squirming rushes, separated by exhausting intervals of hanging on by the skin of their teeth while seas swept over them. By contrast with the open deck, the narrow space beneath the grating represented sanctuary and they were mightily relieved to reach it, untie their lines, and crawl beneath the comforting latticework of teak.

They could not then be swept overboard to drown. Instead, they could drown in relative security. And this they nearly did, for as each sea broke across the ship the after deck filled up and the two men floated under water, prevented by the grille from rising to the surface. Between seas they struggled with the unwieldy chain. It took them two full hours to lever the links into position on the quadrant, and another half-hour to make their way back to the safety of the engine-room companionway. Pynn and his party then completed the repairs by tightening up the turnbuckles.

Lewis had observed the actions of his people with incredulity. In all his time at sea he had seen nothing comparable, and it took a little while for the full import of it to register. But when Pynn was able to announce that the vessel would answer her helm again, Lewis rose to the moment.

His doubts were gone. With no hesitation he gave the orders to get his vessel under way and then, with neat and accurate seamanship, he chose his moment to round her out of the troughs and get her running.

There are few maneuvers more fraught with danger for any vessel, and in particular for a small ship, than the attempt to swing off before the wind in a really heavy following sea. It can be accomplished by a master who not only has flawless judgment, but who also has complete confidence in his vessel. Lewis had always had the skill—and now he had the confidence as well.

By 3 P.M. *Franklin* was again lifting to the mighty seas that were outpacing her and was sliding down their backs as they passed by. She was still in the race, though she had lost her lead.

There was some moderation in the storm as evening came down, black and impenetrable with snow and spume. But towards midnight the wind began to muster all its strength for a new blow. The anemometer on *Franklin's* pilot-house grew frantic, and the wind-speed needle flickered across the dial until the gusts were registering ninety-four miles an hour. No ship could run before so wild a gale and live; and in the early hours of March 12 both *Franklin* and *Willet* were hove-to to ride it out. The difference was that *Willet* lay within half a dozen miles of *Harburg*, while *Franklin* was still thirty miles away.

Reindeer was far astern; and for her the race was done.

As Featherstone drove her through the wicked cross-seas of the previous afternoon, she had begun to pound herself to death. Rising and falling with a terrible motion, she had started to work until her hull was groaning. Planks slid against planks, forcing the caulking out. Her frames recoiled and then expanded as the strain increased. Below decks the sound of wood in agony outcried the wind. She pounded as if impelled by a blind desire to destroy herself.

As dusk fell, Featherstone hove-to some sixty miles off shore. His own driving will could not sustain her any longer, and as the night hours passed he found himself on the horns of an agonizing dilemma. He knew it would be suicide to continue on toward *Harburg*. But he did not dare attempt to bring his vessel round into the teeth of the hurricane in an attempt to run for port, for she was then so heavy in the water that she could not possibly have survived the trial. He could only wait, and pray that dawn would bring a moderation in the gale.

Dawn brought no change. Swept a dozen times, *Reindeer's* decks could no longer withstand the fall of water on them. Her planks had worked so loose that the sea was spurting in between them in swelling gouts that flooded the engine room and stokehold both. The accommodations became little private seas that responded puppetlike to the motion of the parent sea outside.

44

By noon the nature of the old ship's fate was clear to all aboard. Spurting through a hundred seams, the water rose in the stokehold until it hissed against the fires. Her own pumps—running at full capacity, and beyond—could no longer hold their own. Inexorably the water rose, and the cargo hold where the big eight-inch and ten-inch salvage pumps which might have saved her should have been was empty save for the encroaching sea.

They jettisoned the last reserves of bunker coal to lighten her a little, but the water came in faster. The suctions of the bilge pumps choked as the swirling waters rose above the floor plates, laden with a thick sediment of coal dust and ashes. The water in the stokehold rose waist-deep—and it was hot, for it had reached and quenched the fires. Steam pressure fell; the pumps slowed down; the dynamo supplying Sparks with power began to hesitate.

At 2 P.M. on March 12 a new SOS was added to the many that had gone before.

REINDEER TO ALL SHIPS REINDEER TO ALL SHIPS CAN-
NOT REMAIN AFLOAT POSITION 60 MILES BEARING 135
DEGREES FROM SAMBRO LIGHT

There were no further messages from *Reindeer,* for her dynamo had stopped.

At the time *Reindeer* called for help, *Franklin* was more than a hundred and fifty miles to the eastward and could not have turned and bucked the headwind back in time to be of service. In any case, she was committed to *Harburg.* In desperation the manager of the Halifax Shipyard ordered his harbor tugs to attempt the impossible—and they tried —but not one of them was able to get beyond the harbor's mouth. The government customs cutter *Adversus* was also ordered out—but was forced to heave-to ten miles beyond Chebucto Head.

Reindeer's operator had switched to his emergency power supply and he was again able to receive—but not transmit. Featherstone was informed of the failure of the harbor tugs and of the *Adversus.* He took the news with an apparent calm that masked a bleak despair. He had been resigned to losing his ship. Now he had to face the almost certain knowledge that he and his twenty-seven men must go down with her.

There was no more steam, and the pumps had ceased to work. The only warmth in *Reindeer's* hull was in her fast-cooling boilers. She had settled until her decks were nearly awash, and she no longer even tried to rise when the great combers bore down upon her. She could do nothing but lie supine beneath their ceaseless blows.

By 5 P.M. *Reindeer* was a dead hulk; her below-deck spaces almost completely flooded. Her people were crowded into the wheelhouse. Some of them fiddled aimlessly with their life-jackets, fully aware that these could only prolong life for a matter of minutes in that freezing sea. The bosun squatted in a corner holding the ship's dog between his knees. The dog was frightened, and it shivered uncontrollably under the man's careful hands.

The seas were breaking clean over the wheelhouse, and the windows were blurred with running water. Featherstone stood by a starboard window, peering into the storm scud, waiting for the night, which would end all hope. It was difficult to see anything except the patterns of leaden light reflected from dark seas; but suddenly he leaned close to the glass and rubbed his sleeve uselessly against it in an attempt to clear away the water running down its outer face. A gust of wind struck the house; the film of water wavered and then blew clear, and Featherstone gave a great shout and swung across the crowded space to fling open the house door.

"Jump to it, boys!" he cried. "There's a taxi come to take us home for tea!"

The big Canadian Pacific cargo-liner *Montcalm,* out of Liverpool, bound for St. John, New Brunswick, had been fourteen days at sea by March 11. Despite her size and power she had taken sufficient damage from the prolonged gales to decide her master, Captain Rothwell, to run direct for Halifax.

She was some fifty miles off Sambro Light when her Sparks picked up *Reindeer's* SOS. *Montcalm* held on her course while her master waited to see if any other ship could help the dying tug. When it became clear that no other vessel could reach *Reindeer* in time, Rothwell brought his ship around and headed back to sea. It had been no easy decision. *Montcalm* carried sixty passengers and a crew of fifty, and their lives were all in Rothwell's care. The risk to them was real enough, but the death of *Reindeer's* men was sure unless that risk was taken.

To find the almost completely submerged hulk of the salvage ship in that darkening turmoil of wind and water required inspired understanding of the sea—and luck. Rothwell had the understanding. He plotted *Reindeer's* last dead-reckoning position on the chart and then laid off her probable drift. Figuring his own position by DF (radio direction finding), he laid a course to intercept the sinking ship, rang for full speed, and ordered men aloft to be his eyes.

On the outward leg of his search he must have passed within three or four miles of *Reindeer*—but that distance might as well have been four hundred, for she remained invisible. Rothwell held on his course until his intuition told him he had missed his goal. Then the *Montcalm* came about, wallowing like a hippo as she rolled in the troughs. She headed back towards the land, and at 5:15 P.M. with the early winter dusk already closing in, the lookout saw a black and heaving shadow hard on the port bow.

Rothwell had hoped to pick up *Reindeer's* people out of their own boats, but when he saw that these had all been smashed he called for volunteers to man one of *Montcalm's* lifeboats. Second Officer Harry Knight and seven seamen volunteered. The boat was swung out in its davits; Knight and his men scrambled aboard and it was lowered on the vessel's leeward side. The oars were shipped and the falls cast off, but before the boat could get clear of *Montcalm*, it was picked up on a crest and thrown with such force against the mother ship that every seam on the port side was sprung and instantly the boat was half awash. Nevertheless Knight made no attempt to get back aboard *Montcalm*. Setting three men to bailing, he took an oar himself and the half-sinking boat pulled off for the *Reindeer*.

Rothwell saw that Knight would never make it unaided. He had already warned the engine room to stand by, and at his bellowed command down the voice pipe: "Spread oil!" the chief engineer started his pumps and sent a thick black stream into the sea. The oil spread quickly, soon overtook the struggling boat and in a few more minutes had embraced *Reindeer*, four hundred yards to leeward. It made a thin, almost invisible armor against which the seas rose and were miraculously rebuffed. With its protection the boat's crew pulled their hearts out, and the wind helped them along. But they could not steer a course, and they would have been swept helplessly past *Reindeer* if Featherstone had not had the forethought to stream fifty fathoms of Manila line astern of his sinking ship. Knight caught the line fifty yards beyond *Reindeer*, and his boat was soon hauled up to the wreck's taffrail.

Knight counted the men in the tight cluster on the bridge, and was appalled. There were twice as many as he could safely carry—and there was no time to make a second trip, for darkness was upon them. Nevertheless he did not hesitate.

"One at a time," he shouted. "Jump for it!"

Three minutes later the line was dropped. As the boat fell

47

away downwind it was so overladen that it had a bare six inches of freeboard. Oil spray drenched rescuers and rescued alike, and the bosun shoved the dog's head up inside his pea-jacket to keep the oil away.

They rowed and bailed like madmen until *Montcalm* drove down, came broadside to the wind and made a lee. The Jacob's ladder hung ready from her side and, as the light faded, the last man of *Reindeer's* crew climbed to the safety of the *Montcalm's* decks.

Featherstone had one final glimpse of his abandoned ship. She lay awash, heaving ponderously like the dead thing that she was.

First *Bardeleban*, and now *Reindeer* had gone.

Harburg remained afloat and, what was more, she was in tow and bound for Halifax. Struggling mightily, though with small effect, *Willet* had hold of *Harburg* while abeam of her, *Foundation Franklin* hung on her flank, a hungry and a cheated ship. *Franklin* had arrived upon the scene three hours too late, and she had lost the prize.

The knowledge that if she had sailed when *Harburg's* plight was first reported she would have won the race was salt in the bitter disappointment of her crew. Once more the ship herself had been betrayed by too much shore caution.

During the whole of the four days that *Willet* required to bring the prize to port, *Franklin* hung on in the dying hope that luck might break her way. But she was still the dejected and unwanted suitor when *Willet* steamed past Chebucto Head and proudly handed *Harburg* over to the harbor tugs.

7 ❦ THE TURNING POINT

Franklin's effort on behalf of *Harburg* had been magnificent, but they had nevertheless resulted in failure, and the immediate reaction of Foundation Maritime was one of unreasoned irritation. Against the advice of old hands in the business, the company decided to file a claim against *Harburg* for breach of contract, on the grounds that both her master and her agent had agreed to the hiring of *Franklin* before the tug left Halifax. The unlucky German vessel was thereupon arrested pending a hearing of the case.

Under other conditions there might conceivably have been some moral grounds for Foundation's suit, but considering the magnitude of the storm which had battered *Harburg,* and the risk to which she and her people had been exposed, her master obviously had acted correctly in accepting the first salvage tug which reached him.

However, contract law is strict, and the judge who tried the case had no alternative but to award some recompense to Foundation Maritime—even though his sympathy was clearly with the defendants. So the company managed to squeeze some financial benefit out of the affair, but at the cost of further alienating the shipowners, underwriters and Salvage Association men, all of whom were indignant when they heard the story. Thus a fine performance, which might have done much to alter the unfriendly attitudes of these important groups, was sacrificed for a meager, if immediate, advantage.

Nevertheless there were some real compensations. There was the recognition on the part of *Franklin's* people that their vessel would endure almost anything, and could accomplish almost anything. The *Harburg* affair gave them the vitally important faith in their ship, without which they and she would have remained incompatible.

There was another compensation too, one that was apparent to Chadwick almost from the moment *Reindeer I* went down. With her death, one jaw of the pincers which had been squeezing Foundation Maritime had been destroyed. Now Chadwick set about ensuring that this jaw would never be replaced.

Reindeer's primary job had been to keep Halifax Shipyard supplied with vessels for repair. With this in mind, and knowing that the vessel's real owners, Dominion Steel and Coal Company, or Dosco, as it is called throughout the Maritimes, were finding themselves hard pressed for ready money, Chadwick made them a proposal. I'm sure, he said in effect, that you could find a better use for *Reindeer's* insurance money than putting it into a new salvage ship. Suppose we arrange to station *Franklin* at Halifax, and have her bring the casualties to your shipyard—then you'd not need another salvage tug at all.

The suggestion found a warm reception amongst Dosco's directors, who were not marine men, and whose interest lay primarily on the land. And so negotiations were begun to transform Chadwick's offer into a concrete agreement.

Meanwhile *Franklin* had a free hand on the seaboard and the Gulf, and her people proposed to make the most of it.

Their first opportunity to do so came on June 25, when word was received in Montreal that the British freighter *Firby,* laden with grain for England, had gone ashore at Bradore Bay in the Strait of Belle Isle.

This time there was no shilly-shallying. Chadwick took personal command. Having telephoned Lewis at Rimouski with orders to stand by for sea, he contacted *Firby's* Canadian agents. When these gentlemen informed him that they intended to deal with the Quebec Salvage and Wrecking Company, Chadwick reacted by immediately ordering *Franklin* away to the wreck, contract or no.

He was considerably surprised when *Firby's* agents called him back in half an hour. They had suffered an inexplicable change of mind, and now they were willing and anxious to sign the L.O.F.

This sudden *volte-face* seemed to require some explanation. Chadwick promptly telephoned the Salvage Association to ask if they had any details as to *Firby's* situation and condition.

They had indeed. Her master had radioed a full report, and a black one, giving it as his opinion that his ship was a total loss and quite beyond all help. The Quebec Company had seen this message and had thereupon declined to have anything to do with the affair.

It took Chadwick no longer than the time required to hang up the receiver to come to his decision. As he explained afterwards:

"We had nothing to lose. We didn't even have a reputation that could be damaged by a failure. All we had was the hope that somehow we could show those other fellows up, and we knew the only way to do it was to take the kind of chance they'd shied away from."

Franklin's course took her five hundred miles from Rimouski, out through the northern arm of the great Gulf where Labrador and Newfoundland together squeeze the broad waters into the narrow Belle Isle Straits. She had fair weather and she made good time. In mid-morning of June 27 she pushed her bluff bows cautiously into the then uncharted waters of Bradore Bay.

The sight that met Lewis's eyes would have intimidated any man, but it must have been particularly horrifying to a deep-water sailor who was used to lots of sea room.

Bradore Bay is a deep indentation in a bleak and rock-faced coast and it is so heavily infested with reefs that, even in relatively calm weather, the white threat of breaking water covers much of its surface. Inland from it the old Labrador mountains roll away bald and scarred. Clumps of scrub spruce in the few protected hollows only accentuate the air of desolation. It is an uninhabited and almost uninhabitable coast that could not even support the bands of roving Eskimos who once used to pass this way.

But on that June morning in 1932 the bay was by no means empty. Far inshore, and driven hard up at an ungainly angle on a reef, was the black bulk of *Firby* with a wisp of smoke at her funnel. And keeping her close company was a phalanx of icebergs, some of them grounded, but others drifting ponderously about in the onshore breeze.

It took all of Lewis's fortitude and new-found faith in his ship to persuade him to enter that death-trap; but enter it he did. And two hours later, after a nerve-wracking passage of the maze, *Franklin* dropped anchor two hundred yards astern of the stranded vessel.

Firby was a dismal sight. She had been caught in a fierce spring storm during the night of June 24 as she approached the narrows in the Strait. Her master, Captain McLachlan, had been forced to run for shelter; for his ship was old, and with her seven thousand tons of cargo, she was too heavily laden to be easily maneuverable in those tight quarters.

McLachlan tried to make Frigate Harbour, a grandiose name for a tiny anchorage behind a series of inhospitable islands in Bradore Bay; but in darkness and with a snow-storm to blind him further, he missed the passage and fetched up on an uncharted reef. Because of her great momentum the ship had driven up for a hundred feet of her length. Now she lay, hogging badly, with her stern hanging over deep water and the rest of her grinding and groaning on the rocks.

Lewis boarded her and with him was a new employee of the company, a self-styled salvage expert from England who had been hired as *Franklin's* salvage master a few weeks earlier. It is difficult to know just what his qualifications were—but at least he was an optimist. He overrode the pessimistic opinions of Lewis and McLachlan and sent off a blithe message to Montreal to the effect that there was every hope of success. He reported that although number one hold was flooded and tidal, the rest of the ship was holding together well. The job appeared to him to be only a matter of jettisoning the soaked grain in number one, pumping out the water and hauling *Firby* off.

He was a sanguine man. But he was energetic too, and within the hour he had ordered *Franklin's* salvage pumps to be broken out and brought aboard the wreck.

This was easier said than done. The pumps were mostly ancient relics of a bygone era and had been intended for terrestrial use in the first place. They were massive beyond belief. One of them—a fifteen-inch steam centrifugal—weighed nine tons without its fittings. Nevertheless it, and several slightly smaller pumps were hoisted out of the hold, swung onto *Firby's* decks, set up in position and connected to her steam lines.

While this was being done *Franklin's* diver was sent down to inspect the wreck's hull. There was a heavy swell that day and the diver could not venture far under the groaning forward portion of the ship for fear of being pinned. Nevertheless he saw enough to indicate that the salvage master's view of things was highly colored. When he surfaced it was to report that the casualty's entire bottom, for a distance of sixty feet abaft the stem, was a twisted mass of set-up plates, torn bilges, and gaping apertures.

The sea had begun to rise uncomfortably by mid-afternoon, and as the tide came in a number of icebergs heaved themselves clear of anchoring reefs and went on the prowl about the bay. One of them, the size of a four-story building, swung lazily in to have a look at *Franklin's* stern. Lewis watched it anxiously until one of his deck-hands shouted to him:

"Hey, Cap—I think that feller wants a tow!"

Then Lewis decided it was time to move. He took *Franklin* into the meager shelter of Frigate Harbour while the balance of his crew remained aboard *Firby*.

None of them lacked enthusiasm. What they lacked was experience, for not one of them had ever before taken part in a salvage operation of such complexity. This is a fact which should be borne in mind in assessing the results of this adventure.

Work was begun in earnest the next day. Clam buckets from *Franklin's* holds were rigged to *Firby's* cargo derricks, and the jettisoning of grain from number one hold was started. The clam buckets sank down into the soggy mass of swelling wheat, swung up and out, and dumped their loads into the sea. As soon as a space was cleared, the suctions were manhandled into place and the big pumps began to wheeze and clatter and to send great streams of water, mixed with grain, into the scuppers.

There were nearly a thousand tons of wheat in number one, and the discharging was laboriously slow. The pumps began to give trouble almost at once as their suctions began to clog. Thirty different consignments had been loaded in number one, each separated from its neighbor by sheets of cotton known as separation cloths. These cloths had been torn up and dispersed through the cargo by the clams, and the pumps refused to stomach them. The salvors tried improvising wire mesh strainer boxes, but these too soon clogged. Sometimes small bits of cloth passed up a suction to jam an impeller or a valve, so that the whole pump had to be disassembled.

On the second day the pumps began to give evidence of a new and quite inexplicable ailment. One after another, and for no apparent reason, they began to lose their primes. About the same time the salvors working in the hold began to joke about the odor. "Smells like a Halifax beer parlor on a Saturday night," they said. But it was some time before anyone connected the ambrosial smell with the failure of the pumps. It was a lowly stoker who made the discovery that they were now pumping beer, and that it was the gassy "head" on the brew that was causing the pumps to lose their prime. Fermentation of the cargo was not one of the hazards of the salvage game that *Franklin's* people had been warned about.

They pumped and cursed, and clammed and cursed, through three long days, and at the end of that time the salvage master thought they might have lightened her enough and so he called *Franklin* up to give a pull. Lewis brought the tug into position but he was unhappy about it, for the reefs gave him no room to maneuver, and the icebergs were showing an increasingly bovine interest in the operations. Nevertheless *Franklin* tried three times on three high tides—and *Firby* did not budge an inch.

By July 2 McLachlan had decided that there might be a chance to save his ship after all, but that the salvors were not being very efficiently directed toward that end. He found an ally in Lewis, who lived in mortal fear of an onshore blow that might set his vessel in amongst the rocks. Together they drafted a wireless message suggesting that E. J. Biederman, the superintendent of Foundation Maritime, come down and take command. While they waited for him, Lewis decided they had better begin jettisoning dry grain from number two hold, since it was obvious that *Firby* would never come off unless her draft could be drastically reduced.

Before dawn of the following day some five hundred tons of good grain had been shoveled overboard through holes burned in *Firby's* side. The wreck was at last beginning to show some signs of life, and the grating and groaning of her tortured metal on the rocks was becoming increasingly hard on the salvors' nerves.

At first light Lewis came out on *Franklin's* deck and peered apprehensively into an ominous sky. The wind was getting up out of the sou'west. There was the clear threat of a proper blow before the day was done.

He did not need to communicate his fears to the salvage gang or to McLachlan's crew; they were all seamen, and they sensed what was coming. Jettisoning out of number two hold was continued at a feverish pace, for each man understood that unless *Firby* was hauled clear before the storm broke, she would not live to see another dawn.

By 8 o'clock that evening the threat of wind had become a reality, and the sea was rising. *Franklin* backed in until her towing wire could be made fast to *Firby's* after bollards. The gang of men down in number two continued shoveling as if possessed, knowing that every pound sent overboard would help a little. They were all aware that this time it was do or die for *Firby*.

As *Franklin* prepared to pull, there was a brilliant flash of lightning, followed by the keening sound of a high wind rushing through darkness. It seemed as if the tug had heard and understood. She tucked her stern down and in a moment the water under her counter was a white and foaming current. The wire became as rigid as a steel bar and it sang with strain.

Firby did not move.

Franklin worked up to every pound of steam power she possessed; until the safety valves were hissing. She held the strain and, in her frenzy, swung back and forth at the end of her tether like a mad dog struggling to be free. Both funnels belched black smoke so thickly that the quivering wreck upon the reef was almost obscured. *Firby* too had strained her engines and was running them astern at full revolutions. It still was not enough.

The time was then nearly 9 P.M., and hope was all but gone. But in that dark hour the very enemy the salvors dreaded most became their unexpected ally. The seas roared in under *Firby*, lifted her, then dropped her, shuddering, upon the rocks. But as the seas grew bigger they lifted her a little higher too. At 9:24 she suddenly began to move.

She came off in a series of sick lurches, with a crashing impact between each pair of seas. But she came off.

In the flurry of excitement following her release someone aboard *Firby* reached for the telegraph to stop the engines so that she would not back over *Franklin's* wire—but he rang for full-ahead instead. The sudden jerk snatched the towline clean off *Franklin's* winch and stripped the winch gears besides.

Now it was McLachlan's show, for the tug could do nothing further for the moment. With his ship literally sinking under him, he somehow managed to get her turned in those narrow waters and headed out to sea. By that time *Franklin's* crew had been able to rig a tow wire off her towing hook, and with this on Firby's bows, she began to haul the cripple out to open water.

The storm was approaching its full fury by this time, and it was no longer possible even to consider trying to get *Firby* into the shelter of Frigate Harbour, where she could have been beached until underwater repairs had been carried out. But there was not another harbor along that whole coast into which she could go. The only alternative was to try to ease her across ten miles of open bay into the lee of Greenley Island, and then attempt to keep her afloat with pumps until the storm abated.

It was a terrifying journey. The pumps alone were keeping *Firby* up, and they were laboring at full capacity to hold the water in number one at a depth of fifteen feet. Had the water gained five feet more it would undoubtedly have burst the rotten bulkhead into number two, and had that happened, *Firby* would have put her nose under and gone down in fifteen fathoms. Drenched in a driving rain and cut by the flying scud, the three pumpmen nursed their belching engines and prayed that none would clog; while in the echoing darkness of number one the diver and his two helpers struggled to keep the intakes clear.

Down by the head, waterlogged, and trailing her torn bottom plates like fins, *Firby* refused to follow the tug, but lurched off abeam in great heaving surges that eventually carried away the wire again. The storm had become so fierce by then that it was impossible to reconnect the tow. Under her own failing power *Firby* now had to follow where the *Franklin* led; and this she did at a pace of less than two knots. It was dawn again before she came behind the island and dropped her anchor.

Now there was rest and some release of tension for everyone except the pumpmen. These dared not rest. All that day and night, and through the succeeding day, they stayed beside the pumps.

The wind dropped off during the morning of July 6, and at noon a little coastal steamer, chartered by Biederman, poked her nose behind the island. She had been held up for two days by the gale, and Biederman had not expected to find anything except the shattered hulk of *Firby* on the rocks of Bradore Bay when he arrived.

He immediately took over direction of the operation, and late that afternoon *Franklin* towed the cripple back into the bay and anchored her in Frigate Harbour. It had taken *Firby* eleven days to reach the haven she had sought on June the twenty-fourth.

She remained there for a week. On July 7 she was beached on a sandy bar while the work of making her seaworthy enough for the six-hundred-mile tow to the dry docks at Quebec was carried out.

Biederman saw that he could not hope to make the ship even remotely watertight and that there was no possibility of pumping her dry. Calling upon his long experience as a pneumatic-caisson engineer, he thereupon decided upon a risky but novel alternative. His plan was to seal number one hold *from the top*, making it airtight, and then to force in compressed air until there was sufficient pressure to hold the water down to a safe level. Some hundreds of tons of wet and viscous grain, still remaining in the hold, were to be left in position to form a mattress nicely balanced between the pressure of the air above and that of the water below. On this, and on a cushion of air, he thought that *Firby* might conceivably stay afloat until she reached Quebec.

There were innumerable difficulties in the way of putting the plan into effect. First it was discovered that *Firby's* builders had skimped their work and that neither the collision bulkhead nor the bulkhead between number one and number two holds formed watertight (or airtight) connections with the main deck. Worse still, the lower deck plating had been cut away to pass around the transverse frames, leaving still more gaps that had to be plugged. The salvors went to work using sheet lead, wooden wedges and portable welding equipment and by July 15 they thought they had number one completely sealed. Two compressors were brought aboard from *Franklin;* air lines were connected up to valves installed in the strengthened hatch-top of number one and pumping began. Biederman watched the pressure gauges anxiously. They had climbed to three pounds—the minimum pressure needed—and he was about to signify his satisfaction, when there was a long wailing whistle from the ship's innards, and the pressure promptly fell to zero.

The salvors removed the hatch and went below. Exasperated beyond measure they discovered that the builders had again outsmarted them. The spaces between the lapped deck plates and the transverse beams, which are normally plugged with steel wedges, had been plugged with pads of felt instead, and these had been blown out by the increased air pressure.

Sealing these apertures took two more days and it was not until July 17 that the hold was again brought under pressure. This time it held. *Firby* was floated free of her mudbank; *Franklin's* tow wire was connected, and the long voyage to dry-dock was begun.

Firby remained obstinate and difficult until the end. She refused to follow docilely behind her rescuer, but insisted on sheering back and forth until she threatened to put the tug in irons. Once into the St. Lawrence River channel she began to display a passionate affection for the navigation buoys, and she did her best to collect each one she passed. It was with great relief that *Franklin's* people finally led the wayward one into Quebec on July 21 and cast her off.

That was an hour for celebration. Foundation Maritime had successfully completed a most complex and difficult salvage job, against considerable odds, and to the amazement of both the Salvage Association and the Quebec Salvage and

Wrecking Company, both of whom had been frankly sceptical of the early reports of *Franklin's* progress on the job.

The experts had, in fact, been so outspoken in their belief that *Firby* was doomed that her reinsurance rate in London had risen as high as forty-five per cent—which is to say that her underwriters, attempting to spread an almost certain loss, had been offering to pay a premium that represented forty-five per cent of the face values of the policies they held on *Firby* to anyone who would take part, or all, of those policies off their hands.

With *Firby's* rescue, the tide began to change for *Franklin*. There would still be setbacks, but she and her people were now forever free of the strangling doubts which had been for so long laid upon their competence and their abilities. With reasonable luck they could now begin to hope for the kind of future Chadwick had envisaged for his ship.

8 ⚜ CHANGING THE GUARD

DURING THE TEN MONTHS which followed on *Firby's* rescue, Chadwick's negotiations with Dosco had come to fruition. By the terms of the agreement Foundation Maritime took over *Reindeer's* role together with the services of two men who, between them, knew more about Atlantic salvage than anyone in Canada.

These two were Captain Reginald Featherstone and Thomas Nolan.

Nolan was primarily a diver, but he had been in salvage work so long that he was not only an expert at underwater work, but he was fully able to act as general foreman on any kind of salvage job. He was a quiet-spoken, gentle-mannered Newfoundlander—except when he was crossed. At the age of sixteen Tom had gone to work in the iron mines on Belle Isle as a dynamite man; but a premature explosion, which cost him the sight of one eye, decided him on finding a less hazardous profession.

His choice seemed a little odd, for he elected to become a deep-sea diver. When he was unable to find anyone who was willing to teach him this trade, he borrowed an old suit and taught himself.

Tom's qualities as a diver soon became legendary, and remain so to this day. Until he passed the sixty mark he thought nothing of spending ten to fourteen hours a day in his chosen depths. Yet, in all his years he never learned to swim.

Featherstone was an altogether different type. Jut-jawed and domineering, he was a strange mixture of braggadocio and very real ability. His self-assurance and his unconcealed disdain for lesser mortals would have been intolerable in another man but were grudgingly acceptable in Featherstone because he was almost as good as he believed himself to be.

Featherstone's experience with disaster at sea began with the first vessel he commanded—the fast collier *Alice Taylor*. That was in 1916, when Featherstone was just nineteen years old. The *Taylor* was making a passage through the English Channel one winter night when she was rammed amidships by a Norwegian freighter and almost cut in two.

The most sanguine of masters would have assumed that she was doomed, for her wounds seemed mortal. The lascar crew was quite convinced of it and they rushed the boats, only to be turned back at gun-point by Featherstone and his chief officer. Featherstone had already made a decision which was to be typical of him through the years ahead. The fact that the ship had *not yet sunk* was sufficient evidence to persuade him that there was a chance of saving her. The black gang was driven below, still at gun-point, and the *Taylor* began to move again.

Four hours later she lurched sluggishly toward a beach near Weymouth. By then the stokehold and the engine room had flooded to a depth sufficient to drive the engineers and stokers up on deck. But with the last turns of her screw the *Taylor* managed to push her nose up on the sands.

Not content with keeping her afloat Featherstone then turned-to with a British Admiralty salvage gang and helped repair and refloat his vessel. When she came out of dry-dock he took her to sea again.

It was another dirty winter night when the *Taylor* cleared Yarmouth, and she had not proceeded five miles on her way when she struck a mine. Her whole forward portion was blown off; her boats were all smashed by the blast; and her wireless was knocked out. She began to sink at once—this time in earnest.

The weather was so wild that the lifeboat station at Yarmouth neither saw nor heard the explosion. Featherstone soon alerted them, though. He opened fire on the station with his twelve-pounder gun.

Once safe ashore Featherstone decided to try for a change of luck by joining the Admiralty Salvage Section. He was made chief officer of H.M.S. *Reindeer* and by 1918 he had succeeded to her command. He remained with her until the war's end and took part in more than a score of salvage operations.

When Halifax Shipyard bought *Reindeer* from the Admiralty in 1922, Featherstone decided to come over to the new world with her, and until the day she sank under him in 1932 he remained her master as well as being salvage superintendent for the yard.

This was the man who now became salvage master for Foundation Maritime and who was required to work closely with Biederman and Lewis, neither of whom had more than a smattering of practical experience in salvage work. Since it was not in Featherstone's nature to be tolerant of inexperience or of ignorance, the situation was an explosive one.

The battle for individual survival began at once. During late June Chadwick paid a state visit to Rimouski and, in preparation for it, *Franklin* was polished and refurbished until she looked like a private yacht. Resplendent in spotless uniforms the ship's officers greeted Chadwick with the formality and protocol usually reserved for admirals-of-the-fleet. Chadwick was obviously impressed. Turning to his newest employee, who was standing very much in the background, he asked:

"Well, Featherstone. And what do you think of her? A fine ship, eh?"

"Yes," Featherstone replied with a bluntness that outraged Biederman and the vessel's officers. "She's a fine ship all right —for moonlit cruise excursions."

The knives were out in earnest after that, and there was an early opportunity to use them when, on July 4, the British steamer *Marsland* went hard on Vestal Rock in St. John's harbor.

Featherstone knew of the accident the day it happened and he at once wired Montreal for permission to proceed. Permission was not forthcoming. The Montreal office had heard that the casualty's agents in St. John's were attempting to refloat the ship themselves and had no intention of signing a contract with a salvage company.

So Featherstone fumed in Rimouski while the amateurs in St. John's succeeded only in reducing *Marsland's* chances. When they had hauled her over to such an angle that most of her holds were flooded, the Salvage Association men belatedly stepped in and insisted that the *Franklin* be hired.

She and Featherstone arrived on July 8 and the new salvage master made an examination of the wreck. The prospects for successful salvage were depressingly poor. *Marsland* was lying on a submerged rock, broadside to a three-hundred-foot cliff. Her starboard rails were under water. The heavy ocean swell was breaking clean across her and she was almost completely flooded. Nevertheless Featherstone accepted the challenge, and signed the L.O.F.

59

It was at once apparent to his men that he was a driver. Work never ceased, and the onslaught of a heavy blow was no excuse to leave the job. When the breaking seas made it impossible for men to remain above decks, the salvos were sent below to labor through the night in *Marsland's* dark interior. *Franklin*—despite Lewis's protests—was ordered to remain alongside even though she took so much damage that she later had to be dry-docked for repairs.

Led by Tom Nolan the divers were down by day and by night attempting to place timbers in position to seal off the starboard bridge door, which was by then under water. When the swells swept the timbers away, Featherstone ordered special steel doors to be constructed at the St. John's shipyard. These were delivered the following day, and after superhuman efforts they were installed and bolted home.

Through July 10 the salvors worked to such effect that by midnight the foreport of the ship had been sealed and the pumps could be brought into play.

Now Featherstone forced the pace to the limit of human endurance. Denied any real rest for ninety hours, the salvage crew labored like demented beings. By July 12 they had succeeded in lowering the water in the holds sufficiently to give the vessel some buoyancy. The struggle was then at the balance point, and during that night the men worked until they literally collapsed.

But in the morning the pumps began to lose their gains, for *Marsland's* bottom plates were tearing and crushing faster than the damage could be repaired.

With that day's dawn the sea made up and a strong sou'-easter began to blow. By noon *Marsland* had all but disappeared under a veil of spume. The battle had been lost.

When the storm died down on July 15 and *Franklin* returned to salve the gear that had been left on board, she found the wreck crawling with strangers. The doomed ship was surrounded by two score dories bobbing about in the heavy swell while their fishermen owners scrambled over the *Marsland,* helping themselves to anything that could be moved.

Franklin's crew made no attempt to discourage these unofficial salvors. It would have been useless in any case, for there is an ancient tradition on the coasts of Labrador and Newfoundland that once a ship is beyond saving she belongs to the people of the shore.

There is no more honest race of men than these same fishermen, nor is there a braver race. When ships drive onto the hard rocks of their coasts the dory-men will put out in weather that would sink a well-found lifeboat, and will rescue crew and passengers at the most imminent risk to themselves.

Afterwards, while the stranded ship remains intact and while there is a possibility of refloating her, she will be treated as scrupulously as a bride. No fisherman will lay a hand on her even while food that would mean months of sure existence to the shore-dwellers rots in her holds. But on the day that she is pronounced doomed—then she belongs to those upon whose coast she lies.

They swarmed over the *Marsland* in a mood approaching frenzy. They cut her wooden topmasts out of her for use as spars in their little schooners. Two particularly burly characters sized up the mainmast, found that it suited them, and took a stance on either side of it, swinging their axes in unison. Their surprise equaled their pain when they discovered that the mast was made of steel. Reginald Poirier watched with delight, and he remembers that their profanity had a quality that made St. John's harbor reverberate from end to end.

Franklin returned to Rimouski on August 8 with nothing to show for her journey except a pitiful collection of scrap which the fishermen had somehow missed. It was an auspicious moment for the two rival factions at Rimouski to engage in internecine battle in an attempt to fix the blame for the *Marsland* fiasco on one another.

The ensuing struggle lasted for two months and was only resolved when Chadwick suddenly descended on the Montreal office of Foundation Maritime, closed it up tight, and discharged most of the staff. Biederman was finished. The center of gravity now shifted to Rimouski, and to Featherstone.

If Biederman felt bitterness it was justifiable. Although he was no salvage expert he had nevertheless carried the responsibility for the survival of the new company through the desperately difficult early years, and the rescue of *Firby* had been largely his personal success. Many of the failures which the embryo organization had encountered in the first years had been due more to ill luck and inexperience than to bad management; and it is probable that Biederman would, in time, have learned his new trade well. Unfortunately for him, Featherstone was a master of that trade already.

In the first days of December, navigation came to an end on the St. Lawrence and *Franklin* was ordered to sail for Halifax to take up her winter station there. She was abreast of Louisburg on the evening of December 9 when Sparks intercepted a general SOS.

The transmission was so weak that it was barely decipherable, but Sparks was able to obtain the salient facts that the British steamer *Fernmoor* was ashore near Cape Anguille, Newfoundland, and was in urgent need of assistance.

Featherstone replied to her at once:

PROCEEDING YOUR ASSISTANCE FULL SPEED WILL ARRIVE NINE A.M.

At 11 P.M. Sparks picked up a new signal, but even weaker than the first:

FERNMOOR TO FOUNDATION FRANKLIN AM MAKING WATER FAST FEAR LOSS OF POWER WILL BE UNABLE TO COMMUNICATE

The signal faded, and *Fernmoor* went off the air.

All that night *Franklin* drove on at her best speed. The wind began to shift, and before dawn it had gone right round the card into the west—hard on the shore where *Fernmoor* was believed to be. *Franklin* redeemed Featherstone's promise and by 9 o'clock in the morning she had reached Cape Anguille and was steaming along that mountainous and forbidding coast.

There was no sign of the stranded ship. Then, at 11:30 A.M., Sparks caught a faint signal from *Fernmoor's* emergency transmitter and quickly took a DF bearing on it. The direction was north-easterly. *Franklin* picked up speed and an hour later brought *Fernmoor* into view some twenty miles beyond the Cape.

She lay at the foot of a small bay ringed with five-hundred-foot cliffs that rose sheer from the white foam. She was partly obscured by driving snow squalls, but as *Franklin* eased into the bay Featherstone could see that the wreck was broadside on against the cliffs with the seas breaking full over her. His heart sank, for no amount of self-assurance could hide the fact that *Fernmoor* was desperately beset.

Lewis brought *Franklin* in cautiously, for the rocks were near and the wind was rising. He dared not come alongside the wreck, so he held his vessel under half power three hundred yards offshore while Featherstone hung over Sparks's shoulder and talked to *Fernmoor's* captain. The news was black. *Fernmoor* was working and grinding herself to pieces, and all her compartments had already flooded. Her entire crew had spent the night lying under her lee side in open lifeboats, expecting her to break up at any moment. They were suffering badly from exposure, for the temperature was well below freezing point, but until *Franklin* came in sight there had been no hope of escape, for the boats could not have landed below those cliffs, and neither could they have pulled out of the bay in the face of the driving seas and wind.

This time Featherstone could not argue with the inevitable. "Right," he said to Sparks. "Tell them to abandon her at once."

Fifteen minutes after *Franklin's* arrival, *Fernmoor's* exhausted and half-frozen people were being hauled aboard. Their lifeboats were cast adrift, and *Franklin* turned her back on the breaking ship and on one more broken hope for Featherstone. Under full power she headed out to sea and set course towards Sydney, the nearest port at which the thirty-eight survivors of the wreck could obtain medical attention.

The journey back was hard. The wind rose to a full gale and *Franklin* was soon shipping seas both fore and aft. One of the ash-scuttle doors was smashed and the port alleyway and cabins filled with water before she could be brought around and the damage temporarily repaired. Then she began to take water through her forecastle head, and her speed had to be reduced until she was just making headway against the rising seas. It was not until the evening of December 11 that she came thankfully into the shelter of North Sydney harbor.

So the year ended—without a successful salvage operation to Featherstone's credit, and with *Franklin* showing an operational deficit of forbidding proportions.

Biederman was gone, and now Lewis also went—the last of the old guard. And, as with Biederman, Lewis may well have been a bitter man. He had come to a new ship and a new type of work under the worst possible conditions. He had been cautious with *Franklin* at first, but he had proven himself a fine seaman in the end. He was to prove his courage amply enough in the years ahead when, during the Second World War, he was twice sunk in the Atlantic by submarines. The second time saw him adrift on a tiny raft eight hundred miles from shore. Weeks afterwards a fisherman on an Irish beach found the emaciated remains of Captain Lewis, still lashed to the battered raft upon which he had made his final voyage.

9 ❧ MAROONED

IN THE BEGINNING OF 1934 Captain Irwin Power assumed command of *Franklin,* and for the first time she had a skipper who was fully worthy of her.

Power was a big and amiable Nova Scotian out of Yarmouth—that home of famous sailing men. At the age of fifteen he was serving before the mast in square-rigged ships rounding the Horn on voyages between New York and

Hong Kong. A few years later he went into steam with the Allen Line on the trans-Atlantic run, where he worked his way up to second officer during the final years of the First World War.

In 1919 he transferred to the Canadian Government service. Through the next eight years he lived with the North Atlantic in its most savage moods, first aboard a government ice-breaker, and then as chief officer aboard the *Lady Laurier*. In those days one of the *Laurier's* major duties was to assist crippled ships at sea, and during his service with her Power took part in some of the most spectacular ocean rescues of the 1920's.

In 1926 he was posted to another government ship, which had been detailed to spend a winter frozen in the arctic ice. While this vessel was returning south in the following year she was caught in a fearful storm and sustained such heavy damage that her survival was a matter of grave doubt. At the crucial moment of decision her master was suddenly incapacitated. Without hesitation Power took command and by the exercise of consummate seamanship, he nursed the stricken ship into the shelter of an outport on the coast of Labrador.

This exploit was widely reported in the newspapers of the time and Chadwick, looking about for someone who could master the recalcitrant *Foundation Jupiter,* decided that here was his man. Power was hired, and for the next five years he somehow managed to keep the *Jupiter* going about her rightful business; an accomplishment that smacks of the miraculous to those who ever had anything to do with that wayward witch.

Franklin and Power soon had an opportunity to demonstrate the way that they could work together.

On April 1 *Franklin* was lying at her dock in Halifax when a hurricane struck the Nova Scotia seaboard from the east. The wind rose to eighty miles an hour at the weather station on Chebucto Head, and the seas boiled into the harbor entrance with such fury that no merchant ship could leave or enter. *Franklin* lay uneasily, tugging at her mooring as if she knew that this was the kind of weather she was meant to face.

She had not long to wait. Before dawn next morning an SOS boomed into Chebucto radio. It came from the steamer *Incemore,* bound for Halifax from Liverpool with general cargo and with passengers. She had been struck by the hurricane while fifty miles off Sambro Light and had broken her tail shaft. Now she lay completely helpless, drifting rapidly toward the land.

Franklin sailed within the hour. It was a rough passage out, but then a salvage ship is seldom called upon in gentle weather. Power drove her at full revolutions until she corkscrewed through the seas and drenched herself in spray. There was no time to waste in easing her along, for *Incemore* was drifting fast toward the Sambro Ledge.

Incemore's drift had been phenomenal, and was a good measure of the force of the gale. When *Franklin* found her, at 2 P.M., she was just seven miles outside the reefs. Not far off, the freighter *Dominica* was lying hove-to, her lifeboats already swung out, prepared to try to save the *Incemore's* people before that vessel went ashore.

But *Franklin* had arrived. Despite the formidable seas it took Power just forty-five minutes to get his heavy towing wire aboard and start his charge for Halifax. And as dusk came down *Franklin* delivered *Incemore* to the harbor tugs in sheltered waters, and went back to her wharf.

It had been a brief operation, but a most important and rewarding one, for it gave *Franklin's* people, and the salvage staff, hope that the curse had lifted. For the first time in twenty-two long months *Franklin* had really earned her salt.

The belief that luck had turned was an illusion. Or perhaps it was not a question of luck at all, but lack of vision. At any rate Captain Power, the first master who really understood *Franklin* and who could get the best from her, was now transferred to the superintendence of a shore construction job.

Three days after the *Incemore* was docked, *Franklin* was called to sea again—this time to assist the *Liverpool Rover*, which had lost her propeller not far off Louisburg. *Franklin* was slow in leaving for she had a boiler under repair, and when she did get away it was with an unfamiliar hand at her helm.

Once past Cape Canso she encountered a broad ice field, and the new captain cautiously elected to pass outside the pack rather than risk a passage of the open water which ran along the coast. The result of this maneuver was that, when *Franklin* raised the *Liverpool Rover*, there was a barrier of solid ice, five miles wide, between them.

Under Featherstone's urging the new captain reluctantly attempted to force a passage through, but *Franklin* had not gone fifty feet into the pack before she stuck fast. And then she and her people had to suffer the humiliation of sitting helplessly by while the small tug *Cruizer*—out of Sydney—coasted down between ice and land, attached a line to the disabled ship and towed her merrily off to Louisburg.

Franklin returned to Halifax with a seething Featherstone aboard.

Nor was his mood greatly improved by the affair of the *Rutenfjell*, a small Norwegian freighter out of Oslo, which went ashore at Hungry Cove on Cap Breton Island a few weeks later.

Word of the accident was received in Halifax at noon on May 5 and, impelled by the fierce impatience of Featherstone, *Franklin* was away an hour later.

Featherstone did not even wait until contact had been established with the vessel's owners or her agents; nor did he let the presence of an enveloping bank of fog along the whole Nova Scotian coast delay him. He badgered *Franklin's* skipper until that unhappy man found the courage to drive his vessel at full speed for a record passage to the northern tip of Cape Breton, without once having a sight of sun or stars, or of the nearby coasts.

Franklin arrived off *Rutenfjell* at 2 P.M. and half an hour later Featherstone was aboard the wreck and Tom Nolan was already in his diving dress and going over the side. Tom found that the vessel was resting on a mass of granite boulders from her bow to abaft her mainmast, with her forepeak tanks and all the double bottom tanks under her holds tidal and unpumpable.

The chances of successful salvage seemed remote. Nevertheless, Featherstone set the ship's own crew to work jettisoning bagged fertilizer from her holds to lighten her, while as many of the *Franklin's* people as could be spared were set to preparing ground tackle for a quick haul-off.

Men who were on that job remember that Featherstone's mood was by then approaching the savagery of an irritated buffalo. It was hardly safe to approach him with a question. Under his forbidding glare the work went forward with such celerity that by 11 P.M. on the day of *Franklin's* arrival, the ground tackle was set out, the cargo largely jettisoned, and the ship ready for a pull.

By midnight the ground-tackle wire was bar taut to *Rutenfjell* from the two salvage anchors, and a steady strain was being applied through the casualty's winch. The tide was coming in and by 1 A.M. the ship had begun to show some signs of buoyancy. A wave of optimism swept the salvage crew.

But at 1:30 A.M. the weather, which had been fine and almost windless, changed abruptly. Snow began to fall and quickly became a blinding blizzard under the influence of a sudden onshore gale which sprang up almost instantly. The seas rose, and *Rutenfjell* began to heave and bump so alarmingly that Featherstone decided to slack off and wait; but at 5 A.M. the tank tops began to burst, and within minutes the entire ship was flooded, with the exception of the stokehold and the engine room.

Through the next eight days *Franklin* stood off and on. Sometimes her sailors were able to work aboard the wreck—more often not. They salvaged as much cargo as had not been ruined by the seas, but each day that passed saw *Rutenfjell's* position worsen. Nevertheless, Featherstone stubbornly began preparing to repair the hulk. The only remaining hope was to plug enough of the innumerable leaks and holes so that the pumps could hold the water down while the ship was pulled off and hurried to some convenient and sheltered beach.

Tom Nolan was entrusted with the job of ferrying the pumps aboard. The first one—a nine-hundred-pound gasoline-driven monster—was so big it had to be balanced across the thwarts of the little motorboat. It never reached the wreck. Halfway there a sea struck the little boat, which promptly turned turtle and sank, taking the pump with it. It nearly took Nolan as well, but he managed to cling to the upturned keel until help came.

During the next few days an onshore wind made work impossible, but on May 22 the salvors came back once more. But they had hardly begun setting up the pumps when a new gale arose. This time the exasperated and frustrated Featherstone refused to be driven off. *Rutenfjell's* crew availed themselves of the breeches buoy. The motorboat returned to *Franklin* with six of the salvors; but Featherstone, Nolan, and two others stayed aboard. An hour later, when the storm had reached full force and they were ready to abandon ship, they could no longer do so. The seas had grown so high that the motorboat could not return, and the breeches-buoy cable had been parted by the working of the ship.

It was almost as if this was the moment the sea had been waiting for. Through twenty days it had bided its time until it could trap some of the would-be salvors on the wreck. Now that it had succeeded, it set energetically about the business of destroying them.

Rutenfjell lay at the foot of an unscalable cliff. Moreover the reefs on which she lay were only half submerged, and they would have shattered any boat that tried to come amongst them.

The gale's fury was appalling. Before dusk the breaking seas were sending spume right over the clifftop, while *Rutenfjell* herself became invisible to the anxious men aboard the *Franklin,* lying a mile offshore. Finally, as the gale reached near-hurricane force, *Franklin* was herself endangered. She was forced to turn and run clean around the northern tip of Cape Breton to seek shelter under the lee of its western mountains.

The four marooned men now gave up hope of rescue and, having locked themselves into the saloon amidships, prepared to die in comfort. Featherstone and two of the men opened a bottle of the ship's bond and yarned while *Rutenfjell* was breaking up. But Nolan, whose sense of humor was never very subtle, sneaked out on deck, where he armed himself with an old iron pail, with which he began to beat out an alarming and suggestive cacaphony against the deckhouse each time a sea burst across the ship.

The gale continued unabated all that night, and shortly before dawn *Rutenfjell* broke in half just forward of her engine room. That saved the men aboard, for the bow section now drove so hard against the cliff that, during a lull, the four were able to scramble up the remaining twenty feet of rock above her bows and reach safe harbor.

If recollections carry any truth, the castaways were not unduly disturbed by their long night. What did disturb them was the seven-mile walk, through uninhabited bush, up a mountain slope and down again, to join the *Franklin* on the other shore. All four of them were wearing rubber sea-boots, and by the time they arrived at their ship their feet were blistered out of recognition. One of them summed it up succinctly when finally he arrived aboard the *Franklin*.

"I'll take the sea any time," he said with feeling. "She'll drown you maybe; but the land—why, damn it—it can kill you half to death!"

10 🔶 OIL ON TROUBLED SEAS

On november 11 of 1934 a fine new motor-tanker, the M.V. *Cordelia,* eighty-five hundred tons, was approaching the entrance to Canso Strait en route from England for Montreal with a full cargo of refined oil. It was her first trip to Canadian waters and her master was not familiar with the coast. He did not like the look of the Canso approaches, with their multitude of reefs, but even less did he like the look of the weather, for it was blowing up out of the north-east, and there was the promise of a full gale by nightfall.

As dusk came down, *Cordelia* was almost abeam the shoals of Eddy Point. She was in the channel, but she was handling sluggishly, due to the outflowing tidal current and the beam wind. Suddenly the wind gusted up from about forty miles an hour to over seventy. The blast was so violent that the big ship literally blew sideways out of the fairway and before she could be made to answer her helm, she had nosed heavily onto Eddy Reef and had come to a grinding stop. She could make no defense as the wind swung her stern around and drove it aground also.

She had gone ashore under the startled eyes of the keeper of the Eddy Light, and while this gentleman was still considering what action he should take, his telephone began to ring.

"This is Featherstone, Foundation Maritime," the caller said. "Hear there's a ship ashore your way. What sort of shape's she in?"

"Now that feller must 'a had a mighty long telescope," the lightkeeper was later heard to say, "to see her all the way from Halifax! Anyway, I told him she was in a bad fix. The spray was comin' right across her, and you could hear her grindin' away like a gristmill. I told him she was done, unless they got her off darn quick."

When *Cordelia's* SOS crackled in over *Franklin's* radio as the tug lay at her berth in Halifax, Featherstone's first action had been to snatch up Lloyd's Register and the shipping list. He saw from these that this almost-new vessel was one of the most valuable prizes of the decade, and he was determined that she should be his.

No sooner had he concluded his call to the Eddy light-keeper than *Franklin* and Power, who had returned to command the *Franklin,* were ordered out. Featherstone himself was far too impatient to sail with them. Instead, he jumped into his car and set out on one of the hair-raising cross-country rides for which he later became infamous. Tom Nolan sat phlegmatically beside him as the car skittered along the winding roads at seventy and eighty miles an hour, heading for Port Mulgrave on the Canso Strait.

Power also understood the need for haste, but the gale which had stranded *Cordelia* had now become so vicious that it took *Franklin* four long hours even to clear the outer automatic buoy in Halifax fairway. When she weathered it at last and tried to lay a course for Canso, she found herself caught in a beam sea and wind that was as fierce as anything she had yet encountered. She was soon rolling so abominably that she put her bulwarks under twice in twenty minutes.

Power was a very brave man, but he was no fool. He knew that he must either heave-to or run back for shelter—and he had no intention of heaving-to five miles off a lee shore in a hurricane.

So *Franklin* blew back into the harbor and dropped her anchors just inside while her impatient skipper waited for the gale to blow itself out. By 1 A.M. of the following morning his patience was exhausted and so, taking advantage of a lull, he set out again. This time he was able to make an offing before the wind came back. With some sea room between him and the shore he was able to stick it out, but it was eighteen weary hours later before *Franklin* raised Canso Cape.

They picked Featherstone up at Mulgrave docks, quite inarticulate with frustration. He had been unable to persuade any local boat owner to take him to the wreck, and he had almost concluded that *Franklin* had gone ashore herself and that once more he was to be cheated of a prize.

It was full dark on November 12 when he prepared to board *Cordelia* from *Franklin's* motorboat. Only a fanatic, or a man driven beyond all bounds of caution, would have risked boarding her at all; for she and the reefs about her were shrouded in breaking seas. Nevertheless Featherstone and the faithful Nolan succeeded in reaching her. They found that the tanker's forepeak and deep tanks were already flooded, and she was lacerating herself upon the rocks in a manner that must have resulted in her being quickly torn apart if the gale, which had by then abated somewhat, had chosen to renew its onslaught.

Half an hour after boarding her Featherstone was ready to begin his work, but he was stopped short by *Cordelia's* master, who resolutely refused to sign the L.O.F. or any other form of contract until the Salvage Association's representative arrived on the scene to give him an opinion.

One awe-stricken observer of that moment insisted that he could no longer hear *Cordelia* grinding on the rocks, over the sound of Featherstone gnashing his teeth.

Fortunately the wind and seas continued to abate during the night, and, also fortunately, the Salvage Association man from Halifax arrived at dawn—in time to save Featherstone from bursting all his blood vessels. The newcomer did not even delay until he had boarded the ship before giving "his opinion."

"What the devil are you waiting for?" he shouted from the motorboat as he came alongside. "Another onshore gale?"

For an instant Featherstone glared at him in dumb fury, then he became the man that he believed himself to be. His plans were already made and within a quarter of an hour they were being put into effect by a salvage gang that could not have worked any faster if a bullwhip had been snarling about their ears.

Franklin steamed in dangerously close, took *Cordelia's* heavy bower anchor on her own after deck and ran it out some seven hundred feet to seaward in order to prevent the wreck from driving harder on the reef. Returning to *Cordelia*, Power put one end of his ground-tackle wire aboard of her, then ran the wire out to a point fifteen hundred feet astern, where he made it fast to a five-ton salvage anchor. The gang aboard the wreck had meanwhile laid out the purchases which would be made fast to their end of the wire and which would lead to *Cordelia's* biggest steam winch. Almost before the salvage anchor had touched bottom the wire was being rove up taut.

Tom Nolan had gone down to survey the vessel's bottom. He had a hard time of it. There was a five-knot tidal current flowing out of the Strait and it swept him about on the end of his lifeline like a rubber ball. For half an hour he bounced back and forth amongst the "sunkers" on the reef until, tiring of this nonsense, he bent down and caught a large boulder under each arm. With these for ballast he got on with his inspection.

Featherstone was in *Cordelia's* radio room. He had estimated that three thousand tons of oil would have to be removed in order to restore sufficient buoyancy to free the wreck. Having no wish to jettison this valuable cargo, he was sending out a general call in the hope that there might be an empty tanker in the vicinity which could act as a lighter. And now his luck began to change. Almost at once he received an answer from the Imperial Oil tanker *Vancolite*, to the effect that she was even then entering the Strait from the western side, bound for Halifax—in ballast. Even luckier was the presence aboard her of Imperial Oil's marine superintendent, who had the power to authorize *Vancolite* to help the salvors. After a brief radio exchange with Featherstone the superintendent agreed to let *Vancolite* assist, providing that the job entailed no risk to her. Featherstone blithely assured him that there would be no risk worth mentioning.

Vancolite arrived at the scene at 10 A.M., but after a look at the situation her master and the oil company's superintendent became markedly unenthusiastic. *Vancolite* was a big ship, and awkward to maneuver in tight places. Now she was being asked to go in over shoal waters on a lee shore until her stern was only fifty feet away from *Cordelia's*—and just fifty feet clear of the reef itself. There was still a heavy sea running, and the early forecasts were for strong easterly winds. To complicate matters further *Vancolite* would have to be held firmly in place against a five-knot tidal current. If she swung off at all towards the west, she too would go aground.

Probably no one but Featherstone could have persuaded *Vancolite's* people to risk their vessel against such odds. But, in his present mood he could probably have outargued the sea itself. Although with considerable reluctance on her people's part, *Vancolite* was finally committed.

She was far too unhandy to have been brought in stern-first under her own power, yet she had to present her stern to the casualty. The way Featherstone managed this was by having her come in dead slow ahead, and then let go her bower anchors while she was still three lengths off the wreck. When her engines stopped, the ebb current began to swing her in an eastward arc until she was broadside to *Cordelia. Franklin* then nosed in on her starboard quarter and pushed her the rest of the way around until she was again heading out to sea. With *Franklin* remaining in position to hold her up against the current, *Vancolite* then paid out chain and fell back on it until her stern was within spitting distance of *Cordelia's.*

No sooner were the two big ships within reach of one another than the unwieldy oil hoses were slung across the narrow gap. By noon oil was flowing through them from *Cordelia* into *Vancolite.*

After a three-hour struggle with the current and the undertow, Tom Nolan emerged to report that *Cordelia* had not yet suffered vital underwater damage. But she was restless in the grip of the swells, and the more she worked, the more damage she would take. Tom gave her six hours to live—if the weather got no worse. Half an hour later Featherstone was handed a meteorological report. Gale warnings were going up for an easterly blow which could be expected to reach a strength of force eight within five hours.

The salvors redoubled their efforts. Extra hoses were run out until the space between the two tankers looked like a section of an immense spider web. The ground tackle was rove up bar-tight and the wreck's own pumps were run up to maximum speed in an attempt to lower the water in the deep tank. With nothing more to do for the moment Featherstone stood on the deck forward, his hands on a stanchion, feeling the ship for signs of motion and of life.

The wind had already begun to rise before daylight passed. By 8 P.M. it was blowing force 4 and the seas were making-up out of the broad Atlantic with alarming power.

Vancolite's position was becoming very precarious, for the tide had turned and was running in, so that both wind and current were trying to set her westward onto an outlying tongue of Eddy Reef. Her one defense was *Franklin*, now lying with her bow against *Vancolite's* port quarter and with her engines throbbing at full power in the effort to hold the heavy tanker in her place.

As *Cordelia's* oil flowed out through the web of pipes the men aboard all three vessels knew that time was also running out. For *Vancolite's* master the tension was almost unendurable. The rising seas rolled in under his ship so that she lifted heavily to her cables and the oil pipes took a fearsome strain. Men waited. By 9 P.M. it had begun to blow a gale and the outermost points of Eddy Reef were breaking white in the sounding darkness.

Featherstone suddenly straightened from his position by the stanchion.

"She's lifting, boys!" he shouted. "Now give those winches hell!"

There was a hissing clatter as steam swelled in the winch cylinders and the big drums turned. The purchases strained on the ground-tackle wire until it came as taut and hard as a rod of solid steel. Slowly, almost grudgingly—as if she did not want to return to life—*Cordelia* began to grind over the boulders.

Aboard *Vancolite* there was a scene of frantic haste as the pipes were disconnected and the free ends thrown overboard. In their anxiety to get clear, *Vancolite's* officers rang for full speed ahead and, as a result, the big tanker's weigh carried her right over her own anchors before she could be stopped.

Aboard *Cordelia* the ground-tackle wire was humming ominously. But the wreck was moving. Inch by inch she ground her way across the reef until, with a final rumble deep in her laden belly, she slid free. The winch was stopped and she was held steady while her crew ran to get in her bower anchor. But they had not taken in half a fathom of chain when a voice bellowed urgently at them to leave it be. For *Vancolite*, drifting back to get clear of her own anchors, had fouled the ground-tackle wire and had severed it.

The gale might have been waiting for just such a moment, for it took instant charge of *Cordelia* and began to hustle her back onto the reef. But it reckoned without *Franklin,* who was now tied up alongside the rescued ship. Power rang for everything the engines could give him, and white water foamed up under *Franklin's* counter in a cataract of foam.

Slowly *Cordelia's* fatal swing slowed, until at last it stopped. Her crew was desperately hurrying now to bring her up to the bower anchor while *Franklin* strained to hold her off the rocks. The chain came in foot by foot, and as the tanker's bow came round her engines were started and she began to crawl away from the reef which had so nearly been her grave.

The sound and fury had been such that no one man engaged in that rescue obtained a clear idea of what was happening. Each man had acted out of intuitive knowledge. In the darkness and the storm scud they could see little and they could hear less. Yet their instincts had been good. *Cordelia* had been saved.

While Featherstone piloted her to the shelter of Inhabitants Bay, where underwater repairs could be carried out, *Franklin* went to *Vancolite's* assistance.

Vancolite had been forced to remain hanging on the edge of the reef with both anchors down, for there was every probability that the broken ground-tackle wire was still foul of her propellers. She did not dare to try to move away from the thundering proximity of the breakers until the wire was clear.

Although it was now past midnight, and the gale had reached force 7, Tom Nolan climbed into *Franklin's* motorboat and bucked his way in under *Vancolite's* stern. His helper lowered him into the black waters, where he was prepared to spend long hours nibbling away at a Gordian knot of two-inch wire with a hacksaw. But this was *his* moment for some luck. He found that the wire had broken clear of *Vancolite's* screw and that it had done no serious damage to the blades.

Vancolite immediately hauled her anchors and, with *Franklin* at her side, steamed thankfully away from that hungry shore to take refuge with her sister in Inhabitants Bay until the blow was over.

The following day Nolan patched the worst holes in *Cordelia's* bottom, and the Salvage Association man issued a certificate of seaworthiness, so that she was free to continue to Quebec and to dry-dock. She sailed that afternoon, having recovered her oil from *Vancolite* before she left.

The entire operation had taken less than thirty-six hours, and in that short period a ship and cargo valued at one million, one hundred and ten thousand dollars had been saved from certain destruction. Featherstone had good reason for an unwonted joviality as *Franklin* steamed homeward to Halifax that night.

11 ⬦ THE BELGIAN SISTERS: ONE

As 1934 APPROACHED ITS END, the north Atlantic set the stage for an epic combat. It was to be an epic in two parts; and it concerned two sisters of the Belgian merchant fleet.

The first of the sisters was the *Emile Francqui*. She was one of a class of vessels built in the early thirties for the Belgian Maritime Company. They were big, good-looking ships, of six thousand tons, intended for the general carrying trade; but each had accommodations for twelve passengers as well.

The weather encountered by the *Emile Francqui* in the last days of December while she was bound across the Western Ocean for New York was atrociously bad. One particular gale which came to its full stature on December 22 sank seven trawlers and fishing schooners, and three of these went down with all hands. This same gale caught the *Francqui* three hundred and fifty miles south-east of Halifax, and when it had finished with her the big freighter was helpless in the troughs of a mounting sea with her rudder gone.

She did not transmit a general SOS, for her master knew that a sister ship, the *Henri Jaspar*, was somewhere near at hand eastward bound for Antwerp. *Francqui* was able to contact the *Jaspar*, who immediately steamed to her assistance; but the interchange between the two vessels was overheard by Lindsay McManus, *Franklin's* radio operator, who frequently stood listening watches, alert for just such messages, even when the tug was at her berth in Halifax.

McMannus passed the information on to Featherstone, who acted on it with his usual aggressiveness. He radioed:

POWERFUL OCEAN TUG FOUNDATION FRANKLIN OFFERS IMMEDIATE ASSISTANCE PLEASE ADVISE OF YOUR CONDITION

Francqui's reply was not encouraging.

LOST RUDDER PROCEEDING HALIFAX ASSISTANCE STEAMER HENRI JASPAR STEERING ASTERN STOP NO OTHER ASSISTANCE NEEDED

Another man might well have let the matter drop. Not Featherstone. Ten minutes on the telephone told him that *Francqui* was lightly laden and that she would therefore be almost unmanageable if a new gale sprang up. His own instincts told him that such a gale was almost certain at this season and that when it came, *Francqui* would need professional assistance. He ordered McManus to remain on listening watch and to relay to him every message which passed between the two big freighters far at sea.

McManus was kept busy. During the night of February 24 a succession of messages passed between the masters of the ships, most of them relating to the extreme difficulty they were having in keeping the connecting line intact. Despite their best efforts to prevent it, the line parted several times— and this in moderate weather.

Featherstone drew his own conclusions. At dawn he boarded *Franklin* and she put to sea. She was barely clear of the harbor when Featherstone dispatched a second signal:

FOUNDATION FRANKLIN WILL MEET YOU TOMORROW MORNING AND ASSIST YOU INTO HARBOR

Nor was he the least bit disconcerted by the reply:

WILL REQUIRE NO REPEAT NO TOWING BEFORE ANCHORING CHEBUCTO HEAD

Captain Degryse of the *Francqui* sounded very certain of himself, and well he might, for the weather on that day was positively tranquil. The gale had died out completely on the twenty-fifth and by the time *Franklin* came in sight of the casualty early the next morning, the sea was almost calm. Only the deep and ever-present ocean swell testified to the transience of this moment of peace.

When Featherstone came alongside the *Francqui* at 9 A.M., he found her making fair progress toward Halifax under her own power, with the *Henri Jaspar* on a line astern acting as a rudder. Nothing daunted by this brave sight, Featherstone signaled to Degryse:

SUGGEST YOU LET FRANKLIN TAKE HOLD OF YOU BEFORE MAKING COASTLINE STOP WITHOUT PREJUDICE SALVAGE CLAIMS OF HENRI JASPAR

It was a well-phrased signal, and a wise one; but Degryse, poor innocent, believing himself in no more danger from the sea, chose to ignore it.

Franklin now took station abeam of the casualty and jogged amiably along without further remark until noon, when McManus received the weather report from Chebucto Radio. It was what Featherstone had anticipated:

ALL SHIPS SOUTHEAST TO SOUTHWEST WINDS INCREASING TO GALES WITH SNOW TONIGHT TURNING TO SLEET TOMORROW

McManus was instructed to find out if Degryse had also heard the report. When the Belgian admitted that he had not, it was politely relayed to him, together with a supplementary report which was received half an hour later:

STORM SIGNAL NUMBER THREE INDICATING A HEAVY GALE FROM EASTERLY BEGINNING THIS EVENING ALL SHIPS SHOULD TAKE PRECAUTIONS

Degryse declined to comment on either of these messages, other than to thank McManus; so Featherstone needled him.

IN VIEW OF HEAVY GALE WARNINGS SUGGEST YOU DO UTMOST AND INCREASE YOUR SPEED OR LET US CONNECT UP BEFORE DARK

Again the message was acutely phrased. *Francqui* obviously did not dare increase her speed for that would endanger the line to *Jaspar*. The alternative, then, was to take *Franklin's* wire at once.

This signal had some effect. It precipitated a flurry of messages between *Francqui* and *Jaspar*, the gist of which was that *Jaspar* was unwilling to share the salvage with the tug and saw no reason why she should. Degryse inclined to the same opinion, but he was nevertheless becoming slightly uneasy about the prospects if he *should* be caught close to the coast by an onshore gale. He sent Featherstone a casual request for information as to how *Franklin* would connect, supposing that it should be necessary.

Featherstone's reply was terse:

WILL SHOW YOU HOW

He had no further time to waste, for he was well aware that the need to get a wire on *Francqui* was no longer simply a matter of obtaining a salvage job—it was fast becoming a matter directly affecting the chances of survival of the crippled ship. He knew that if the gale struck *Francqui* as she approached the coast and if, as was quite possible, *Franklin* was then unable to get a line aboard her due to wind and darkness, the rudderless freighter would be driven onto the rocks despite the best the *Jaspar* could do to hold her off. The probable outcome of further delay was all too obvious to Featherstone; but Degryse, who did not know the coast, remained irresolute. Eventually, and it was then 3:30 P.M., he tried to compromise with his unease by offering to take *Franklin's* wire when they got abeam of Sambro Lightship, from which point the *Jaspar* would not be able to assist in any case. Featherstone replied:

IF GALE BREAKS YOU WILL NOT WEATHER SAMBRO WITH-OUT MORE HELP FOR YOUR OWN SAFETY TAKE OUR WIRE NOW

Still Degryse shied away from the decision. It was not until the wind abruptly began to freshen out of the east at 4:30 P.M. that he gave in and radioed:

ACCEPT LLOYDS FORM NO CURE NO PAY COME ALONG-SIDE GIVE US YOUR TOWLINE

Franklin was at his side almost before the message could be acknowledged. Sambro was then only twelve miles off, and the sky was already black and angry in the east. The ships were well to the south of the harbor fairway and it was clear that even with the best of luck they would have difficulty weathering the Sambro ledges before they could turn into sheltered waters. It was going to be a near thing.

The wire was put across to *Francqui* in record time. *Franklin* immediately began to work up speed and at 4:50 P.M. the tow was under weigh with *Franklin* ahead and *Jaspar* still clinging to the line astern. *Jaspar* did not hold on long. As the quick seas began to lurch in from the east the strain on her manila grew, and at 5:30 her line parted. She made no attempt to replace it. It would have been waste effort anyway, for that morning, in a flat calm, it had taken her three hours to float a line down to the *Francqui* by means of buoys. In any event *Jaspar* was now most anxious on her own account to claw away from that waiting coast. With a long farewell blast on her whistle she turned and headed out to sea.

Jaspar's haste was pardonable. By 6 P.M. the easterly wind had become a full gale, blowing force 8, and the seas were becoming particularly sharp and ugly, for the vessels were now well in over the shallow coastal banks. Driving rain and the onset of darkness obscured the fury of the grey waters and from *Franklin's* bridge only occasional blurred glimpses could be caught of *Francqui*, who was wallowing almost broadside-to at the end of the tow wire. *Franklin's* course was roughly northward, in an effort to compensate for the eastward drift of the big freighter toward the reefs, which were then less than five miles distant, and straight to leeward.

By 8 P.M., in an impenetrable darkness, the gale was howling at seventy miles an hour full upon the shore, and the men in *Franklin's* pilot-house could almost feel the unseen presence of the ill-omened Sisters Reef close on the port beam. With her great freeboard acting as a sail, *Francqui* was now being blown off nearly at right angles to *Franklin's* course, and the tug had to alter, and keep on altering, until her head was pointing almost out to sea again, in an effort to hold the Belgian clear of the thundering rocks.

Franklin was now laboring and straining terribly. The beam seas were breaking clean across her deck and over the boat-deck too. Occasionally a giant in the pack rose up so high above her that it broke down her funnels and filled the stokehold with stinking steam. Nevertheless she was holding her own—and a little more. Yard by yard she was edging the casualty past the surging breakers of the Sisters.

The thoughts of the people aboard the tug were concentrated on the towing wire. It was a new one of inch and three-quarter steel and strong enough for almost any task, but it was being fearfully abused. The salvors knew that there was the gravest danger it would begin to chafe at *Francqui's* bows unless a perpetual watch was kept upon it, and unless it was kept smothered in grease. They knew that if a single strand let go, the wire would part; and if that happened *Francqui* would be doomed and so, in all likelihood, would everyone aboard her.

Featherstone could evaluate every risk he could foresee. He had complete faith in his own ship and in her gear. But he could not watch that wire where it rose out of the seas to grip the *Francqui's* bitts.

At 9:20 he radioed Degryse:

WATCH OUR TOWLINE CLOSE FOR CHAFING AT YOUR BOW

Degryse did not reply to this directly, instead he radioed:

WE REQUIRE MORE ASSISTANCE ARE THERE MORE SALVAGE BOATS CLOSE BY

Featherstone smelled the scent of incipient panic in those words. He knew that it was vital to calm Degryse, so he dispatched a soothing, if not entirely accurate message in return:

WE ARE SLOWLY WORKING YOU TO WINDWARD OF CHEBUCTO HEAD AND TRYING TO AVOID TOO GREAT STRAIN ON WIRE STOP NO SALVAGE TUGS EXCEPT GOVERNMENT STEAMERS BUT WILL ASK THEIR ASSISTANCE

That single word, except, contained the subterfuge, for Featherstone was well aware that only one ship in Halifax, the *Lady Laurier,* could hope to live at all on such a night; and that her help, at best, must be limited to the attempt at saving life if *Franklin* sank or if, as a last resort, *Francqui's* people tried to abandon their ship before she struck.

Featherstone now sent off a signal to R. J. Nelson, manager of Halifax Shipyard, who was acting as *Franklin's* shore agent. Once again the message was most carefully worded, for Degryse would undoubtedly intercept it. It read:

HEAVY SOUTHEAST GALES REQUEST IMMEDIATE ASSIST-ANCE GOVERNMENT STEAMER STAND BY WE ARE STRAIN-ING TOWLINE AND PUNISHING FRANKLIN OFF CHEBUCTO HEAD JASPAR BROKE LINE AND DEPARTED SEAWARD

Nelson, who had been Featherstone's employer in salvage work for almost twenty years, was quick to read between the lines. He knew that the admission by Featherstone that his ship was being "punished" was tantamount to the admission by another man that she was in danger of going down. He moved swiftly. Within five minutes he had the government agent on the telephone with an urgent request that the *Lady Laurier* put out to sea at once.

The government man replied, with all due apologies, that he had not the authority to send the *Lady Laurier* to sea, and that he would require specific instructions from Ottawa to do so.

Nelson wasted no more time on this bureaucratic nonsense. He immediately telephoned the Belgian Consul at Halifax, and that dignitary called the Department of External Affairs in Ottawa. Half an hour later Nelson was informed that the *Lady Laurier* was getting up steam and would be ready to sail in two hours time.

That was something accomplished, but not enough. Nelson got in touch with the local owners of the two big new harbor tugs, the *Banscot* and *Banshee*, and hired them. The tugs put out at once, but neither of them got beyond the harbor mouth. Their masters put back into shelter claiming, with justification, that it would have been suicide to attempt to go "outside."

Featherstone had not expected any aid to reach him and he had planned accordingly. Knowing that the tow wire might let go at any moment (and that it could not, in any circumstances, remain intact much longer), he also knew that he would only hasten this inevitable moment if he continued to try and haul the *Francqui* off the shore. The only chance, as Featherstone saw it, was to edge the crippled vessel in *toward* the coast so that, by easing the strain on the wire, and with the assistance of the gale, he might hope to get *Franqui* over good holding grounds before the wire parted. There was only one such patch of mud and clay bottom on that entire stretch of coast, and it lay somewhere ahead and close inshore. The rest was rock, upon which no anchor would have held in such a storm.

It was a calculated risk, but such a one as few men would have cared to take. By 10 P.M. the wind was gusting eighty miles an hour and *Franklin* was being continually swept from end to end. The rain had changed to a driven, bitter snow that mixed with the salt spray and froze over the deck and bridge. The shore remained invisible, but it was close . . . so close that Degryse could hear Bell Rock and Duncan Reef breaking close beneath his lee.

That fearsome sound drove him to transmit a frantic message begging Featherstone to haul him out to sea.

Featherstone ignored the message.

Then, at 10:30, Degryse could stand the tension no longer. His radio began to crackle out a general SOS.

STEAMER EMILE FRANCQUI TO ALL SHIPS . . . EMILE FRANCQUI TO ALL SHIPS . . . AM TWO MILES SOUTHEAST CHEBUCTO HEAD NEED IMMEDIATE ASSISTANCE AM DRIFTING ONTO SHORE. . . .

Featherstone listened to that call, but he gave no sign that it disturbed him, and he held *Franklin* to her course. He was utterly preoccupied with the problem of locating a patch of mud hidden under fifteen fathoms of rolling water, on a winter night when nothing could be seen of the world about him except salt spray and squalls of snow.

At 10:45 he turned his eyes from the inscrutable sea and glanced quickly at the chart; then he scribbled a message for the *Franqui* and a deck-hand braved the seas sweeping over the boat-deck to get it to McManus in his little radio shack.

MASTER EMILE FRANCQUI WE ARE PULLING HARD AND MAKING PROGRESS BUT IF WIRE PARTS DROP BOTH AN-CHORS AND STEAM UP TO THEM YOU ARE NOW OVER GOOD HOLDING GROUND

Featherstone's confidence was not shared by anyone aboard the *Franklin*—and certainly not by Degryse. As one of *Franklin's* officers remembered it:

"If Featherstone knew where we was at just then, he was the only man in the whole damn world who did—and maybe they would have had to guess in Heaven, too!"

Ten minutes after that message was dispatched *Franklin* gave a sudden sickening leap as she breasted a huge sea. Without being told, every soul aboard knew that the wire had gone.

Although he must have believed his ship was doomed, Degryse nevertheless obeyed instructions. He let go both anchors with a run and then, with his engines at half-ahead, steamed up to them. At the same time he dispatched a pathetic signal to Featherstone:

ARE YOU LEAVING ME

The reply came back instantly:

WE ARE STAYING WITH YOU NO MATTER WHAT AND WILL GET A NEW LINE ON YOU WHEN THE TIME IS RIGHT

Featherstone's decision to remain upon the scene seemed suicidal to some of his officers. One of them said as much, but he was silenced by half a dozen words which left him dumb.

Franklin was still afloat. She would remain that way. This —Featherstone. And more than this, she would do the impossible if need be and get a line on *Franqui* if that vessel began to drag her anchors. If *Francqui* held, then *Franklin* would stand by and wait for dawn and less desperate weather, to reconnect.

INFORM AT ONCE IF YOU BEGIN TO DRAG, radioed Feather-stone, and then hove the *Franklin* to.

And now, in a frightful paroxysm, the gale rose to its climax. On shore the weather station clocked the gusts at up to one hundred miles an hour, and at sea the wind had be-come an element as tangible as the grey waters of the Atlantic. It bore down upon the two ships and bludgeoned them unmercifully and without respite until, at 11:30 P.M., its strength began to fail. That was the longest interval in time that most of *Franklin's* men had ever lived through—

what it must have been to the passengers and crew of the
Emile Francqui can be imagined only dimly.

As the wind began to falter Featherstone again asked
Francqui how she was, and the reply came back:

WE ARE HOLDING FIRM

The crisis was over. Chebucto Radio came on the air to
inform Featherstone that the heavy gale warning had now
been changed to strong gales from the south-west—offshore.
The wind was dropping fast before the change, as the eye of
the storm passed overhead. Featherstone radioed Degryse:

YOU ARE SAFE NOW WE ARE READYING ANOTHER WIRE
BUT STILL SHIPPING SEAS FORE AND AFT WILL GET LINE
TO YOU AS SOON AS POSSIBLE

While his men were laboring in the alleyways to lay out
a new wire, Featherstone ordered *Franklin* to be brought
around out of the wind so she could run down toward the
Francqui. The helmsman watched his chance, but as he spun
the wheel hard-over, an unsuspected giant loomed out of the
darkness and broke full on *Franklin's* starboard side, almost
burying her beneath it. Gamely the little ship turned and came
up to it—but slowly, slowly. And at that crucial instant the
steering-chain, stretched by the abuse of the long struggle,
slipped free of the rudder quadrant.

Featherstone himself leaped from the bridge to the foredeck and fought his way hand over hand along the weather
rail to reach the anchor windlass. He knocked off the brake
and the chain roared out, sending a stream of sparks into
the wind. There was a dreadful waiting minute. and then the
anchor caught, dragged a few hundred feet and caught again
—*Franklin's* head came up out of the trough in answer, and
she lay into wind and sea once more.

The *Lady Laurier* arrived soon afterwards, having been
unable to make any headway until the wind began to drop.
Now, at Featherstone's request, she hove-to nearby while the
salvage men endeavored to restore their vessel's helm.

Tom Nolan and his diving attendant, Alan Macdonald, volunteered to go aft and try to replace the chain while Featherstone and a fireman clung to the turnbuckles on either side
amidships, ready to slacken and then tighten them again as
was required.

Tom and his companion crawled across the after deck
like a pair of seals on a wave-washed rock, for the deck
space had become a part of the North Atlantic. When they
reached the grating in the stern they found it to be so thickly
coated in ice that there was only room for one man to
crawl under it. Following on the change in wind, the tem-

perature had plummeted far below freezing. Spray froze on the two men's faces until they were masked in ice.

Alan crawled under the grating while Tom braced himself and clung to his companion's legs. Inside the narrow space Alan struggled with his bare hands to get the heavy chain back where it belonged. The quadrant, with the full weight of the rudder behind it, swung murderously back and forth within inches of his head. For half an hour he lay there waiting his moment, until at last he managed to lever the chain back into place. A kick of Macdonald's foot told Nolan that the job was done, and a hoarse Newfoundland voice broke through the sound of wind and seas.

"Tighten them goddamn bottles—she's back on!"

At 2 A.M. on December 27 *Franklin* hauled up her anchor and once more was under weigh.

Despite querulous complaints from the *Lady Laurier,* who was not enjoying the buffeting of the devilish cross-sea which had risen with the new southwesterly gale, Featherstone was in no hurry now. *Francqui* was no longer in any danger, and he felt it was better to wait until the easterly seas had fallen off a little. So wait he did, through a succession of blinding snow squalls, until the daylight came and the westerly began to smooth the seas. Only then did *Franklin* put her wire aboard the casualty and, with the *Lady Laurier* astern to steer, she proceeded for Halifax.

So they came up the harbor that morning: three ice-encrusted vessels hard-done-by at the hands of man's oldest and most implacable adversary. And the little ship who led them blew her whistle as she came, so that the sound of it rolled back from the great citadel in the city's heart to tell the people of that port of victory.

12 🦋 THE BELGIAN SISTERS: TWO

IN JANUARY OF 1935 *Franklin* had just refloated a small freighter from an island off Newfoundland when she was ordered back to Halifax, where the large and valuable passenger-freighter *Silveryew* had driven onto Mars Rock.

Franklin was preceded to the scene by Chadwick, who had come down posthaste from Montreal hoping to obtain an L.O.F. contract in *Franklin's* absence and hold it for her arrival; but he was a few hours too late. The Salvage Association representative had already advised *Silveryew's* master to sign a contract with a local tug-boat company.

Chadwick's appearance (he was accompanied by Irwin Power) was not welcomed. He and Power boarded the stricken ship to find themselves being pointedly ignored.

Phlegmatically they adjourned to the dining saloon, where they were treated to a seven-course dinner, complete with wines, by a dejected steward, who explained sadly:

"The passengers have all gone ashore and the officers are all up on the bridge figuring how to get us off. Sandwiches was all they wanted—and me with the best dinner of the voyage and not a soul to eat it. Please, gentlemen, *do* have a little more."

He had not been completely deserted, however. One passenger had remained on the vessel. She was an elderly lady completing a world cruise. When the lifeboats were launched she had resolutely refused to enter them. She explained matter-of-factly that she would probably never again have the chance to be shipwrecked, and she had no intention of allowing herself to be deprived of that experience.

By the time *Franklin* arrived, after bulling her way through a pea-soup fog at full speed all the way from Newfoundland, the would-be salvors who had signed the L.O.F. had begun to realize that they had bitten off more than they could chew.

Featherstone now boarded the ship and began making one of his apparently perfunctory examinations. While he was about it, the rival salvors approached Chadwick and, with a lordly condescension that fooled no one, announced that they were prepared to hire some of *Franklin's* salvage gear. Apologetically Chadwick explained that he really could not risk his valuable equipment in the hands of amateurs. However, he added, *if* the rival salvors were prepared to include Foundation Maritime in the L.O.F. contract on the basis of equal pay for equal work, then something *might* be arranged.

The salvage representative, who was only concerned with freeing the ship before an onshore wind destroyed her, swung his weight behind Foundation Maritime and the opposition salvors were reluctantly forced to accept Chadwick's terms.

As for the ship—Featherstone took her off on the next high tide by pumping her forward tanks and then juggling water ballast in her other tanks while *Franklin* towed. He made it look so easy that his rivals probably felt rather sick. In any event they never again attempted to engage in salvage in competition with Foundation Maritime.

After the *Silveryew* there was a month of inactivity culminating in the second episode in the affair of the Belgian sisters.

It began on March 25 when the Canadian trawler *Kerlew*, homeward bound from the Grand Banks, encountered a small and sorry-looking tramp steamer wallowing in the swells several hundred miles from land and flying international distress signals.

Kerlew altered course to investigate. When she had closed to megaphone range she learned that the distressed ship was the *Longbird*, out of Bermuda, bound for New York and twelve days overdue (as well as being more than two hundred miles off course) as a result of leaking boiler tubes which had left her all but helpless in the grip of a series of spring gales.

Kerlew was unable to tow the casualty, but she radioed an SOS for *Longbird*, whose own radio was out of action. The message was picked up by the Department of Transport stations ashore and was relayed directly to the Royal Canadian Mounted Police Headquarters in Halifax. There is some mystery as to why Foundation Maritime—the legitimate commercial salvors on the coast—were not also notified. At any rate the R.C.M.P. promptly dispatched their police-cutter *Preventer*, with orders to take *Longbird* in tow.

If anyone had hoped to keep Foundation in the dark the hope was a hollow one. Chadwick had always had a penchant for cloak-and-dagger work, and early in Foundation Martime's history he had laid the groundwork for a system of unofficial "agents" who were paid to report all marine casualties to his headquarters. Combined with this he had also invented a complicated company code whose use was mandatory during salvage operations.

Preventer had hardly cast off her lines before Featherstone not only knew of her departure, but also knew where she was bound and why. He promptly telephoned *Longbird's* agents in New York, told them that their vessel was in distress, and offered to assist. He made no mention of *Preventer*, but then of course he did not know, officially, that she had sailed. *Longbird's* agents were duly grateful for the information about their missing ship and they authorized *Franklin* to go and get her under the L.O.F.

Like most professional salvors Featherstone regarded government vessels, which engaged in rescue work as a sort of part-time hobby, with intense dislike. Consequently he had few scruples when it came to protecting his company's interests from such "unfair" competition.

Under command of Captain Power *Franklin* sailed three hours behind *Preventer*. Once clear of the harbor, Power dispatched an innocuous-sounding message to the police vessel:

UNDERSTAND YOU ARE LOOKING FOR LONGBIRD PLEASE ADVISE AREA YOU INTEND TO SEARCH AND IF YOU LOCATE HER

To which *Preventer* replied suspiciously:

SEARCHING SOUTH OF GIVEN LOCATION WHAT ARE YOUR
INTENTIONS

Power answered innocently;

ENDEAVORING TO LOCATE LONGBIRD PROVISION HIM AND
GIVE ASSISTANCE IF REQUIRED

Preventer made no reply to this, but no reply was needed. During the first transmission from the R.C.M.P. vessel, McManus had been operating his direction finder. Power now knew which way to go.

Both ships had then been at sea for some time and the wind, which had been light earlier in the day, was making up into a moderate westerly gale. *Preventer* was easing up as the seas grew heavier; but *Franklin* was driving so hard that she was taking water fore and aft. If it was possible, Power intended to reach the *Longbird* first.

His hopes were dashed at 5 P.M. when McManus intercepted a message from *Preventer* to her base in Halifax.

HAVE LOCATED LONGBIRD NOW IN TOW

It was a brief transmission, but not brief enough to elude McManus's vigilance on the DF set. He passed a bearing to Power, and *Franklin* altered to an interception course.

Power knew that once the connection had been made, *Longbird* would hang on to *Preventer* like grim death, for her master would have the choice of a free tow to port behind the cutter or an expensive tow behind *Franklin*. Therefore, in order to get the job, Power had to separate the two vessels. There was one circumstance that favored him: *Longbird* was virtually deaf without her radio, and this meant that *Preventer* was the key. Somehow she had to be persuaded to relinquish her prize.

Power opened his campaign:

GOOD WORK PREVENTER PLEASE ADVISE YOUR POSI-
TION COURSE AND SPEED WILL MEET YOU AND TAKE OVER
TOW

Preventer refused to bite. Her reply was immediate and unfriendly.

MY INSTRUCTIONS ARE TO TOW LONGBIRD IN TO HALIFAX

With the failure of his opening play, Power prepared to unlimber heavier artillery. Using the company code he radioed Featherstone a full report of the situation, suggesting that he take the matter up on a higher level.

Featherstone entered the fray with gusto. He telephoned R.C.M.P. Headquarters staff and, having first congratulated

them on *Preventer's* work, he asked if they were aware that
they were interfering with a commercial contract which had
been made between Foundation Maritime and *Longbird's*
agents. This was a bombshell. Interference with free commercial enterprise can cause a government no end of embar-
rassment, even when it is not an election year.

Featherstone rang off, and gave the bomb time to explode
before he called again. "I've just heard from Captain Power,"
he explained, "that *Preventer* refuses to relinquish the tow
except under direct orders from your office. Perhaps you
could straighten this little matter out for us?"

It was 8 P.M. when Power came in sight of *Longbird*.
At almost the same instant McManus reported to him that the
cutter had received instructions from Halifax to hand over
the tow.

Preventer's master took the reverse with good grace. He
prepared to release *Longbird*, but it was immediately apparent
that *Longbird* had no intention of being released. Her skipper
had observed *Franklin's* arrival on the scene with indignation
and dismay. To *Preventer's* repeated request that he cast off
the cutter's line, he turned a blind eye and a deaf ear. But
to *Franklin* he signaled, using his lamp:

I DO NOT WANT ANY TUG I AM IN GOOD SHAPE AND CAN
GET TO PORT ON MY OWN IF NECESSARY GO AWAY

Shortly thereafter *Preventer's* master dispatched a somewhat plaintive message to Power:

HE WONT LET GO AND ITS MY LINE AND WORTH
FIVE HUNDRED DOLLARS WHAT DO YOU THINK WE SHOULD
DO

Power was ready for that one. In fact he had been de-
bating whether or not to make a suggestion before he was
asked for it. Now he signaled:

FOUNDATION MARITIME WILL MAKE GOOD ALL GEAR
LOST OR DAMAGED IN CONNECTION WITH THIS JOB

The official report does not detail the events that followed this transmission. It merely records that at 9:40 P.M.
Preventer's line mysteriously carried away at her stern, and
that she then swung off to starboard and took station half
a mile away.

Power was close in under *Longbird's* quarter when the
line "carried away" and he had his searchlight trained on
Longbird's stern, for he had noted that this unhappy ship was
turning over her propeller as if to demonstrate that she
really *was* able to look after herself. Power was still watching closely when *Longbird* overran the broken Manila
rope and wound it so firmly around her screw that it looked

like a gigantic piece of knitting. The screw stopped dead. Power turned to his mate, John Pynn.

"Poor chap," he said sympathetically. "He's gone and got his propeller all fouled up."

Franklin now came in close and Power yelled: "Stand by to catch our heaving line!" Which brought a scurrilous reply, the gist of which was that *Longbird* did not need or want a tow and in fact wanted nothing from *Franklin* except some food. Come dawn, said *Longbird's* master, he would start up his engine and run for Halifax.

Power understood. *Longbird's* master knew that his propeller was inextricably fouled (though he did *not* know that Power knew it too). He believed that if he could persuade Power to give up and go away, he could then signal to *Preventer,* who was still in visual range, give the excuse that *Franklin* had abandoned *Longbird* and ask the cutter for another tow.

Power remained impeccably polite, as was his habit. Despite the high seas he launched a dory and sent a load of food over to the casualty—and then he settled down to wait.

He was a patient man.

At 7 A.M. the following day *Longbird's* master knew that he was beaten. With an ill grace he took *Franklin's* wire at last, but he was determined to make things as difficult for Power as possible. Despite the fact that the L.O.F. contract called for "delivery to the nearest safe port," he insisted that he be towed all the way to New York.

Power was willing to humor him. "All right," he cried through his megaphone, "New York it is."

Franklin eased forward to take the strain, and then she swung slowly on course for Ambrose Lightship, five hundred miles away. Power sighed contentedly and went below to his cabin for a little rest.

Twenty minutes later he was disturbed by McManus, bearing an electrifying message which he had just intercepted.

It was an SOS from the steamer *Jean Jadot,* reporting herself disabled six hundred miles east of Halifax and asking urgently for aid.

"I could have kicked myself good and proper," says Power as he recalls that moment. "There I'd been working for a day and a night to get myself fast to a great, useless lump of iron, and now I was tight to her and couldn't get away. I knew the *Jadot.* She was a sister to the *Emile Francqui,* and about as valuable a merchant ship as you could find on the Atlantic in those years.

"I just had to get shed of the *Longbird* somehow. I almost wished she'd sink. Then I remembered that she still had no radio, and I got a kind of faint idea what to do. I had

McManus call direct to her owners in New York. I told them I had their ship in tow for New York at the master's orders, but that with the head-sea and all, it was going to cost them three times as much as to take her into Halifax. I asked them if they concurred in the master's choice of port. Well, sir, they came booming back. 'Take her to Halifax,' they said, 'and be damned to what the master says.' "

Power had not underestimated the economical ways of a ship's owner.

When *Longbird's* captain noticed the sudden change of course he almost went berserk. Blowing his steam whistle and howling through his megaphone, he demanded to know what in the name of all the furies was going on. Power waited for the din to die down, then politely explained that they were proceeding to Halifax on the owners' orders.

And that was that.

With less than a hundred miles to go before he could be rid of *Longbird,* Power dispatched a message to the *Jean Jadot.*

POWERFUL OCEAN TUG FOUNDATION FRANKLIN SAILING
TO YOUR ASSISTANCE

It was a little premature, but Power was never a man to let the grass, or the seaweed either, grow underneath his feet.

The *Jean Jadot* had put out from Antwerp on March 16, bound for New York with a cargo of general merchandise valued at a million and a half dollars. Her master, Captain Sadi Gonthier, was expecting a hard passage, for March is always a bad month on the North Atlantic. Accordingly, he had prepared for heavy weather and his vessel was as sea-worthy as good seamen could make her. Gonthier was not particularly disturbed when he met head winds and heavy seas almost as soon as Bishop's Rock and Europe lay astern. He had only one worry and that concerned his vessel's rudder, for as *Emile Francqui* had shown a few months earlier and as he had already discovered for himself, the design of the rudder in all five of the sisters was defective. Gonthier took no chances; he ordered relieving tackle rigged to the steering gear on the first day out in order to ease the strain on it.

For the next eight days *Jean Jadot* fought the age-old battle of a merchantman against the sea. The weather was wild throughout that time and the ship labored heavily, on some days making no more than a hundred miles of westing. She met almost incessant head gales and a sea that at times almost stopped her in her tracks. Nevertheless she held doggedly to her course, and in the afternoon of March 25 the skies cleared long enough for Gonthier to get a sight and to confirm his position as forty-three degrees north, fifty-two degrees west—about three hundred miles southeast of Newfoundland. During that afternoon the wind began to abate and the seas dropped a little. *Jadot* worked her speed up to six knots, and her people began to relax from the long tension.

Their relief was premature. By 11 P.M. the sou'west wind had again risen to gale force, and at midnight of March 25 the *Jadot* suddenly refused to answer her helm and began to steam in a great arc to port.

Gonthier guessed what had happened, but all the same the bosun was lowered over the stern on the end of a long ladder. When he climbed up again—half drowned—it was to report that the sole piece appeared to have broken off and that the rudder itself was jammed immovably to port.

So the *Jadot* was crippled even as her sister had been crippled in these same waters in December of the previous year; but this time there was no assistance near at hand. At 4 A.M. on March 26 Gonthier sent off a general SOS.

Two ships replied. One was the *Audania,* a freighter outbound for Southampton and several hundred miles away. The other was the United States Coast Guard cutter *Mendota,* on ice patrol a hundred miles to the northward. *Mendota* radioed:

COMING TO YOUR ASSISTANCE WILL REACH YOUR POSITION LATE THIS AFTERNOON IF NOT HELD UP BY WEATHER

Mendota was as good as her word and at 3 P.M. she came over the horizon and bore down on the crippled freighter. *Mendota's* master was dismayed to see how large the *Jean Jadot* was, for the little Coast Guard ship was not designed for towing. Furthermore, *Mendota* had been on patrol for several days and she had none too much fuel oil left.

Nevertheless she was prepared to do what she could. In order to conserve fuel *Mendota's* master suggested that he put a line on *Jadot's* stern and act as a floating rudder, while *Jadot* used her own engines to drive her towards Halifax, which was the nearest port.

The attempt was made, but it proved futile. The jammed rudder caused the *Jadot* to carry such a heavy port helm that *Mendota* could not hold her on her course. At midnight the attempt was abandoned and *Mendota* cast off, circled *Jadot,* and put a towline on the cripple's bow. Now it became a straight contest of strength, with *Mendota* struggling to pull *Jadot* along the course for Halifax against the resistance of the jammed rudder and against a mounting headwind and a massive head sea.

Power had dispatched his message to the *Jadot* before he knew that *Mendota* was already at the scene. A code message from Featherstone informed him that they had been forestalled, but Featherstone also made it clear that he was not much worried about the eventual results. He did not think *Mendota* could complete the job, and he was ready to confirm Power's offer as soon as something was heard from Gonthier.

However, Gonthier was quite content with his free tow and so he ignored Power's message for a full day, during which time *Franklin* steamed into Halifax, cast off the *Longbird* as if she had been a leper, and hurried back to sea again. She was fifty miles off shore when Gonthier finally radioed:

AM IN GOOD HANDS SUGGEST YOU MAKE OFFER TO TOW ME FROM HALIFAX TO NEW YORK ON DAILY RATE OF HIRE.

If he had thought to discourage Fountain Maritime with this, he was mistaken. Featherstone immediately replied:

THANK YOU FRANKLIN ALREADY EN ROUTE TO BRING YOU IN WILL ALSO OFFER TOW NEW YORK

To which Gonthier, realizing that he was faced with a tenacious type, responded abruptly:

I DO NOT ASK YOU TO COME OUT AND I ACCEPT NO OBLIGATION

This merely elicited the suave response:

WE ALWAYS ENDEAVOR TO ASSIST SHIPPING WILL BE ON HAND TO RENDER ASSISTANCE IF REQUIRED

It is possible that Featherstone's messages were not directed entirely to Gonthier's ears, for he well knew that *Mendota* would also be receiving them. Foundation's salvage master was a man of cunning. He was not at all surprised when, an hour after the dispatch of this final message from Halifax, *Mendota* contacted Gonthier to say:

MY FUEL SUPPLY TOO LOW TO GET YOU IN STOP MAKE ARRANGEMENTS FOR TUG TO TAKE YOU IN TOW AS SOON AS POSSIBLE

Now, unlike *Longbird's* master, Gonthier knew how to accept the inevitable. At 1 A.M. on March 28 he radioed *Franklin:*

NOON GMT 400 MILES FROM HALIFAX STOP MENDOTA FUEL LOW WILL YOU AGREE LLOYDS OPEN FORM TOW US HALIFAX SAFE ANCHORAGE

In Halifax Featherstone grinned cheerfully, while aboard

Foundation Franklin Captain Power ordered the mate to get the towing gear laid out on the after deck.

It was a fine day when *Franklin* came alongside the *Jean Jadot*. The wind was light, the sky was clear, and only the lifting seas reminded men that this was the ocean of great gales.

Power put his little ship in so close alongside the freighter that John Pynn was able to throw a heaving line onto the *Jadot's* forecastle. The line was followed by a bridle composed of two two-inch wires, each a hundred and fifty feet in length, that came together at a shackle which was connected to *Franklin's* towing wire some distance off the *Jadot's* bow. Gonthier and Powers, with memories of the *Emile Francqui* incident fresh in both their minds, were anxious that the *Jadot* keep her anchor cables free—in case.

At midnight on March 28, some three hundred and fifty miles east-sou'east of Halifax, the tow began. After saluting the two ships and wishing them good luck, *Mendota* bore off toward that port to fill her empty bunkers.

For the rest of the night things went well. *Franklin* had to strain a little to control *Jadot's* constant tendency to sheer to port; but the weather was moderate and, to Gonthier at least, it looked as if the balance of the trip would be uneventful. Power was not so sanguine. He knew that there is no such thing as uneventful weather off those coasts.

His pessimism was confirmed shortly before noon on March 29 when the wind began to make up out of the sou'east —and make up fast and hard. By 1 P.M. it was gusting sixty miles an hour. The skies grew black and the seas, which had never relapsed into quiescence, were rising with new vigor. Snow flurries drove out of the low scudding clouds and *Franklin* settled her stern a little deeper, as if preparing herself for the struggle which she knew must come.

Gonthier's optimism had meanwhile turned to mounting apprehension. A glance at his chart showed him that Sable Island, that place of death for ships and men, lay only thirty miles to the nor'west, and a glance out at the driven smoke from his funnel showed him that the wind was slowly but steadily backing into the east—direct for Sable's sands. He knew that thirty miles of sea room—or twenty to the shoals which are as deadly as the isle itself—is no more than four or five hours' drift for a disabled vessel in a gale of wind.

Gonthier did not need a reminder from Power asking him to "watch the wire where it passes through your chocks." He was a good seaman, and he knew that the life of his ship depended on the slender wire stretching over his bows. Despite the mounting gale, and seas which were already breaking over *Jadot's* forecastle, two men went forward every half-hour to grease the tow-line and to see that it was sound.

Meanwhile *Franklin* had all but disappeared from Gonthier's view. Only occasionally, when she mounted to a crest and hung poised for an instant before plunging to the trough below, could he catch a glimpse of her. As the gale raged on, *Franklin* finally became invisible. Gonthier knew that she was there, half a mile ahead of him, only because the towing wire still had a strain upon it.

Franklin's people appreciated the danger of Sable even better than did Gonthier. Despite the fact that *Franklin's* stern, dragged down by the great strain upon the cable, was often completely submerged, men still went aft every few minutes to check the bulldog grips and to spread grease on the taffrail. For the rest, *Franklin's* crew clung to anything that would support them and hung on. She rolled until at times it seemed as if she would never come up again. Taking the gale full on her port beam she staggered under the impact of the seas until her decks ran white and the whole vessel looked like a half-awash reef.

Those were forty-eight desperate hours from midnight on the twenty-ninth until midnight on the thirty-first. As *Franklin* struggled to drag the *Jean Jadot* past waiting Sable, the wind kept shifting as if in league with the Graveyard sands, so that it always blew toward them. At dawn on March 31 Sable lay only sixteen miles to the nor'west and the offshore banks were not ten miles away.

At this crucial moment Gonthier discovered that the port leg of the towing bridle, which was receiving the lion's share of the strain due to *Jadot's* wild sheering to port, had chafed and was starting to strand. He radioed *Franklin*. Power immediately stopped his engines and let *Franklin* swing inert into the troughs so that the strain would come off the wire and give Gonthier's men a chance to haul the bridle in a little. It was a dangerous maneuver, but less dangerous than to risk losing the link between the two embattled ships, which, once lost, could hardly have been renewed in time to cheat the sands.

Jadot's crew worked against time to haul the bridle in so that a new section would bear on the chocks; but the big freighter was blowing fast to starboard and inexorably she began to drag the bight of the cable under *Franklin's* stern. There was nothing Power could do about it. If he started his engines in order to escape the trap, he knew he would part the stranded wire at *Jadot's* bow. If he remained stopped, there was every likelihood that the bight would sweep under his counter and foul his propeller blades. He kept the engines

93

stopped. The wire came under, and they could hear it all through the little vessel as it rasped against the blades.

The moment the work aboard the *Jadot* was completed Power called Gonthier and asked him to start his vessel's engines and ease her forward in order to allow the bight to sink deep below *Franklin's* stern. It was uncertain how *Jadot* would react as she gained headway but, considering her jammed rudder, there was a possibility that she would come far enough up to port to let the cable sag. While both crews watched intently the possibility became a reality, and an hour after she had stopped her engines, *Franklin* again got under weigh. It was none too soon. Their drift had carried the two vessels three miles closer to the Sable shoals.

Franklin again took up her tow at full power and by 2 P.M. on the thirty-first she and her charge were in the clear. Then it was as if the sea gave up its efforts to take the *Jean Jadot*. The wind, which had swelled to a full northerly gale, began to fall light. *Jadot's* jammed rudder broke loose and sank, so that the ship was no longer being forced out almost abeam of the tug. Now she fell meekly in astern of *Franklin*, and through a moderating sea, came in toward the land. On the evening of April 1 the second of the two sisters entered Halifax harbor—her ordeal done.

The *Jean Jadot* and the *Emile Francqui* owed their lives to *Foundation Franklin*. Their owners, Cie Maritime Belge, were not hesitant in acknowledging the debt; but at the same time Foundation Maritime owed much to the two Belgian sisters.

The salvage awards on the two vessels were huge by comparison with most of those the company had received from earlier jobs. The account books showed such a well-blown credit balance that even the sceptics in the Montreal headquarters who had long whispered of Chadwick's folly were impressed.

Of even greater importance was the fact that these two remarkable exploits firmly established the company's reputation for offshore rescue work—even as *Firby* and *Cordelia* had already established it for onshore salvage. By the late spring of 1935 a phrase had been born which was to recur time and time again in newspapers across Canada through the next decade.

Canadian Press. Halifax. Tonight the powerful tug Foundation Franklin steamed out of this port under forced draft on another rescue mission into the North Atlantic. . . .

Franklin had found her way, and she had also found the men whom she could trust: Irwin Power on her bridge;

John Pynn as chief officer; tough little John Sommers, chief in the engine room; Reginald Poirier as second engineer; Lindsay McManus in the radio shack; and Tom Nolan wherever he was needed. They and the deck-hands and the black gang were men to gladden the heart of a Frobisher or a Drake. They and their vessel were as one—indomitable and able spirits all.

13   COLLISION

IN THE SPRING OF 1935 Foundation Maritime displayed its new-found confidence by digging its roots into the Maritimes. Although the titular head office remained in Montreal the heart of the company now beat in a single tiny room in a dockside building on the Dartmouth shore of Halifax harbor, where Featherstone, one chair, one deal table, and an attractive young secretary named Minnie Milsom were installed.

When she recalls those early months of 1935, Minnie does so with gusto, and with regret that they are gone. Probably no company in modern history ever operated with such a minimum of paper work, and few have ever had the carefree attitude of Foundation Maritime's first independent office.

It was a good time for *Franklin* too. Power and Pynn looked after her with as much loving care as if she had been their joint possession, while Sommers and Poirier kept the engine room with a pride and competence that would have earned the respect of a Royal Navy chief petty officer.

These four, together with McManus and Nolan, were the only permanent crew. At the conclusion of each job the deck-hands and stokers were paid off and sent ashore as an economy measure. But this no longer weighed against the vessel's efficiency as it had done in the early days when *Franklin* had no name. Now her reputation stood at apogee, and she had but to blow her sonorous whistle—which was now a familiar sound to the residents of Halifax and Dartmouth—to bring thirty or forty good seamen scurrying to the docks anxious to serve in her.

By now the company had become somewhat inured to the uncertainties of salvage in the North Atlantic. It could even accept with some degree of equanimity the inevitable failures. When *Franklin* sailed four hundred miles to the assistance of the storm-damaged steamer *Tower Bridge* and, on arrival, was told that no tug was needed after all, no one was particularly distressed. The old nagging fear of the headsman was gone. The ship's officers and the salvage staff remained unworried when, through no fault of their own, their efforts failed to show a profit.

May of 1935 was a bad month for ice. The bulging pack sagged southward until it had sealed off the Cabot Straits and almost all the ports of Cape Breton Island as far down as the Canso Gut. It trapped many ships in Sydney and Louisburg and not all of these were content to wait until the ice withdrew. On May 8 the four-thousand-ton British collier *Langleeridge*, fully laden with Cape Breton coal, decided to put to sea from Louisburg. She had barely got clear of the harbor when she was beset, but stubbornly her skipper drove her on, clinging close to the shore in the hope of finding open water. He clung too close, for in the evening of that day his ship ran hard up on a submerged reef known as Bull Rock.

Her situation was not serious at first. She had taken little damage, for she had been steaming dead slow. The ice, which lay only a few hundred yards to seaward of her, held down the perpetual Atlantic swell so that she was not set to working on the rock. Her master radioed Louisburg and the government icebreaker *N. B. Maclean* was ordered to her assistance from a position in the pack some thirty miles off Guion Island.

The message was also relayed to Halifax and *Franklin* sounded her whistle, signed on a crew, and sailed north.

But now the wind began to rise and blow on shore. By the time *Franklin* was off Cape Canso the ice had set against the land and the little salvage ship was herself beset. But Power was not afraid of ice. He eased his vessel into the pack and kept her moving. The ice crunched against her bow and rasped along her plates, but she came on.

By the next day *Franklin* was in sight of Guion Island and a few hours later she entered a lane of freshly shattered ice, which testified to the recent passage of a powerful ship. Following the lane, Power soon raised his goal—and saw that *Langleeridge* was done. The ice had already killed her. Driving irresistibly inshore the pack had shoved her over Bull Rock, tearing her bottom out, and then had gripped and crushed her sides until she was almost broken in two. The *N. B. Maclean* had already taken off the crew and had then gone back to Louisburg, leaving the wreck abandoned to the sea and ice.

Although there was no value in the hulk itself there was a chance that favorable weather might make possible some cargo and general salvage, and so Foundation Maritime signed a contract with the Salvage Association representative on a basis of fifty-five per cent to the company and forty-five per cent to the underwriters, of the value of anything that could be saved. Then for two full weeks *Franklin* worked against the ice. Each morning she would try to leave Louisburg. Sometimes she would get to *Langleeridge* and sometimes she would be driven back. It was soon clear that nothing could be done about the cargo of coal, for barges to carry it could not have survived the pack. On favorable days *Franklin* would lie as close as possible while her crew ferried over to the wreck in dories and brought off what they could carry. In the end they salved twenty-four hundred dollars worth of such items as dried fish, canned pig-feet stew, red paint, saloon chairs, and oil lanterns. And that, minus forty-five per cent, was all that the company received for two weeks' labor in the ice. On May 22 *Langleeridge* gave up the ghost and slid off the rock to disappear for good.

Franklin came back to Halifax and paid off her crew. On the *next* job, perhaps . . .

That next job came before a month had passed.

During the night of June 16 the forty-five-thousand-ton passenger liner *Empress of Britain,* flagship of the Canadian Pacific Steamship Company, was on her way down-river from Quebec outward bound for Southampton. As she entered the Gulf and laid a course for the Cabot Straits, the fog, which had been thickening all that day, suddenly closed down to blot out all visibility. The *Empress* reduced speed a little, sounded her siren at one-minute intervals, and kept her course to clear the Bird Rocks off the Magdalen Islands. The big ship was in a hurry and, despite the lack of visibility, she was moving fast when, out of the grey murk ahead, there loomed the formless mass of another vessel.

It was too late for either ship to take evasive action, and the sharp prow of the liner sliced into the other vessel just forward of her collision bulkhead.

Aboard the collier *Kafiristan* there had been only a moment's warning—an insufficient time for a group of men at work on the foredeck to escape. They were cut down where they stood and the bodies of three of them went down in the steel coffin which was *Kafiristan's* bow, and which was completely sheared away.

The *Empress* stopped her engines and her boats put back, guided to the stricken ship by the cries of the injured men who still lay upon her decks. As the boats came alongside they were met by a billowing cloud of acrid smoke, for *Kafiristan* had taken fire. For an hour the *Empress's* boats' crews and the *Kafiristan's* survivors fought the blaze, eventually subduing it. By then another Canadian Pacific ship, the freighter *Beaverford,* had felt her way to the scene and the *Empress,* in the imperious way of liners, took back her boats and resumed her course for England.

The people remaining aboard *Kafiristan* now had time to take stock of the damage. They found that the collision bulkhead was still holding, but that its outer edges had been weakened and strained where the ship's shell plating had been sliced through by the liner's prow. Water was pouring into number one hold and mixing with the cargo of nine thousand tons of slack coal. The bilge pumps were holding it in check, but only just; and they were already showing symptoms of clogging with coal dust.

Fortunately the night was calm. At midnight the *Beaverford* put a Manila line on the stern of the crippled ship and took her in tow for Sydney, the nearest port. For a time all went fairly well, and the *Lord Strathcona,* which had put out from Quebec at the first news of the accident, was deceived into thinking that she would not be needed and so turned back.

In Halifax Featherstone had also heard the news, and he had immediately radioed *Kafiristan* to offer *Franklin's* services. Receiving no reply he deduced that the situation might well be more dangerous than the shore stations knew, and with his usual penchant for a gamble he ordered *Franklin* to sail anyway.

Franklin left Halifax at 3 A.M. on June 17. She had been at sea only an hour when Featherstone, who sailed with her, intercepted a message from the disabled ship directed to the Dominion Coal Company at Louisburg, which held the charter on *Kafiristan.* The message amply confirmed Featherstone's suspicions. It said:

IMPERATIVE HAVE TUG AT ONCE FROM LOUISBURG MAY NOT LAST UNTIL FOUNDATION FRANKLIN REACHES US

Franklin was not going to arrive too late if she or her people could help it. Down in the engine room Chief Sommers drove his stokers with a lethal tongue until the steam pressure rose above the safety limits. It was thick along the coast that night but *Franklin* might as well have been coasting that dangerous shore in blinding sunlight for all the notice that she took of navigation hazards. She drove headlong, quivering in every plate.

Meanwhile *Beaverford* was still trying to get *Kafiristan* to port; but despite the fact that *Beaverford* was a big, twin-screw vessel, she was having little success. She herself was cumbersome and hard to maneuver, and *Kafiristan,* towing stern-first to ease the pressure on the collision bulkhead, sheered heavily from side to side. The resulting strain on the relatively light ropes which *Beaverford* possessed caused them to part with frustrating frequency. Nevertheless, the tow had made some progress when, towards noon on June 17, the fog blew away and the sky began to darken ominously. At noon Captain Busby of *Kafiristan* dispatched this message to *Foundation Franklin:*

POSITION 2½ MILES FROM BIRD ROCKS AM BARELY
KEEPING WATER NO. 1 HOLD UNDER CONTROL STOP PRO-
CEEDING TOWARD SYDNEY IN TOW BEAVERFORD BUT
MAKING SLOW PROGRESS AS SHIP SHEERING BADLY AND
PARTING ROPES STOP HOPE YOU CAN REACH ME SOON

Featherstone hoped so too, but once more it seemed as if
a conspiracy of the elements would cheat the *Franklin*. At
midnight she was rounding Sactari when the wind, which had
been light and puffy all the day, began to make up from
the north. The sea immediately began to rise and *Kafiristan*
radioed urgently:

NOW OFF CAPE NORTH PROCEEDING DEAD SLOW STOP
WHEN CAN YOU GET HERE MAKE ALL POSSIBLE SPEED

It was a superfluous request. *Franklin* was already straining for every revolution that her engine could provide.

By 1 A.M. on June 18 the wind had settled into the north-
west and was blowing hard. *Beaverford* and *Kafiristan* were
then only five miles off the rock-bound coast of Cape North,
and as the seas increased it became clear that *Beaverford*
must stop towing or part her last sound line. Once parted she
could not be reconnected, for it was by then impossible to
stream a buoy and messenger line down to *Kafiristan*. So
both ships stopped. They lay there while the wind and current set them inexorably toward the rocks.

Meanwhile the harbor tug *Cruizer* had put to sea from
Sydney, but she had been unable to locate *Kafiristan* in the
darkness of the rain-swept night. Then at 3 A.M., the straining
lookouts on the crippled vessel glimpsed first one, then two
lights bearing down on them. *Foundation Franklin* had arrived, with *Cruizer* in her wake.

Franklin was greeted by this message from Busby:

CAN YOU LEND ME ANY MEN TO HANDLE THE TOW WIRE
AS MOST OF MY DECK HANDS WERE KILLED OR INJURED
AND THE REMAINDER ARE EXHAUSTED

To which Featherstone instantly replied, as if to show his
contempt for the rising wind and sea:

WILL PUT A CREW ABOARD SOMEHOW

Franklin edged in toward the two stopped vessels which
were by then less than two miles offshore: *Beaverford* was
still connected, but by so short a line that her proximity
made it impossible for *Franklin* to maneuver alongside
Kafiristan in order to transfer men to her. Featherstone
therefore contacted *Beaverford's* master and asked him to
take in his line and steam out of the way. *Beaverford's*
captain was unwilling. His thoughts may have been on the

99

prospects of a salvage award. At any rate, it was not until another precious hour had elapsed that he could be persuaded to relinquish the sinking ship. By then the wind and waves were considerably higher, and the business of laying *Franklin* alongside the injured collier had become extremely dangerous.

Nevertheless, *Franklin's* temporary master (Power had been unable to sail due to illness), Captain Benjamin Pope, skillfully maneuvered the tug in close. At the crucial moment when the two ships lay side by side, Featherstone, Tom Nolan, and three other salvage men leaped from their own vessel and caught a net hung over *Kafiristan's* side. After clambering up to the casualty's deck, the five men ran aft and caught a heaving line from *Franklin*. Helped by *Kafiristan's* survivors they then hauled the heavy towing wire aboard and made it fast. The whole operation had consumed exactly sixteen minutes.

It was a hair-raising exploit and, as the salvage arbitrator in London later wrote, "it was accomplished by a display of courage that only escaped foolhardiness by virtue of the skill with which it was performed."

On this occasion no towing bridle was employed; instead, one hundred and fifty feet of two-inch wire made fast to *Kafiristan's* stern was shackled to one hundred fathoms of fifteen-inch manila rope, which was in turn shackled to *Franklin's* towing wire. The function of the intermediate streach of manila was to serve as a spring and to absorb the shocks which might otherwise have snapped even the tough tow-line.

The wire was no sooner fast than *Franklin* began to take a strain on it and *Kafiristan's* began to draw slowly away from the breaking rocks of the Cape Breton coast.

Meanwhile Featherstone had gone below with his salvage gang; and the five men were soon sloshing about in the Stygian blackness of number one hold. They found seven feet of water there, and the slack coal was swirling about uneasily. Largely by feel they checked the inner face of the vital collision bulkhead. Their hands encountered a hundred hard jets of cold sea water gushing through sprung seams and loosened rivets. Featherstone realized that the ship would sink before a harbor could be reached unless the inflow could be slowed.

He wasted not a moment. Dragooning those members of *Kafiristan's* crew who could still stand, he set them to fetching lumber from the ship's storeroom. Tom Nolan and his assistant lowered themselves into the hold, and standing shoulder deep in water, they began building a coffer dam inside the bulkhead; shoring it with timbers as the wooden wall rose slowly upward. When the dam was completed the salvors hung themselves over the jagged outer edges of the deck, and by means of turnbuckles and lengths of chain they tied the torn shell plates of the vessel's sides together so that they would be held tightly against the edges of the collision bulkhead.

Featherstone had judged the situation accurately. Within a few minutes after the completion of the coffer dam the ship's bilge pumps, hopelessly clogged with coal dust, gave up the struggle.

Franklin was towing her heart out, but the bulk behind her kept sheering wildly. At length Featherstone signaled the *Cruizer* to take a line off the wreck's bow in order to act as a floating rudder. *Cruizer* steamed in and the salvage crew hove out a line to her. A few minutes later she had fallen back and was taking the strain.

Kafiristan followed a little better after that, but she was still filling fast. As the little flotilla entered Sydney harbor at 9 P.M. on June 19, she was so far down by the head that the seas were lapping across her decks, and water was standing twenty feet deep in number one.

But the worst was over. They were in sheltered waters and it was only a matter of half an hour until *Franklin* could relinquish the tow wire, come alongside, and hoist her big salvage pumps aboard the collier. After that there was only the routine of starting up the pumps, and *Kafiristan* was safe.

It had been a near thing, but this time *Franklin* and her people had won the toss. They had not, however, won a total victory. The result of the arbitration of the case was to prove heartbreaking.

When the case was heard, the Canadian Pacific hired the best lawyers they could get to state the case for the *Beaverford* and to belittle the work done by *Foundation Franklin*. These lawyers were ably assisted by the owners of *Kafiristan*, for it was to the mutual advantage of both these parties to endeavor to squeeze Foundation Maritime's payments down to the smallest possible figure. It was suspected then, and later officially acknowledged, that the *Empress of Britain* had been substantially at fault in the collision, and it was therefore thought that the Canadian Pacific Steamship Lines would have to pay not only for *Kafiristan's* damages, but also the salvage costs, in part at least. Since *Beaverford* was a Canadian Pacific vessel, any salvage award given to her owners would be of double value, for the C.P.S. would then be paying itself for the cost of *Kafiristan's* salvage, while at the same time it would be cutting down the amount payable to the upstart rivals, Foundation Maritime. The arbitrator was therefore asked to believe that *Kafiristan* had been in no real danger either of driving ashore or of sinking, that *Beaverford* could have completed the salvage easily enough, but had been unjustly "dispossessed" by *Foundation Franklin,* and that Featherstone never did build a coffer dam inside the sinking ship.

Unfortunately these arguments were ably put, and the outcome was that *Franklin* only received about one-third of the award which precedent should have ensured for her.

14 ❧ DEAD MAN'S ROCK

ALTHOUGH THE DEPRESSION was still being keenly felt in Canada's Maritime Provinces in 1935, at least one major company was still doing a good business. This was Dominion Steel and Coal Company—the colossus which overstrode much of Nova Scotia and which, to all intents and purposes, was the financial master of Cape Breton Island.

Dosco owned or controlled most of the coal mines in the province, and to get its coal to the buyers it was Dosco's policy to charter a fleet of ships each spring. Most of these vessels were from England, where there were far more bottoms than there was cargo to be carried in them and where vessels could consequently be chartered for a pittance.

Kafiristan was one of Dosco's chartered fleet, and another of these hard-driven ships was the *Berwindlea,* fifty-two hundred tons, out of Aberdeen. *Berwindlea* had crossed the Atlantic in the early spring of 1935, and through the summer and autumn she had been almost constantly at work hauling slack coal through the Gulf and up the St. Lawrence River. In mid-October she was free at last, for her charter had expired. She and her weary crew were ready to sail for home; but first she had a cargo of pulp to load at Dalhousie for delivery in England.

It was a clean cargo, and *Berwindlea's* people were in a good mood as she put out from Dalhousie on October 22. The lateness of the season and the prevalence of autumnal gales and heavy fog did not dismay them. They were homeward bound.

Berwindlea's master was in a hurry. His ship would only log seven or eight knots, and Aberdeen was a long way off. He wished to make the best time possible while he remained in the relatively sheltered waters of the Gulf, for he knew that the winter storms on the open sea would strive against his vessel for every mile she made.

As darkness fell on October 22 it brought with it a black,

impenetrable pall of fog. *Berwindlea* drove into it and disappeared. Her navigation lights glowed feebly, each contained in a hemisphere of fog not ten feet in diameter. The mate upon the bridge could not see the foredeck of the ship, and members of the crew vanished from each other's ken before five paces intervened between them.

The night was calm, but cold. There was no sound except the rusty *blat* of *Berwindlea's* whistle as it tried to pierce the fog, but which was blanketed and absorbed almost as it left the whistle's throat.

The course line laid out on the chart in the wheelhouse began to waver. The little penciled crosses which represented *Berwindlea's* position became fewer and less firmly placed. Dead-reckoning alone was an uncertain pilot on such a night.

At 3:50 A.M. the master, Captain Williams, stood at the chart table with the officer of the watch beside him. They stared intently at the last dead-reckoning position. It showed *Berwindlea* on course and ten miles south of the dangerous nest of islands called the Magdalens. Williams was uneasy. It was not much of an offing on such a night, and he was contemplating ordering the vessel's head to be brought a little more toward the south when, without any warning, *Berwindlea* went on.

Men who have spent their lives sailing the Gulf make no pretense of familiarity with the strange currents which flow through it. *Berwindlea's* people—strangers all—had no way of knowing in advance what the current had been doing to their ship that night. But now they knew what it had done.

Berwindlea took the ground with a great shudder and the sound of crumpling steel.

In the engine room the chief was already starting up the bilge pumps even before the frightful shuddering of the initial shock was over. The bosun, thrown to the deck by the impact, had already regained his feet and had begun to turn forward to sound the wells, even before the order to do so reached him from the bridge. The moment of confusion which is close to panic and which always seizes on a ship at such a time was short-lived. It was succeeded by a questioning silence broken only by occasional hails from the officers to the men who had gone forward. It was a period of fantastic tension, of hope struggling with the fear of what must soon be known.

The destruction of the ship began within ten minutes of the time she struck. The bosun's measurements showed water rising fast in number one and number two holds, and when the pumps not only failed to reduce the flooding but were powerless even to slow its rapid rise, it was obvious that not only the vessel's bottom, but her inner bottom too was ruptured.

Captain Williams listened grimly to the reports of his officers, then, at 4:15 A.M., he ordered Sparks to make his call. At 4:20 the international distress frequency woke to life.

At 9 A.M. Featherstone in Halifax received a telegram from one of his "intelligence sources":

SS BERWINDLEA REPORTED ASHORE DEAD MANS ROCK MAGDALEN ISLANDS STOP BELIEVED FLOODED FORWARD BUT NO IMMEDIATE DANGER PRESENT WEATHER STOP FULLY LADEN PULP

Featherstone considered the information for fifteen minutes. He knew that this late in the season good weather in the Gulf could not be expected to last for more than two or three days. He was familiar with Dead Man's Rock and he knew that a ship on that exposed pinnacle would be doomed by any gale which blew. There was no time for him to try to make arrangements with the ship's agents. There was, perhaps, just enough time to save the ship if *Franklin* sailed at once.

So *Franklin* sailed "under forced draft," as the papers would have it. Once more Power was on her bridge: but Featherstone intended to proceed by train to Canso Gut and meet the *Franklin* there, for he wanted to collect Drake, the local Salvage Association man, en route.

Franklin had thick fog and heavy weather all the way north, but she picked up Featherstone and Drake at Mulgrave at 3 A.M. on October 24 and by 4 P.M. of that day she had reached Dead Man's Rock.

The islet is a forbidding sight at the best of times. The craggy peak of a submerged mountain rising abruptly out of the waters, its area is only a few acres. Its shores are so precipitous that there is only one spot where boats may safely land; and this lies on the opposite side to the cliff where *Berwindlea* had driven ashore. Men seldom visit Dead Man's Rock, but on the north shore there is a tiny turf and stone shack where fishermen, or shipwrecked sailors, may find some meager shelter.

The place has a hard reputation—as hard as its name; but neither its reputation nor its name meant much to Featherstone. What counted in his mind was the terribly hazardous position of any vessel ashore upon it.

As *Franklin* came in Featherstone saw that the light north wind which had been blowing all that morning had kicked up such a sea that even on the lee side of the rock where *Berwindlea* lay, a boat could not safely be launched. What must inevitably happen in the event of a real gale rising from the south, the east or west was brutally apparent.

As things stood Featherstone considered it too dangerous

to attempt a landing, so *Franklin* withdrew into the lee of Amherst Island for the night. During those hours Featherstone was in radio contact with Williams, and he learned some of the details of the problem which he faced.

Berwindlea was flooded and tidal in number one and number two tanks (open to the sea in these), while her forepeak tanks and most of the remaining double bottom tanks were also flooded. Mercifully the engine room was still dry, but there was every prospect that it too would flood unless the weather moderated soon. On this score Featherstone and Power were not immediately worried. Knowing the signs by instinct they expected the northerly to fall light with darkness, and they hoped they would then have a period of a day, or perhaps two, before the wind came round through east to south and began to blow.

Featherstone and Power made their plan. Williams was ordered to flood his deep tanks in order to hold *Berwindlea* firmly on the rocks and prevent her from working. At dawn *Franklin* would come in, lay two sets of ground tackle off *Berwindlea's* stern, land an air compressor on her and, after blowing the forward tanks and pumping the after ones, would try to take her off with her own winches.

Impelled by the knowledge that time was against them, the salvors went to work at dawn with demoniac energy. Within five hours both sets of ground tackle had been laid out. Featherstone, Tom Nolan and Drake went aboard *Berwindlea* and supervised the reeving and setting-up of the purchases. Nolan's helper, Alan Macdonald, brought *Franklin's* little motorboat in through the surf with a two-ton air compressor balanced across the gunwales and safely delivered it aboard the wreck. Nolan went over the side to make an underwater examination and to begin patching, if this proved feasible. Having fully assessed the situation, Featherstone radioed an urgent request to Sydney for a small coastal vessel which could bring out stevedores and coal, and which could take off bulk pulp if jettisoning proved necessary. The coal was particularly needed since *Berwindlea's* bunkers were low—her master having intended to bunker at Sydney before setting out across the North Atlantic.

Everything was in readiness for the first attempt to refloat the big ship at evening high tide, when Featherstone made a shocking discovery.

During her summer season *Berwindlea* had been unloaded, not with her own deck gear, but with shore equipment. Consequently her engineers had removed certain vital valves from the deck winches in order to prevent corrosion —and these valves had never been replaced. No one had thought about the matter until late afternoon on October

25, when Featherstone called for steam on the winches in order to take the preliminary strain on the ground tackle.

When the discovery was made that the winches were useless, it was too late to search out the missing valves and install them in time to make use of that evening's tide. Nothing more could be done until the following day.

Meanwhile Power, aboard *Franklin* lying at anchor half a mile offshore, had heard some disquieting news on the standard broadcast radio. A violent hurricane had cut a swath of destruction across Haiti on October 23, killing more than two thousand people. The track the hurricane was following had not yet been plotted with any certainty, but Power knew that it might well run northeast over the Maritimes—as Caribbean hurricanes so often do.

With this possibility in mind, Power watched with increasing apprehension as the afternoon waned and as the wind came out of the east, then switched freakishly to the southwest and began to rise. Power kept his fears to himself until 4:45 P.M. when he radioed Featherstone:

WIND AND SEA RISING FAST SUSPECT HURRICANE TRACK WILL COME THIS WAY SUGGEST YOU ABANDON BERWIND-LEA AT ONCE

Featherstone was not infallible. He could make mistakes; and when he did they were monumental. He made one now.

Irritated by the affair of the winches and by the fact that he had been robbed of a quick success by such a trivial matter, he made up his mind to stay aboard *Berwindlea* and have another try at dawn. He did not think much of the hurricane scare. In his experience a south-west gale was not likely to last more than a few hours.

Whether or not they were influenced by Featherstone's example, the officers and crew of *Berwindlea* also elected to remain aboard their ship. Drake too decided to stay, while Nolan had no thought of leaving if Featherstone remained.

At 5:30 P.M. Alan Macdonald was told to return to *Franklin* with the motorboat. It was none too soon. While rounding *Berwindlea's* stern Macdonald was caught in the surf and his boat was nearly swamped. Damaged and leaking badly it barely managed to get him back to *Foundation Franklin's* side.

Contrary to Featherstone's expectations the gale did not slack off. Instead it mounted with a ferocity that was terrifying. At 9 P.M. *Franklin* began dragging both her anchors and was forced to heave them in and stand offshore into the teeth of a force 8 gale and a wild and savage sea. She rose to most of the big ones, but she took it green across her decks many times that night.

Clamped in the vise of the rocks, *Berwindlea* could do nothing but accept her punishment. By midnight she was being swept from end to end and spray was breaking high above her mast-heads against the glistening rocks of the cliff face.

Berwindlea had her crew accommodations aft, while her bridge and officers' quarters were well forward of amidships. Her boats were aft as well and the only communication between the poop and the bridge was over the open decks.

By midnight this route had been closed. Black water was falling on the decks to a depth of six feet. The stanchions of her rails were smashed, and the rails themselves carried away. Her starboard boat was shattered in its chocks. Her hatches began to break under the ponderous impact of the seas and she began to flood in number three and number four holds.

Her crew were now besieged in their quarters aft and dared not open a door or port. Forward, in the bridge structure, the officers with Featherstone, Nolan and Drake were marooned in a more ugly position—close to the destroying rocks.

By midnight the ship had begun to work so much that the sound of her plates grinding and gnashing on the rocks rose clearly above the high-pitched scream of wind and the sonorous thunder of the breaking seas.

Franklin was now hove-to some miles off shore and barely able to hold her own. Emergency weather reports were coming in steadily from the government stations, and these were increasingly ominous. The hurricane had indeed tracked up the American seaboard, and the center of that whirlpool of tortured air was rapidly approaching the Maritimes. Already the distress frequency was crackling with calls and McManus was logging them between his attempts to keep in touch with *Berwindlea's* young operator.

At 3:30 A.M. on October 26 there was no answer to McManus's signals. He fought his way to the bridge to tell Power, and found the skipper peering shoreward through the driving murk with his night glasses. There was no need for Sparks's message. Power had seen the dim glow of *Berwindlea's* lights suddenly go out.

Aboard *Berwindlea* both the ground-tackle wires had parted under the strain imposed by that irresistible sea, and the ship had swung broadside, tearing her belly out as she was flung across the reefs. She heeled over and the seas flooded into her engine room; the lights flickered once and then went out. Within half an hour she was flooded in every compartment and her doom was sealed.

That she did not break up immediately was tribute to her Scottish builders. Any lesser ship must have quickly gone to pieces under the merciless assault of the mounting seas; yet *Berwindlea* hung on, a shell of a thing, her bottom gone and her side plates buckling until her deck was hogged like a boar's back. She was dead, but not yet destroyed.

The storm-wracked daylight hours of October 26 were an ordeal that drove one officer mad, and that led the crew to the panic act of attempting to launch the remaining boat. It was swept from them like a chip and only a miracle spared the men who launched it. They crawled back into their prison and hung on.

At dawn the radio operator managed to get his emergency power working, and communications with *Franklin* were restored. It was a desperately anxious Power who talked to Featherstone, but though he was immeasurably relieved to hear that the men aboard the wreck were still alive, Power was driven half-distracted by the fact that he could do nothing for them. Until the hurricane had passed it was all that he could do to keep *Franklin* afloat; any attempt to venture close to Dead Man's Rock would have been suicidal. Standing three miles offshore he could not see *Berwindlea* at all. He could only see a succession of gargantuan columns of white spray such as might mark the seas which break across a submerged reef in a great gale.

The news upon the distress frequency was as chilling as the spectacle before Power's eyes. The steamer *Vardulia*, the same ship which had rescued the crew of the *Aggersund* off Newfoundland in that memorable spring of 1932, had called for help from several hundred miles east of Halifax, and then had not been heard again. She had gone down and taken her crew of thirty-seven with her. Nor was she alone. The Nova Scotian three-masted schooner *Esthonia*, from Barbados to Shelburne, also died that day, although her crew of ten were saved.

As the number of distress calls mounted, Power's frustration increased. Several times he sailed *Franklin* dangerously close to the foam-sheathed rock, but each time he was forced away before he had come close enough even to see *Berwindlea* through the driven spume.

Aboard the doomed vessel there were two kinds of men. There were those who saw death at arm's length, and who were afraid of him. And there were those who could not see him, either because they lacked understanding of their plight, or because they were too preoccupied to notice. Featherstone and Nolan belonged to this latter group. With a cigar thrusting aggressively out of his heavy jaw, Featherstone still would not admit defeat. Plan after plan to save not just the men but the ship as well went through his mind, and the notes in his little pocket notebook grew numerous as plan after plan had to be abandoned.

Not until noon of October 26 would he accept the fact of *Berwindlea's* loss; and then he concentrated his efforts on how to save her people. He knew that no boat could live in the hell's brew about *Berwindlea,* and that it would be death to try to leave her until there was a lull. He made plans for the moment when she would go under. He began a long and reasoned discussion with the ship's officers as to the relative merits of rafts and boats versus ladders, as life-saving gear; and he was irritated when the distracted officers refused to listen with the proper degree of attention to the niceties of his arguments. Somewhat grumpily he left them to their fears and turned to the phlegmatic Nolan.

"Best way in the world to leave a wreck on a lee shore —a ladder. Hold you up fine as you go through the surf, then with any kind of luck you can use it to bridge the breakers so you don't get bashed to bits. After that you can use it to climb up the cliffs. You get a ladder ready, Tom."

Tom routed out a ladder, but not because he thought it would be needed. He was not worried by their plight, for as a Newfoundlander born and bred he had long since learned never to worry in advance about what the sea might do to him. What bothered him at the moment was the problem of finding grub; and he was considerably disgruntled by the steward's failure to provide an adequate grub locker in the officers' saloon.

The day passed in different ways for different men. Some were silent and withdrawn as soldiers are before the battle which they suspect will be their last. Some were violent in their futile rage. Some concentrated all their effort in the attempt to achieve sufficient self-control to fool their fellows. The madman screamed insensate things at sea and wind.

The hurricane continued unabated all that day and into the next night. At 1:30 A.M. on October 27 *Berwindlea* began to go. She split amidships, separating the two little groups of men one from the other, and the bow section began to settle steadily as she broke up below the waterline.

The salvage men and the ship's officers were soon driven out of the saloon by the invading waters. They made their way to the bridge—and the waters followed until they were knee deep. For a time the thundering breakers drove over the bridge structure as if it were no more than a piece of flotsam, and then, temporarily content with the destruction they had wrought, they slowly began to lose their fury. At long last the gale began to ease.

It was now or never for the men aboard the wreck and at 2 A.M. *Franklin* radioed a general SOS on their behalf, which was picked up and immediately rebroadcast by the powerful government station on nearby Grindstone Island.

SS BERWINDLEA ASHORE DEAD MANS ISLAND URGENTLY NEEDS ASSISTANCE SHIP WITH LARGE LIFEBOATS

There was no immediate reply, for there were few ships left at sea that night. A few minutes after sending the SOS Featherstone, his mind as agile as ever, radioed Power with a suggestion of his own.

DO YOU THINK YOU COULD LAND SOME MEN AT THAT SHACK ON THE LEE SIDE OF THE ISLAND AND CROSS THIS SIDE AND RIG LINES FOR A BREECHES BUOY FROM THE CLIFF

To which Power replied:

DONT THINK POSSIBLE LAND BOAT NOW BUT WILL DO SO AT DAYLIGHT IF HUMANLY POSSIBLE

This message was interrupted by a call from a strange voice. It belonged to a rare bird, the Japanese freighter *England Maru,* who reported herself as being abreast of East Point, Prince Edward Island, and able and willing to come to *Berwindlea's* assistance.

Her message brought a surge of hope, for it was a voice from a world that the survivors on the wreck had all but despaired of knowing once again. With the Gulf swept almost clear of shipping by the hurricane they had come to think of themselves as utterly abandoned. So *England Maru's* message brought hope, though of a tenuous kind, for they knew she could not reach them until late the following morning—and there was every likelihood that *Berwindlea* would have vanished before then.

Featherstone put the feelings of all of them into this brief message to Power:

THANK JAP BUT WE ARE RELYING ON WHAT YOU CAN DO WITH SHORE PARTY

Nothing can better tell the story of the next few hours than the radio log kept by McManus. It is vivid, for it is truth.

England Maru to *Berwindlea:* WE ARE PROCEEDING YOU FULL SPEED BUT ONLY MAKE SIX KNOTS IN HEAVY SEA GOOD WISHES

Franklin to Grindstone Radio: DO YOU KNOW OR CAN YOU FIND OUT FROM FISHERMEN IF MEN CAN WALK AROUND BEACH OF DEAD MANS OR MUST THEY GO OVER TOP TO CROSS

Grindstone to *Franklin:* SORRY DONT KNOW AND CANT GET INFORMATION ALL PHONES DOWN

Berwindlea to *Franklin:* WHERE ARE YOU MAKE ALL POSSIBLE SPEED

Franklin to *Berwindlea:* AM NOW ABEAM ISLAND COMING AROUND AND UP LEE SIDE

Franklin to *Berwindlea:* GETTING BOAT READY UNDER COMMAND DOBSON WHO WILL HAVE SIGNAL FLAGS TO TALK FROM BEACH HOW ARE YOU AND HOW IS SHIP IS SHE BREAKING UP FAST

Berwindlea to *Franklin:* GLAD NEWS FROM YOU WE ARE WELL ALL HOPE IS IN YOUR EFFORTS THIS SHIP IN BAD WAY BREAKING BACK BUCKLING AND BATHED IN GREAT SEAS EVERY FEW MOMENTS

England Maru to *Berwindlea* via Grindstone: 28 MILES FROM YOU PROCEEDING BEST

Franklin to *Berwindlea:* BOAT OVER WITH MEN MAKING FOR ISLAND

Berwindlea to *Franklin:* ARE THEY MAKING GOOD PROGRESS

Franklin to *Berwindlea:* BOAT BEING SWEPT INTO BREAKERS THEY ARE ON EDGE OF BREAKERS WILL BE SWAMPED THEY ARE MAKING BIG EFFORT TO PULL CLEAR [And five minutes later] BOAT ESCAPED BREAKERS IMPOSSIBLE FOR THEM TO LAND AND LIVE SEAS SWEEPING BROADSIDE ON BEACH

Berwindlea to *Franklin:* FEATHERSTONE SAYS COME BACK STAND BY TO WINDWARD OF US AND COOPERATE WITH JAP STEAMER THERE MAY BE SLIM CHANCE FOR BOAT TO ROUND OUR STERN AND LEE SIDE STOP THERE IS A ROCK ON SHIPS PORT SIDE AMIDSHIPS RIGHT AGAINST HER

Franklin to *Berwindlea:* HAVE YOU ANY BOATS LEFT AND CAN YOU LAUNCH THEM OUT

Berwindlea to *Franklin:* BOAT SMASHED BUT WILL TRY IT IF ALL ELSE FAILS

These messages cover only three hours in time; but that was a decade in the lives of those concerned.

Power's attempt to land a boat upon the north side of

111

the island had been nobly prosecuted. Second Officer Dobson (who was to die a few years later as a destroyer commander in the war), with three deck-hands and two firemen—all volunteers—had put off from *Franklin* in a twelve-foot boat. During the launching a sea had swept the little craft so hard against *Franklin's* bulwarks that it was half stove-in before it took the water. Once afloat it was at the mercy of the great seas, for the hope that Dead Man's Rock could provide a lee in the face of the hurricane was a delusion. There were three miles to pull in order to reach the roaring shingle beach. Dobson and his men were exhausted before they reached the line of surf. Dobson himself knew that there was little possibility of his crew's surviving an attempt to enter the surf, yet he decided they should try. The lifeboat was immediately caught, spun end-for-end and almost swamped. Half-full and leaking badly, it was still two hundred yards from land. There remained only the hope that the boat's crew could save themselves. With the strength of desperation they pulled clear of the surf and then dropped their oars in a state of near collapse as the wind carried their boat clear of the islet and out into the Gulf. *Franklin* bore down upon them, and was able to retrieve them by a near-miracle of seamanship on Power's part. The broken boat was left to drift away.

All this took place between dawn and 6 A.M. *Franklin* then fought her way back around the islet and stood by the *Berwindlea*; but she was now completely helpless to assist the shipwrecked men, for she had only the motorboat left and, apart from the hull damage it had sustained earlier, its engine would no longer run.

It was at this juncture that the distant smoke of the *England Maru* came into sight. Power and the Japanese master were in radio communication and by 9 A.M., when the freighter was close upon the scene, they had devised a plan. It was an incredibly risky one that could only succeed if *England Maru's* big boat could be so packed with oarsmen that they could defy the wind and surf.

With a quality of seamanship that could hardly be believed, the Japanese skipper, Captain Honja, maneuvered his big vessel (she was light and therefore doubly hard to handle) broadside to the islet and less than half a mile from *Berwindlea*.

Honja then launched his biggest boat, a thirty-footer, and manned it with twenty oarsmen. Despite the bitter cold of that October morning the Japanese sailors were naked to the waist. They took up the stroke and made for the waiting *Franklin*, who was hove-to in *England Maru's* lee, halfway between her and the wreck.

Chanting in unison and rowing like superhuman beings, the Japanese crew slipped under the shelter of *Franklin's* lee, while Power eased his tug inshore.

Two hundred yards off *Berwindlea*, *Franklin* stopped. Not even Power dared to take her farther in. Now the lifeboat was on its own. It did not hesitate but plunged straight into the breaking seas that rose as high as *Berwindlea's* foretop.

The boat shot under the wreck's stern, seeking her lee side, but found instead a pinnacle of rock thrust into *Berwindlea's* belly that made a cul-de-sac from which there could be no escape. Second Officer Anto cried one shrill order, and in the last instant the men reversed their stroke and the boat came out alive.

Anto now took the only alternative. He brought his fragile craft in against *Berwindlea's* weather side. Bosun Okabe leaped to the boat's gunwale to prevent her being crushed against the wreck and with his own body took the shock of impact. It smashed seven of his ribs and nearly killed him— but he saved the boat.

The people on *Berwindlea's* after-part swarmed over the rails as one man. They had not far to drop, for already the after deck of the dying ship was awash. The lifeboat leaped away on a receding sea and pulled for safety.

Leaving her cargo of half-frozen survivors on *Franklin's* deck, the Japanese boat went back again—this time right into the surf in an attempt to reach the little group marooned on *Berwindlea's* bridge. She reached them too, but just how she did it no man can tell. Featherstone, his cigar still in his mouth, was amongst the last to leave and he recalls that moment in strange fashion.

"It wasn't the sea and the gale that bothered me just then. It was the seals. There must have been a thousand of them hanging about the wreck, just waiting to see us drown. They kept popping their silly heads up and staring, as if we were some kind of circus for their special benefit."

He was most indignant about those seals.

He was indignant too about the loss of *Berwindlea*, but philosophical as well. The loss of the ship pointed his favorite moral.

"Salvage on these coasts is always a knife-edge proposition. One little thing goes wrong, and you've lost out. There are no second chances. The wind and water sees to that."

The wind and water saw to *Berwindlea*. Within three days nothing remained of her except a frieze of flotsam on the beach of Dead Man's Rock.

15 🐦 CHICKEN FEATHERS

SEVERAL MONTHS OF INACTIVITY followed on the heels of the *Berwindlea* disaster. With the exception of a few mundane towing jobs, *Franklin* lay idle at her new wharf in Halifax. From the nearby docks four harbor tugs which had recently been purchased by the company bustled out busily to assist freighters and liners coming into or leaving the port. But it was a dreary time for *Franklin* and for her people.

Then in early April, with the opening of navigation in the Gulf and river, *Franklin* was dispatched to a temporary station at Port Hawksbury in the Gut of Canso, from which port she was available both for open ocean work and for emergencies in the Gulf. She had only a few days to wait before her first call, for on April 25 a violent gale swept out of the north-west and in a matter of hours had disabled three freighters on the northern great-circle route. One of these, the Russian steamer *Ivanhoe*, radioed a general SOS. *Franklin* sailed within an hour of its receipt, although *Ivanhoe* was then nine hundred miles east of Nova Scotia and at the extreme limit of *Franklin's* towing range. In any event the distance did not matter, for *Ivanhoe* was taken in tow by the Polish liner *Pilsudski* while *Franklin* was still five hundred miles away.

Power turned for home, but he had not run more than an hour when he was diverted to the aid of the British freighter *Rushpool*, which was seven hundred miles east of Halifax with a damaged rudder. *Franklin* came smartly about and was soon making good speed toward the new casualty. Then *Rushpool* radioed that she no longer needed help, having effected emergency repairs.

"We came home empty-handed," Power said later. "But the old girl needed a romp to loosen her up a bit."

It had been quite a romp—six days at sea and more than twelve hundred miles of heavy weather. But as far as Foundation Maritime was concerned that kind of romp could be depressingly expensive. When, on June 24 *Franklin* found a paying job, her owners were considerably relieved.

On June 19 the French diesel-electric vessel *Spitzberg*, out of Fécamp for St. Pierre and Miquelon with a cargo of Scotch whisky and French wines, was lying at her St. Pierre dock when fire broke out aboard. The fire quickly got out of control, and in an effort to save the ship the sea cocks were opened and she was allowed to sink. Her people evidently had underestimated the depth of water at the docks, for instead of settling to her gunwales, *Spitzberg* went right on down out of sight. For a week the local authorities tried to raise her without success. Finally they were forced to appeal to Foundation Maritime.

Franklin sailed, with Featherstone aboard to direct the job. According to her log *Franklin* made one of the fastest passages in her history. There is some reason to believe that her phenomenal speed was connected with the persistent rumors that *Spitzberg* had sunk before her precious cargo had been taken off.

The hopeful and anticipatory expressions of her crew changed to one of common gloom when, on arrival at St. Pierre, they found that *Spitzberg* had been unladen two weeks earlier, and at the time of her sinking she had been taking on six thousand quintals of dried fish.

They went to work on her with a kind of disappointed frenzy that resulted in the *Spitzberg's* being floated inside of forty-eight hours. Tom Nolan dived to plug her openings and close off the sea cocks; and pumpman Buck Dassylva drove his big centrifugals with such fury that *Spitzberg* popped up like a cork.

The company considered the operation eminently successful. And so it was financially; but *Franklin's* crew recall the incident with a retrospective gloom that the years have not mellowed. "Oh by damn!" Buck said. "If *only* she had sunk two weeks before!"

Shortly after the raising of *Spitzberg* there occurred a strange affair from which the aura of mystery has never been satisfactorily dispelled.

On July 13 Featherstone received a phone call from the Nova Scotian village of Lockport to the effect that a ship was hard aground on Emulous reef and had apparently been aground there for some forty-eight hours. The vessel had not sent out an SOS, and news of her was so scanty that Featherstone was at first inclined to suspect a hoax, until confirmation of the stranding was received a few hours later.

Knowing the coast as he did, Featherstone realized that the time which had already elapsed might well have doomed the vessel. There was certainly no time left to spare. Loading Tom Nolan, Buck Dassylva, Alan Macdonald and another man into his new Airflow Chrysler, Featherstone set off for Lockport, having ordered Power to bring *Franklin* along at her best speed.

Featherstone was a notoriously uninhibited driver. As he rounded one of the dangerous curves in the coast road near Mahone Bay he saw ahead of him the high box of an ancient Hudson. Both cars were over the middle line, and both swung hard to port. But the old Hudson, with her upright steering wheel, needed a dozen turns to put enough helm on her to get clear and there was insufficient time for that. The cars collided head on. The occupants of the Hudson were both badly injured, but it looked at first as if Featherstone and his passengers had escaped serious damage. It was not until he tried to lift the hood of his own car that Featherstone discovered his right arm was broken. Nolan found that he had a number of broken ribs, while the other salvage men were able to claim a wide variety of lesser injuries.

An hour later they were all in the hospital. Featherstone's arm was set in plaster and he was ordered into bed. Instead he went straight through the ward, out the back door, hailed a cab, and within minutes was again on his way to Lockport.

Two hours later he was scrambling up the side of the stricken freighter, hauling himself aloft with one arm and his teeth.

The situation was as he had suspected. The vessel was in a hopeless condition. She had been light when she went on and had driven far up the reef. Two days of punishment by the eternal swells had damaged her so badly that she could never float again.

The mystery of why the ship had remained silent during the hours when she might have been saved remains officially unsolved. But seafaring men profess to know the answer. It is closely related, so they say, to the combination of an old ship—and a large insurance policy.

A somewhat similar experience was in store for *Franklin* and her people in November of 1936. The ship involved this time was the *Delphi*, an ancient Greek tramp of five thousand tons that had been banging around the world for nearly thirty years. *Delphi* went ashore on the low and muddy beach of Escouminac Point, New Brunswick, on November 19, during a moderate blow from the nor'west. She was undamaged, for the bottom there is soft, but she drove in across nearly a mile of shoal water. Despite the obvious fact that she required a powerful tug and ground tackle in order to get free, her people perversely decided to pump out all her tanks in an effort to refloat her. The predictable result was that she promptly drove two hundred yards closer to dry land and ended up—at low tide—with hardly enough water under her to float a dory.

At the time a report of her difficulty was being received in Halifax, Power and *Franklin* were at Charlottetown, Prince Edward Island, where they had just refloated the stranded steamer *Marine Trader* in the smart time of seven hours. Power was ordered to sail for *Delphi* while Featherstone made his way to her by car from Halifax. Driving at an aver-

116

age speed of seventy miles an hour (despite the fact that his right arm was still in a sling) Featherstone soon reached Chatham, the nearest town to Escouminac. Turning down a sand track leading to the point, he had gone about ten miles when he found the trail blocked by *Delphi's* crew accompanied by three women and several goats, and with a collection of miscellaneous property balanced on their heads or cradled in their arms.

Having identified this strange cortege Featherstone realized that he must reverse the human tide, for if *Delphi* was to be saved her crew would be required. But the Greeks were adamant in their refusal to return to her. *"Fini*—no good!" they shouted when he suggested they turn back.

"Perhaps you're right," Featherstone replied sagaciously. "But it's a long way to the nearest town and your women look tired. Tell them to get in, and pile your luggage on the car, and I'll give you some help."

The unwary castaways did as they were told. They were appalled when Featherstone, instead of turning around for Chatham, gunned his motor and went careening on down the road toward Escouminac. There was nothing that the crew could do but follow him back to their ship.

Featherstone arrived at the *Delphi* to find Power already in possession. *Franklin* had come booming up from Charlottetown some hours earlier and had anchored as close to the wreck as possible—which was not very close, for the shallows kept her a mile and a half off shore. Forcing his way through the ice Power had come in to her in the motorboat, only to discover that the Greek vessel had been abandoned by everyone except the officers and the cook. Power met this problem by moving aboard the *Delphi* with his own salvage gang, in order to begin the job of freeing her.

He found that being *Delphi's* guest was a memorable experience. The ship was so old that she did not even have electric lights and her saloon was lit by dim oil lamps. This was a good thing. "Otherwise," says Power, "I would have starved to death, for I would have been able to *see* the grub they put before me."

Like most good Greeks, *Delphi's* people were canny about waste. When thirty chickens, quartered on the forecastle froze to death the first night Power was aboard, the cook immediately boiled the lot and served them complete with innards. He took off *some* of the feathers, but not enough.

Delphi was owned by her officers on a share basis; and these officers were convinced that she would never float again, and they showed no desire to be unconvinced. They were unco-operative as far as salvage work was concerned, but they were friendly. When Featherstone arrived, a light

117

snack of boiled chicken was brought in for him, and the skipper lit a hookah pipe and passed it amiably around. The Greeks did not even wish to talk about salvage. However, one of them had heard of the recent birth of the famous Dionne quintuplets, and he was deeply interested in that. Turning to his wife he said accusingly:

"See what fine women these French Canadians are? One try—five baby! With you, five thousand try—*no* baby!"

His wife was not one to accept this sort of thing in silence and Featherstone and Power beat a hasty withdrawal.

The refloating of the *Delphi* took place on November 20 under Power's direction. He eased *Franklin* in beyond the three-fathom line, and there he anchored with no more than two feet of water under his keel while the motorboat took a messenger line to the stranded ship. It was a bitter cold day and ice was rafting thickly off shore and threatening to close in at any time. *Delphi* herself was completely sheathed in ice; and with her propeller almost out of water she looked like a hopeless case.

It took several hours for *Delphi* to haul in the tow wire from the tug. The distance was three quarters of a mile, and the weight of the wire alone was so great that her old winches could hardly drag it along the bottom. Power did what he could to help it along by lashing empty oil barrels to the wire at intervals of a hundred yards as it went off his after deck. When the entire three thousand feet were out, the salvage foreman radioed from aboard the *Delphi* that they had not yet hauled in the towing bridle. There was no more wire available so Power took a serious risk; he upped *Franklin's* anchor and allowed *Delphi* to winch *Franklin* into even shallower water. When *Franklin* was actually bumping bottom the salvage gang finally got hold of the bridle, cast off the messenger line, and made fast.

It was now late in the evening and a nor'west wind was getting up. Snow squalls drove down over the freezing water as Power rang for full-ahead and *Franklin's* engines whistled and throbbed. The little vessel's stern sat down deeper as the strain of the wire came on her, and her propeller sent great rushing gouts of mud and water out astern. She strained until her frames were creaking, but she would probably not have succeeded in releasing the *Delphi* had not the onshore wind already built up a moderate sea. The waves, lifting under the Greek, provided just enough extra buoyancy; and reluctantly she began to move over the sand and shingle into deeper water.

Once she had been pulled to safety *Delphi* cast off the wire, saluted her rescuer with three long blasts of her horn, and set course for Sydney. The Straits were no place in which to linger, for during the early hours of that night two other ships had become frozen in the ice not thirty miles away.

Franklin recovered her tow wire after a twelve-hour struggle to free it from the mud and boulders of the Escouminac flats, then she sailed for Charlottetown. But before she reached that haven she intercepted a radio call.

SS DELPHI REPORTED ASHORE ON REEF ENTRANCE TO SYDNEY HARBOR

Power and his mate stared at each other for a moment. Then Power grinned, "Oh no he don't," he cried as he rang down for full speed. "Not after what we've put up with."

With the memory of the chickens still vivid in his mind he hastened to the rescue of the unwilling one, announcing his intentions with a forceful radio message.

No one will ever know if it was *Franklin's* persistence or a particularly high tide, but *Delphi* inexplicably refloated herself some time before Power could arrive upon the scene. She was standing smartly out to sea before *Franklin* steamed into Sydney harbor.

Nevertheless she fulfilled her death-wish in the end. Not three weeks later she went hard-on at the mouth of a South American river—a good safe distance from *Franklin's* bailiwick. And there her bones remain.

16 ❦ A WILD-GOOSE CHASE

FEBRUARY HAD ALWAYS TAKEN pride of place as being the most inclement month on the approaches to the continent, but February of 1938 was more violent than any of its predecessors for thirty years. It began with a full-blown hurricane and went on from there to try to make its opening days seem like an idyllic June.

The calls for aid from ships at sea provided convincing proof of its success.

On February 8 the British steamer *Dalcray* radioed an SOS from a position off Cape Race, reporting that she was leaking badly as a result of strained and sprung shell plates. *Franklin* had been lying at her dock with steam up and a full crew aboard ever since the month began. She steamed out to assist *Dalcray* on twenty minutes' notice. By midday on February 10 she was closing with the casualty when *Dalcray's* master radioed to the effect that the leaks had been brought under control, and that he expected to be able to limp into St. John's without assistance.

Power was not unduly disappointed. The two-day outward

journey had convinced him that it was going to be a busy month, for neither he nor any of his crew had ever been to sea in weather quite as turbulent. *Franklin* came about for Halifax, but she had only been under weigh for half an hour when McManus brought Power a new distress signal.

This call was from the American steamer *Hyacinth City*, outbound for Europe with twelve passengers, full cargo holds, and a deck cargo of logs. While passing over the submerged mountain peak of Flemish Cap, some four hundred miles east of Newfoundland, she had lost her propeller and had begun to suffer serious structural damage from the seas.

Power acknowledged her message and swung his vessel onto the new course.

He remembers the rest of that adventure in intimate detail. He has good reason to.

"It was blowing a hard gale of wind when we got the message from *Hyacinth City*, and it had been blowing the same gale for six solid days so that the sea was bigger than a man could well believe. After we came about and headed out again, the wind began to blow harder. The old anemometer on the flying bridge was spinning so fast the needle wouldn't follow, and it kept on jumping about as if it just didn't believe the wind could blow that hard.

"I kept *Franklin* going at pretty near full revolutions, for I thought we had this fellow sure, and I didn't want him to sink before we got to him. Anybody who didn't know the old *Franklin* would have thought I was going to drive her under; but none of us worried. We knew what she could do —or thought we did.

"We'd been running for him about two days and were getting close, when Sparks intercepted a message from the *Hyacinth City's* master to her owners in New Orleans telling them that *Franklin* was on the way. That was just routine; but their answer wasn't. They came right back at him with orders that he wasn't to take a wire from any tug except a Yank. 'Under no circumstances' was the way they put it.

"I can't say that I was worried much by that. One look out the wheelhouse at those big grey fellows roaring all the way in from Ireland should have been enough to make any master forget the orders of a bunch of landlubbers in plush chairs ashore.

"I sent a message to the *Hyacinth* right off, and never let on I'd heard the call from her owners. I made it sound like everything was set between us. I told him we'd come up to weather and then shoot a line across his forecastle, then he was to haul in our wire and shackle it to one of his anchor chains.

120

"He fooled me, though. He came back to say he was sorry. He'd like nothing better than to take our wire, but his owners wouldn't let him. He said he'd give his arm to be able to tie onto the *Franklin*, but he didn't dare go against his orders.

"I still wasn't worried. I knew the nearest Yankee tugs were Merritt-Chapman's in New York, and they would have had a thousand miles to steam to reach the casualty—even if they would have put to sea at all in that kind of weather. I kept on coming, figuring that something would break our way.

"On the morning of the eighteenth it looked as if we were going to get some luck. We were already close enough for Sparks to get a good DF bearing on the casualty. We began to run it down and just when we raised him on the horizon, Sparks got an emergency weather warning from Halifax. 'Heavy north-west gales increasing to hurricane force by noon,' it said. 'All ships take precautions.'

" 'Well, by golly,' I thought to myself. 'I've got him now.'

"We came up alongside and I told him that in view of the emergency warning he had better let us put a line on right away so we could hold him up to windward until the blow was over. But of course I knew—and I guess he did too—that once I got a line on him I wasn't likely to let go.

"The poor fellow pretty nearly cried. He wanted my wire the way a baby wants a bottle. He knew what he'd have to stand up to in a few hours' time, and considering the damage his ship had already taken, he didn't even know if she'd live through it. All the same he still wouldn't go against his owners' orders.

"I tried every way I knew to change his mind. I told him that if his passengers got hurt or killed, he'd be responsible. I tried to make him see the sense of ignoring his orders and doing what he could to save his ship. He agreed with everything I said—but when it came to taking the wire from me, he just wouldn't budge.

"We must have argued back and forth about an hour—and then the weather broke.

"Now, things had been bad enough before, and we'd already had so much misery that we were getting used to it; but this was the kind of storm that a man never could get used to until the day he died. It came in on top of one of the biggest seas I'd ever seen, and it got behind them and pushed them up until they weren't seas at all but water mountains. It gusted up to ninety miles an hour, and never fell off below eighty for six hours. It was cold too. The temperature in the wheelhouse stood around freezing point, and on deck it must have been down close to zero. Ice started to form, but luckily for us the seas were so fierce that they kept it swept off before it could get thick enough to make us list.

"Once it started in to blow we couldn't see beyond the vessel's rails for spray and sleet. The *Hyacinth City* blew off so fast that within an hour she was five miles to leeward— being bigger, she was drifting faster than the *Franklin*. The last I saw of her she was lying in the troughs—one minute clean out of sight and the next she was hove up on a crest higher than her spars; then rolling off into the trough again. She was being swept from end to end until you couldn't tell if she was a ship at all or just a mass of foam.

"Around 2 P.M. I came out of my cabin under the bridge wing and tried to get up to the wheelhouse. I got to the ladder and had my hands on it when *Franklin* began to climb one of those seas. She put her nose up in the air till I thought she was going to go right over on her back. My feet swung off the deck, and for about half a minute I was hanging by my hands at right angles to the ladder. I looked up and I could see the crest so far above me that it was nearly overhead. Then it went under her and we started down. I don't know what speed she was making, but it felt like riding an elevator. You'd have swore that when she hit the bottom of the trough she'd have kept on going until she struck mud a thousand fathoms down. But not the *Franklin*. At the bottom of the trough she lifted as pretty as a gull and started up again.

"The seas were so big and so steep that it was almost calm air in the troughs, and at the same time the hurricane was slicing the whole crests right off the tops of the waves overhead. They were the biggest seas I'd ever seen; some of them must have been nearly fifty feet.

"Once I got into the wheelhouse I stayed put. There was no value in trying to run around the decks that day. Mc-Manus was shut up in his radio shack, hoping it wouldn't be carried right off the boat-deck. He was talking to the operator on the *Hyacinth City* and every now and again he'd shout the news to me through the voice pipe.

"That ship was in trouble. Her deck load carried away and her cargo began to shift and she took on a bad list. One of her passengers got flung across his cabin so hard he broke an arm, and the rest of the passengers were pretty close to mutiny. They were making all the trouble they could to force the captain to take the *Franklin's* wire—but it was too late then.

"By midnight we were still hove-to, and we were forty miles away from the *Hyacinth* when Sparks got another SOS. It came through so loud it nearly took the ears off him. He peered through the port, half expecting to see the other ship poking its nose up to his door.

"This fellow was a Latvian, the *Everhope*. His steam steering gear had broken down and he was in the troughs. There was no way to figure exactly where anyone was that night, in terms of distance, but McManus got a bearing on him and I radioed that we were coming to his assistance at full speed.

"Maybe that was stretching it a little. He was upwind from us, and the best we could do against the gale and seas was about half a knot. Even then we were getting a terrific beating and the *Franklin* was taking it green both fore and aft. The hardest thing was to keep her dead into it. The wheelsmen had to watch her like a pair of hawks—there were two men on the wheel—for if she'd ever started to fall off, nothing could have kept her from broaching.

"I don't think there was a ship anywhere around that night that wasn't hove-to, no matter how big she was, except for *Franklin*. We were under weigh; but we weren't making any record passage of it.

"We kept the old girl charging up and down for six straight hours, and we'd gone maybe three or four miles when the Latvian comes on the air to tell us he's got his steering engine fixed and is hove-to himself, and doesn't need us any more.

"We weren't mad about that at all. We hove-to again and waited for the gale to blow itself out. It was no night for cruising. Before dawn came McManus told me that two big liners three hundred miles east of us, were hove-to as well.

"I don't know if the liner passengers were more comfortable than we were, but I know we got more exercise. Everybody had to hang on to something with one arm at least. If that gale had lasted for a week we'd have had muscles like weight lifters. There was no question of sleeping or even of lying down. The best thing was to get up against a stanchion and wrap yourself around it like an ivy vine.

"Just about dawn Sparks picked up another call, but it was so weak he couldn't read the details—just the SOS came through. I told him to send off a reply anyway, saying we were on our way to help and that we were in this fellow's vicinity. We *might* have been too, for all anyone could tell. Sparks called and called, but couldn't raise him until finally the *Queen Mary* picked up our signals and offered to relay them along. She said she was stopped herself, and it takes quite a storm to hold her back.

"She was as good as her word. With her powerful transmitter she contacted the disabled ship and found it was a Norwegian called the *Victo* who'd lost her propeller about seven hundred miles south-east of us, off near the Azores. Lost propellers were getting pretty common by then. The reason for that particular kind of trouble was that even the big ships were pitching so badly that their screws were out of the water and racing one minute, then away deep under and laboring the next. That put a terrible strain on the shafts and on the screws themselves.

"For us to go off to the *Victo* meant we had to come around and run pretty well straight before the gale; and that was a risky business. All the same I was getting pretty tired of false alarms and so I thought we'd chance it. I wouldn't have tried it with any ship except the *Franklin*, and even with her it was a near thing. My Lord! When she was half-way round and broadside to those seas, I couldn't see why she didn't roll right over.

"But we got around; and then the big ones came booming up astern of us and we began to run. We must have been making thirty knots when we went down the seas. There never was a twin-screw destroyer that could have caught us then.

"We had to watch her twice as careful so she wouldn't broach. But she was the greatest little thing to run. She had quite a flair onto her bows and when she hit the bottom of a trough she'd just drive down so far, and then she'd lift so fast she'd throw you off your feet if you weren't ready for it. It wasn't often she'd bury herself, not even when we were pushing her. We *were* pushing her then, for we had seven hundred miles to go.

"We ran for twenty-two hours and then Sparks got a message through from the *Queen Mary*. A Dutch tug out of the Azores had reached the *Victo* and was standing by to give her a wire when the weather moderated. That let us out, but we couldn't turn back yet. It's one thing to turn a ship out of a howling gale, but it's worse to try and head her up into one. We just had to keep on running and wait our chance.

"The biggest seas most generally run in threes; and if you watch them close you may get a little lull behind the third one. *Franklin* was about as quick on her feet as any ship I ever knew, and if there was no time wasted she could be brought round in time to catch the lull. I called down the pipe to John Sommers to stand by, and he was waiting with his hands on the steam wheel to give her power when I said.

"We watched our chance all that night and most of the next day until along about noon I saw a lull. I rang for full-ahead and the wheelsman spun the wheel hard over. John gave her everything he had and she came around just as if she knew there wouldn't be a second chance. She came as nice and pretty as a man could ask—but she was no more than head into it again when three of the big ones rolled right down on top of us. They were just a mite too late.

"The gale had eased a trifle, but now it came back full and we hove-to again. *Hyacinth City* was sending out new calls for help, and Sparks picked up a message that a Merrit-Chapman tug was just about ready to set out for her. The tug had a thousand miles to go—about two weeks' steaming in that kind of weather. I thought maybe *Hyacinth's* skipper would see reason now, so I called him and told him we were still around.

"He sounded desperate when he came back, but he still wouldn't go against his owners. He must have been scared to death of them, or maybe it was because a master's berth was hard to come by in those days.

"Thirty hours later the weather began to let up a bit and we got under weigh for home. We had to, for we had been out two weeks and we were getting short of coal. But not three hours later a message comes through from Featherstone telling us to stand by, that there was another ship in trouble, and we should try and get to her. We hove-to again and waited.

"The wind had almost dropped out by then, but the sea was still running as big as ever and we were getting pretty sick of the cricks in our neck we got from watching the big ones go by. Finally Featherstone comes back on the air; he had the name of the ship, but no position for her and no call sign either. MacManus couldn't find her listed in his book and so he began calling her name alone. He worked for an hour with no luck, and then some freighter halfway across the ocean relayed his message for him. She came back to us just at dusk to say the crippled ship we wanted was a hundred miles off the coast of Ireland.

"Ireland was a mite too far. We told Featherstone so and started for home. Then, believe it or not, we got another call.

"This one was from a ship called the *Scottish Musician* that had broken down a hundred and eighty miles east of Bermuda. We called her and she said for us to come.

"I got hold of old John and asked him if we had enough bunkers to make Bermuda, figuring that we could bunker there and then go on to the *Musician*. John answered 'Maybe,' which was about all you could hope for, so I decided to try.

"We came around again and we had run about seven hours when damned if the *Musician* didn't call us back to say she'd made repairs and could get in to Bermuda on her own.

"We headed home once more, but we were pretty doubtful if we'd make it. It looked as if we might have to get a tow ourselves, for we still had better than eight hundred miles to go.

"Two days later we ran into another gale, but we didn't dare heave-to. We had to ease along for port with John nursing her, and counting every lump of coal that went into the fires.

"It was real dirty weather too; thick of rain, and dark. We were coming along slowly when there was a little break in the muck, and dead ahead of us I saw a big ship, hove-to. We came up on her, hoping that she needed help and praying that she didn't. It was the *Everhope*. She was still trying to get to port and having to heave-to with every gale.

"Luckily she didn't need us, for we never could have got her in before our coal gave out.

"In fact we just got in ourselves. There was about two ton of coal left in the bunkers when we raised Sambro after eighteen days at sea, six distress calls—and not a thing to show for it."

There was some compensation for Power and his people in a wireless message which McManus intercepted on the day following *Franklin's* arrival home. It was addressed to the *Hyacinth City* from a New York tug, and it was to the effect that the tug was just then clearing Ambrose Lightship —and hoped to reach the casualty within ten days.

Power's account of that epic voyage well illustrates the frustrations which the salvors faced in those last years before the war; but it gives little insight into life aboard the *Franklin* during a hard passage.

Recalling this same voyage, Reg Poirier describes conditions in the engine room as being good compared to what the deck people had to endure. At that it hardly sounds idyllic. There were just two engineer officers, Sommers and Poirier, and they stood watch on, watch off, four hours' sleep, four hours' work, for the entire eighteen days. The engine room and stokehold were closed off as tight as could be, and the only fresh air was the draft for the fires. The temperature in the tiny stokehold never fell below one hundred and twenty degrees and at times it went to one hundred and thirty. With the ship battened down tight, the ashes could not be spilled overboard through the chutes and so they accumulated until both alleyways and every spare inch of stokehold space were jammed with them. Because of the fire risk the ashes had to be wet down with salt water, and the resultant stinking steam and dust filled the entire ship.

The accommodation deck was sealed as tightly as dogged

doors could make it, and there was nowhere for the stench of ashes, bilge, and engine oil to escape. It became a tangible substance. Men lived in it, breathed it, and became a part of it. During the gales—and that was most of the time—no fire could be kept in the galley stove and there was no hot food or drink for anyone. The crew's quarters in the forecastle were sealed like a coffin, and were as dark and chill; and the exaggerated motion over the ship's forefoot was such that even Newfoundland seamen became deathly sick and stayed that way for days on end.

Yet these men survived an experience which would have been an almost unendurable ordeal to ordinary men—and they survived it without particular comment; and most of them forgot about it a day after they were back in port. They saw nothing unique in it, for this was the way of life aboard the North Atlantic salvage ships.

17 ✥ APPROACH TO WAR

THE THREAT OF WAR had grown heavy over half a world and men were being stirred from the somnolence of the depression years either by fear or by the hope of profits. Long-idle machines were starting up, and factories had begun to hum with a muted murmur which would soon become a roar. Maritime traffic, which had been no more than a trickle since the debacle of 1929, quickened in a matter of months into a beginning flood. The ship lanes of the Western Ocean began to grow crowded with vessels bound for North America to take on cargoes of nickel, copper, iron ore, and manufactured goods of a kind that could be turned to warlike uses.

It was a time when old ships, laid up for a decade, were hurriedly refittted and sent back to sea. Creaking and limping, they toiled over the North Atlantic—and many of them inevitably came to grief. For *Franklin*, they marked the beginning of an era of almost ceaseless labor.

That era began on January 18, 1939, when the steamer *Black Condor* broke down off Sable and radioed for help. *Franklin* and Power went out to her, but were forestalled by a U.S. Coast Guard vessel. They had hardly returned to harbor when they were sent to assist the American freighter *Gro* six hundred miles east from Halifax. Power conned his little vessel through some of the worst weather of a bad winter, and through ice that bulged far south of Sable, only to find that the damaged ship was another *Hyacinth City*. She would have no tug except one that flew the U.S. flag. Power turned back, but he had only proceeded for six hours when McManus picked up an SOS from a six-thousand-ton British ship, the *Cornerbrook*, outbound for England with newsprint. *Cornerbrook* was then seventy-five miles off Cape Race with her steering gear disabled, and he was suffering increasing structural damage from the heavy seas. She was not fussy about the nationality of the tug that came for her. Power took her in tow and brought her home.

Now John Pynn took command and sailed for Prince Edward Island to help refloat the steamer *Nandi*, which had driven ashore on the broad sands of West Point the previous autumn, and which was eventually refloated by means of a mile-long channel dredged by the *Jupiter* from the beach to deep water.

Franklin was called away before this job was concluded, to rescue the *Gerda Toft*, a Norwegian that had lost her propeller over Flemish Cap four hundred miles east of Newfoundland. That twelve-hundred-mile passage was completed on May 13, and on May 15 *Franklin* sailed to assist the ten-thousand-ton tanker *Britamer*, whose engines had failed her in the narrow and dangerous waters of Northumberland Strait. *Franklin* safely delivered this big ship to another tug at the entrance of Halifax harbor and then, without entering herself, turned and made again for the *Nandi*, which she refloated five days later.

Scarcely a week after the *Nandi* had been freed, *Franklin* was at work on the scrap-laden British steamer *Penolver*, which had sunk in Louisburg harbor after hitting a submerged rock. The pumping, patching and lifting of this ship took a month of unremitting labor. But there was no respite. A few days later *Franklin* and Power were busy refloating the Dutch motor vessel *Bernhardt* from ill-famed Cerberus Rock.

Then on September 9, 1939, Canada officially declared herself at war with Germany.

It is doubtful that this declaration caused the German General Staff much initial alarm; for Canada was one of the least warlike nations in those days. Her Army consisted of three under-strength infantry battalions and some fragments of supporting arms. Her Air Force had a dozen or so planes, mostly of museum vintage; while the Navy could probably have been outweighed by the Royal Navy of Siam.

Nevertheless Canada had fighting men; and these volunteered so enthusiastically that before Christmas an entire infantry division was on its way to England. She also possessed nearly limitless resources of raw materials which, together with a latent capacity for industrial development, were eventually to transform her into one of the major Allied arms factories. In addition to all this, and of more immediate importance, Canada's doors swung open on the neutral United States, which was prepared to sell weapons and the machines with which to make them.

There was much that Canada could contribute, even in the early months of war, but these contributions could reach Europe only over the bridge of ships which spanned the North Atlantic, and whose western terminal was Halifax.

Throughout the next five years Halifax (anonymous behind the censor's "An Eastern Canadian Port") was to receive, to harbor and dispatch a volume of shipping which was not equaled by any other port on the Atlantic seaboard of the continent. The *Queens—Elizabeth* and *Mary*—became almost as familiar to the people of Halifax as were the harbor tugs. Eventually the freighters, tankers and warships of fifty nations were to come crowding into Bedford Basin in their thousands; to lie in endless rows, drab and shoddy in their camouflage, and hungry for the cargoes which might win the war.

But when it all began in September of 1939, Halifax was almost totally unprepared for the gargantuan task ahead. The port lacked adequate dockage facilities, harbor tugs, seaward and anti-submarine defenses, and the mechanisms to control and supervise the mighty flow of vessels which would soon come funneling in past Chebucto Head. On the water there was no organized authority to take command, for the Navy was only a shadow with hardly enough boats of any kind even to begin a training program.

Halifax, like the rest of Canada, had been caught napping. Nevertheless there were a few men who had not been drugged into stupor by the wish for peace. One of them was Chadwick, who, a year before war was declared, had already drawn up detailed plans for the deployment of his private forces. "Chadwick's Navy"— that sardonic joke of a decade earlier—was about to come into its own.

With the outbreak of war most of the nations concerned had automatically taken over control of their respective salvage services. Thus the British Admiralty had assumed command of all salvage and rescue work in home waters, under direct naval supervision; and it had officered the commercial salvage vessels with naval personnel. Overnight most salvage fleets became auxiliaries of the naval forces. It was not so in Canada.

The Royal Canadian Navy did indeed make an attempt to absorb Foundation Maritime, but it met such stubborn resistance that the attempt came to nothing. Chadwick took his case directly to the Canadian Cabinet and when he had pointed out that the Canadian Navy had quite enough to do to get to *be* a navy, while the Foundation salvage fleet was already a fleet in being, he won his point. Having established a precedent he clung tenaciously to it throughout the war years so that in the end Foundation Maritime was probably the only private company in the Western world fully engaged in war work which was never under government control. Later on when the United States belatedly entered the struggle, this situation seemed so inexplicable to the Americans that they actually made a move to absorb Foundation Maritime themselves and integrate it into their own salvage service. The mere suggestion of this brought Chadwick charging into Washington where, after a series of interviews with various highly-placed officials during which he talked pointedly of national sovereignty, he not only squelched this plan but emerged from the battle with a contract that must be unique in American history. By its terms Foundation Martime was not only to be free and unfettered in its work for American owned or chartered vessels, but in cases where U.S. naval forces were also involved in the salvage job the civilian captain of the Foundation tug was to be in over-all command, and was empowered to issue orders to the U.S. Navy. As a contract it was flagrantly illegal, for it violated the U.S. Constitution. As a fact it worked very well indeed, and the company's subsequent relations with the U.S. Navy were on the whole far better than its relations with the Canadian Navy.

However, Chadwick had been somewhat premature when he had talked of "his fleet in being." When the war began, the salvage fleet which was eventually to become responsible for most of the rescue and salvage work on the northeastern approaches to the continent consisted of the *Franklin*, the cantankerous *Jupiter*, and five harbor tugs. Of these, only *Franklin* could operate safely and with efficiency at sea.

But having won his point at Ottawa, Chadwick was not going to lose it by default. By September 15 he had every available man scouring the docks and harbors of the country for more vessels. It was then too late to build new ones, and it was even too late to hope to buy good secondhand ones. Some people thought it was probably too late to do anything at all about enlarging the salvage fleet. The company's experience with its first new purchase seemed to confirm this opinion.

An eighty-foot tug, reputedly of "ocean-going" stature, but of uncertain vintage, had been bought sight unseen at Quebec, and Power was dispatched with *Franklin* to bring her down to Halifax for refit.

"She was a desperate-looking thing," Power recalls. "She was built of wood and she had been laid up for fifteen years.

I got out my knife to test her timbers and at the first hack I took at her, my knife went clean in to the hilt."

Nevertheless it was his job to tow her east and so a wire was put on her forward winch—the bollards could not be trusted—and the tow began.

The weather stayed fair and the sea was smooth as they came down toward Cap Chat on the second night of the voyage. Power had just gone to his room for a sleep, when he was awakened by Pynn.

"Cap," the mate said gently, "best you come and take a look astern. We can't seem to see that tug no more."

Power scrambled up to the bridge—but even through the night glasses he could see no tug. And that was more than passing strange, for the tow wire was still taut across the stern, with a strain upon it.

Power ordered *Franklin* brought about in a wide circle, and as she steamed westward again he saw that they were sailing through a mess of floating planks. There *was* no tug.

They hauled in the tow wire, and at the end of it they found the winch—complete. They had pulled the bow off the ancient vessel and she had come apart. For some time past they had been dragging five tons of iron along the bottom of the Gulf.

As the autumn waned, the vessel situation became increasingly desperate. Chadwick's scouts were unable to locate a single tug which was for sale, except for those which were so old that no one wanted them at all. Driven by desperation the company bought any number of these sad relics, the very names of which are still sufficient to make their unhappy wartime skippers shudder with distaste. Most of those resurrected ghosts never went to work. One of them gave up and sank at the Foundation docks and had to be raised, towed out to sea, and left to sink again in less congested waters. One of them burned before her refit was complete—and that was lucky for her prospective crew. Most of them were soon towed in behind McNab's island, to lie with the other rotting hulks in that graveyard of old ships.

There were two exceptions—exceptions which made it possible for Chadwick to uphold his brag.

The first was the *Aranmore*. She was an iron ship, built in Scotland in 1888 as a coast-wise passenger vessel in the Irish Sea. When her usefulness in those waters came to an end she was "sold foreign" and brought out to Canada to fill the lowly role of a cattle boat upon the river and the Gulf. She probably would have ended her days in that unromantic trade had not the advent of the First World War impelled the Canadian Government to buy her and refit her as a light-tender. She served in this capacity until 1937, when she was finally retired. By that time her tanktops under the boilers were rusted through, and she could no longer pass her annual steamship inspections. She was saved from destruction only because scrap prices were so low that it would not have paid a wrecker to break her up.

Then came the new war. Chadwick found her at her berth in Montreal one winter day, and Power was told to go and have a look at her. His report was favorable. The old vessel's iron shell plates were as sound as the day they had been forged, and her Scotch boiler and triple-expansion engine were of the sort that never wear out. Chadwick bought her from the government for a token payment of one dollar, and the old girl went back to sea again after a three months' overhaul.

Fitted with towing gear and with salvage equipment, she worked from 1940 until the war's end under Captain Power; and her record was one that the most modern salvage ship afloat could hardly have surpassed. She and the *Franklin* were two old vessels out of another age. Belching black coal smoke across the grey Atlantic they showed the sleek new diesel tugs of the modern era what real ships were. And the outport Newfoundlanders, Nova Scotians, and Cape Breton-ers who manned them showed the union-bound mechanics who served aboard the world's merchant fleets and the hidebound sailors of the Canadian and United States naval vessels what real seamen were.

Aranmore and *Franklin* were assisted by yet another able relic resurrected from the bone yard—the *Foundation Security* (built in 1905 as a barge tow-boat)—and by the little harbor tugs, which, half the time, were worked as ocean-going vessels.

The result of all their efforts was that during the war years the company was responsible for the salvage of one hundred and thirty-two vessels with a gross aggregate tonnage in excess of half a million; for the salvage of war cargoes totaling two thirds of this amount; and for the rescue of nearly a thousand men.

It did other notable things as well. When war broke out, the Canadian Navy could not begin to carry out all of its proper duties and some of the most important of these devolved on Foundation Maritime. Foremost amongst them was the design, building, and laying of anti-submarine nets across the mouths of Halifax, Shelburne, Sydney and Gaspé harbors. This was a tremendous task, which British naval authorities later conceded would have required a full six months of work by their technicians, but which Foundation

Maritime's crews, under the direction of the versatile Captain Power, accomplished in half that time.

Power, that man of many talents, turned over his command of *Foundation Franklin* to Captain Pynn during this period. When the nets were all in place he went back to sea again—but as commander of the *Aranmore,* and insofar as this book is concerned, his subsequent feats must be passed over.

By late October enemy submarines were being reported in Canadian coastal waters, and in early November the German battleship *Deutschland* seized and sank two ships not far off Sable Island.

War was becoming a reality and in the first wild flurry of reaction the lights along the seaboard coasts were hurriedly extinguished for fear they might aid the enemy. Merchant ships received sealed instructions, which they often found were quite impossible to follow, and they were ordered to sail blacked-out. The combination of a huge and sudden influx of vessels (most of whose masters had never sailed these waters before), together with the blackout, the lack of lighthouses, and an enforced radio silence, combined to make navigation several times more dangerous than it had always been in these unfriendly waters. The confusion in the shipping lanes and in the harbors grew apace, and the number of resulting accidents at first did more damage to the Allied cause than did the enemy's U-boats.

Franklin had been fully prepared to take her place in the war at sea before September finished. She had been fitted with blackout gear; her radio transmitter had been sealed; she had been given her battle paint (which is to say that she was now a solid black, unrelieved even by the company colors on her funnels), and she had also been armed with two .30/30 sporting rifles.

Defensive armaments were considered necessary, for at that time there were no Canadian naval ships available even to escort the merchantmen. Thus, when *Franklin* sailed she had to be prepared to hold her own against the *Deutschland* and the U-boats too. Whether or not her armament was adequate was a moot point, but at least, as one of her officers remarked, "We could have held off a herd of seals if they'd got nasty-like."

When *Franklin* sailed on her first wartime mission the question of armaments remained academic. For it was not the new enemy, but the old familiar one with which she had to battle.

The *Selje* was a brand-new Norwegian ship of twelve thousand tons dead weight which had been chartered by

Dosco to carry iron ore from that company's mines at Wabana, in Newfoundland, to the mills at Sydney. Outward bound from Sydney in early November, *Selje* encountered an onshore blow thirty miles south-west of St. Pierre and Miquelon, and in the ensuing struggle she lost her propeller and began to drift toward the shore.

Immediately her SOS was heard in Halifax and *Franklin* sailed. Pynn drove his vessel, for he knew it would only be a matter of hours before *Selje* would be ashore.

Franklin made good progress until 4 P.M. on November 6, when a heavy storm blew up out of the south-west. By then she was close enough to get a DF bearing on *Selje*, and to hear from the casualty's master that the big ore ship was less than six miles off a lee shore and drifting fast toward it. It was clearly no time to ease *Franklin* down. Pynn kept her at it and she corkscrewed through the beam sea like a porpoise. At 10 P.M. she raised the *Selje*, who, in defiance of the potential danger from submarines, was using all her searchlights to assist her in avoiding the all-too-real dangers of the St. Pierre reefs.

"It was safe enough for her to do that," one of *Franklin's* crew said later. "No U-boat commander in his right mind would have gone near her. Only a damn-fool tug-boat skipper would have tried to go in close."

Pynn was anything but a damn fool; nevertheless it was a stupendous risk he took that night as he worked *Franklin* in against the lee shore within sound of the breakers, in darkness and in a gale of wind. It was very nearly a footless risk too, for *Selje* was rolling and pitching with such abandon that it proved almost impossible to get a line aboard her. The first three tries with the rocket gun were failures, and it began to look as if she must go on the rocks.

Attempts to get a line aboard her from the seaward side having failed, Pynn decided to double the stakes. He took *Franklin inside* the *Selje*, feeling his way blind through the nests of "sunkers" that made St. Pierre a sailor's horror. He did not take this risk out of bravado, for he was normally a cautious man. He took it because he was aware that if the *Selje* went ashore on that wild night her crew would perish with her.

As *Franklin* went in, one of her engineers stuck his head up out of the engine room companionway to see what was going on. He ducked quickly back inside again.

"I couldn't bear to watch," he said. "When seas begin to break *offshore* from you, it's time to go and get yourself a hooker of something strong."

In a last attempt to save herself *Selje* had dropped her anchors—but they were not holding. The anchor chains put an

134

extra obstacle in *Franklin's* way and made Pynn's job still more difficult. Yet somehow he maneuvered his little ship into position, and once more the rocket gun blasted its lurid streak of flame into the black sky.

This time the gap was bridged. The Norwegian seamen on *Selje's* forcastle threw themselves on the fragile line as it snaked past them, and within minutes had hauled the manila messenger aboard their ship.

They were good seamen. Carefully—for if the line had broken, their last hope would have been gone—they brought the wire bridles over and made them fast. Then *Franklin* eased out from under *Selje's* bow, swung her head straight into the gale, and took the strain.

For in interminable time it seemed as if she would not get clear. Being light, *Selje* towered up out of the white seas like a cliff of steel and gave the gale an immense expanse to push against. *Franklin's* engines labored at full revolutions and her propeller shaft rumbled until she shook all over like a dog; but still the *Selje* would not leave the edge of her own grave.

Four hours after the tow began, Gallantry Head loomed up in the dawn scud less than two miles to leeward. Pynn was no longer trying to lay a course for Halifax. He was concentrating every effort on clawing away from that lee shore. Down in the stokehold the half-naked stokers shoveled coal until the furnaces roared like the gale itself. John Sommers watched his steam gauges and hoped that the safety valves were screwed down tighter than the regulations said they ought to be.

Franklin strained her heart out through fifty hours of that south-west gale, and at the end of that time she had pulled *Selje* exactly six miles off St. Pierre!

Only then did Pynn dare alter course for Halifax; but with the change in course he found the going not one whit easier. Through the ninth, tenth, and eleventh of November *Franklin* strained like a chained animal; and she made good one hundred miles in those three days and nights.

At noon on the twelfth one leg of the bridle on *Selje's* bow let go. The sudden strain as the other leg took the full weight of the tow was too much for the main towing wire and it parted with a banshee screech just off *Franklin's* rail.

For the first time Pynn used his radio. He called Halifax (which had heard nothing from him for seven days, and did not know if either *Selje* or *Franklin* was still afloat) to say that he had burned two hundred and fifty tons of coal since November 5 and that he must come into Louisburg for bunkers before attempting to reconnect to *Selje*. "Send out another tug to help," he asked.

They sent out the little harbor tug *Banscot,* under command of Captain Turner.

Turner is a phlegmatic man, as befits a tug-boat skipper of thirty years' experience; but he was not phlegmatic about the *Selje* job. To this day he can recall the shape and location of every sea he met on his voyage out. He knew them all so intimately; for every one of them came aboard *Banscot* to call.

Banscot stayed afloat only because she was so tightly sealed that she would have popped back to the surface from twenty fathoms down. As things were she seldom saw the light of day. "Water was coming down her funnel," recalls her chief engineer, "like the flow out of the main Halifax sewer pipe."

With fresh bunkers aboard *Franklin* returned to her charge and grimly put another line aboard, while *Banscot* did the same. And on November 17 the two tugs brought their prize through the submarine nets and into Halifax.

18 ❖ TOO CLOSE IN—AND TOO FAR OUT

ALTHOUGH HALIFAX HARBOR is one of the finest on the eastern coast, the approaches to it are not without their dangers. With the additional hazards of submarine nets, the blackout, the absence of the usual navigation aids, and the colossal increase in the numbers of working ships, it was inevitable that some of the vessels seeking its safe haven would find themselves in trouble. Thrumcap Shoal, Mars Rock, the Sambro Ledges, and the rest of the obstacles in the approaches were all to exact their special tolls before the war was done; but Thrumcap was the first to claim its dues.

The night of March 23, 1940, was miserably cold. The inevitable fog stood between land and sea, amorphous and yet of such substance that not even the onshore gale could dissipate it.

The submarine-boom gates were closed and the two gate boats were lost islands in an abysmal deep. No ships were moving. From Chebucto Head the dull throb of the diaphones was felt, rather than heard, against the whine of wind.

As midnight approached, the office of the Naval Control station grew somnolent with inactivity. Two vessels which had been due into Halifax that evening had not arrived, and were not now to be expected until the dawn brought clearing visibility. Both were presumably hove-to well off shore, waiting out the storm.

That presumption held good for only one of them.

The other, the large tanker *El Ciervo*, had had enough of the North Atlantic and she was driving hard—and blind—for port. Her cargo tanks were filled with Admiralty fuel oil destined to bunker the Royal Navy vessels which were beginning to use Halifax as a convoy base. It was a particularly vital cargo and *El Ciervo's* master was anxious to get it into harbor. He did not know Halifax, but he had his charts and he believed that they would see him through.

Two hours before dawn on the twenty-third Featherstone was roused from sleep by an urgent telephone call from Naval Control. The message was brief enough; a tanker called *El Ciervo* had broken radio silence a few minutes earlier to report that she had driven up on Devil's Island off the entrance to the harbor and was in dire need of help.

Featherstone was at the docks in fifteen minutes. He found *Franklin* crowded with busy men, for she had blown down her boilers the previous evening for cleaning and her people had been working the night through to complete the job. They were not yet finished, and *Franklin* could not sail for several hours. Featherstone boarded the *Banscot* instead and set out into the fog-shrouded darkness of the harbor.

He found the tanker just at dawn, after an agonizing search. She was not on Devil's Island. She was halfway across the infinitely more dangerous Thrumcap Shoal—a mile-long shingle and boulder reef exposed to the full surge of the open sea.

El Ciervo must have had a death wish in her soul, for she had run on the shoal within three minutes of the highest water recorded in Halifax that winter. She had gone on at ten knots running before the gale and, with the tremendous momentum imparted by her twelve thousand tons of dead weight, she had driven so far up that she lacked ten feet of draft ever to float again.

When Featherstone reached her she was being heavily assailed. Spray was breaking clear across her superstructure and it was lavishly mixed with bunker oil that was flowing thickly out of shattered cargo tanks. Thrumcap was breaking white and ugly in its triumph, and warning off the little tug.

Banscot was not dismayed. Captain Turner backed her in right over the shoals that reached up through the hungry foam. At exactly the right instant Featherstone jumped from the taff-rail, caught a swinging rope ladder, and went scrambling up the oil-smeared sides of the big ship. Before Thrumcap could avenge this insolence, *Banscot* was gone again.

It was a grim situation which confronted Featherstone aboard *El Ciervo*. The tanker had already sustained such heavy underwater damage that all of her port cargo tanks were open to the sea while numbers one and two tanks were not only open, but were tidal on both port and starboard sides. Only the engine room seemed reasonably tight, but there was no telling when it too would flood, for the big ship was grinding savagely upon the boulders of the reef.

The weather was promising to help her die. It was then blowing force seven and there was every indication that the wind would make up as the day advanced.

Standing on her spray-swept bridge, Featherstone considered how he might circumvent this would-be suicide. He knew that unless she could be lightened she was done. But he could not make use of the vessel's cargo pumps to jettison the oil, for the main pump room was flooded. Nor could salvage pumps be brought aboard, for no vessel big enough to handle them could have approached within several hundred yards. As Featherstone saw it there was but one solution to the problem. If Tom Nolan could get aboard, he could perhaps descend into the flooded pump room, open the valves, and allow the cargo to drain out of the fractured tanks by gravity as the tide fell.

Franklin arrived (on one boiler) at 10 A.M. She hove-to a quarter of a mile off the reef while Nolan, his tender and his diving gear were lowered into the dory. *El Ciervo's* people watched with incredulity. They could not believe that so small a boat—or any boat—could pass through such a surf and live. When they were told that Tom could not swim, they thought he must be mad.

Twenty minutes later when they had snatched him—dory and all—out of the heaving foam at their vessel's side, one of them could not contain his curiosity.

"How in the name of God," he asked, "can you take that kind of risk when you can't even swim?"

Tom thought it a foolish question, for, as he had often pointed out, not even a seal could stay afloat in the kind of sea that was needed to pitch a Newfoundlander out of a dory.

Tom dressed and went down into the flooded darkness of the tanker's belly. By feel alone he found his way through the unfamiliar intricacies of the ship, located the valves, and opened them one by one.

As the tide ebbed, the viscous oil oozed out into the sea where a portion of it was picked up by the breakers and flung back on *El Ciervo's* decks until the entire ship was thickly coated.

Meanwhile Turner and *Banscot* were again baiting Thrumcap. Backing and filling like a skittish colt, the little tug gradually eased her stern in toward the wreck until she found a break in the defenses and was able to get a heaving line onto *El Ciervo's* deck. Then she scuttled out of danger, delivered her end to *Franklin*, and stood off as the messenger was hauled back to the tanker. When the wire was fast, *Franklin* took a strain; but that was a forlorn hope, for no one believed the big ship would move—nor did she budge an inch. *Franklin* had to cast off the wire and withdraw to deeper waters.

The gale continued unabated for the balance of the day. The stranded ship continued to "creak and shake like an old Model T." Crew and salvors alike were marooned aboard, for as the sea rose it prevented even the intrepid little *Banscot* from again closing with the wreck. She and *Franklin* stood by as near as possible, since *El Ciervo* seemed about to break up momentarily and the tugs might have had some slim chance of saving lives if this had happened.

Featherstone was counting on a slackening of the gale which would allow *Franklin* to transship pumps and air compressors; but instead of slackening, the gale gradually grew worse. The temperature began to plummet and a rich slush of freezing sea water and coagulating oil formed thickly on the casualty's decks and superstructure.

Before dawn on the twenty-fifth all of the remaining cargo tanks had fractured and the entire vessel, save for the engine room, was open to the sea and tidal. She was then beyond saving by the usual methods of patching and pumping. The only remaning hope for her was that her hatches and decks might be sealed tightly enough to contain compressed air, and that the compressors and ground-tackle gear could somehow be landed on her from one of the tugs.

Banscot was game to try. She came in shortly after noon with the purchases for the ground tackle. *El Ciervo* had no cargo winches, and *Banscot* had no lifting gear. Consequently the heavy equipment had to be transhipped by man power alone—one piece at a time—whenever *Banscot* rose on a crest to the level of *El Ciervo's* after deck. Turner's skill in maneuvering his tug under these conditions was remarkable, but the operation was too dangerous to continue and so *Banscot* was ordered off.

Toward evening there was some moderation in the storm and three volunteers, in the ubiquitous dory, undertook to get another messenger line from *Franklin* to the wreck in preparation for the laying of ground tackle. But the sea was too rough to allow *Franklin* to swing the five-ton salvage anchors over her sides without seriously endangering her, and this attempt also had to be abandoned.

In Halifax the secrecy which had shrouded the early part of the operation had been dissipated, and seamen gathered on the docks to discuss *El Ciervo's* situation. They gave her only the slimmest chance of surviving. And there was a growing apprehension that unless the people were taken off her soon they would be lost as she broke up. She had already taken more punishment than any ship should have to bear, and it was obvious that she was living on borrowed time. If the wind, which had gone westerly, continued around into the north-east, it would make short shrift of her.

But her people could not be taken off that day or during the following night. It was not until late morning of March 26 that *Banscot* was again able to come in close, and by then there was a reviving hope that the vessel herself might yet be saved. Featherstone refused to abandon her and, moved by his example, her own people chose to remain also.

Those men aboard the wreck had not been idle. For three days and nights they had labored under Featherstone's directions and in the face of frightful difficulties from the freezing slime of oil and from the breaking seas to make her airtight above the water line. By morning of the twenty-seventh they were near complete exhaustion. Nevertheless they somehow found reserves for one last effort as they laid out the purchases for the ground tackle and completed the sealing of the hatches and other deck openings.

Meanwhile Pynn had managed to get the salvage anchors down, though at the imminent risk of having *Franklin's* sides stove-in as the great masses of iron swayed and pirouetted from the boom. When they were in place at last, *Franklin* took a wilder risk and steamed in toward the wreck, bringing the air compressors. *Franklin* drew fourteen feet of water. There was a depth of fourteen and a half feet off *El Ciervo's* stern, and the seas were running high. As she came around under the overhang of the wreck's counter *Franklin* struck bottom with a shudder that went through her every frame. She lifted and struck again—and yet again, so that the men in her engine room looked up toward the deck with longing eyes. Nevertheless Pynn held her on the shoal until the compressors had been swung up and over onto *El Ciervo's* deck. Only then did she back clear. Pynn's relief must be imagined when Sommers came on deck to tell him that the old ship's iron plates had given with the shock instead of fracturing, and that she was still sound.

Aboard *El Ciervo* conditions had grown worse. The wreck had begun to list to starboard and she had settled so that she was being swept from end to end. As fast as a compressor was lashed into position a breaking sea would tear it loose and send its two tons of dead weight slithering across the canted and oily decks. The compressor engines were inundated in freezing salt spray so that they could not be kept in operation for more than a few minutes at a time.

By evening the wind had begun to rise again and the seas (which had never stilled) renewed their assault upon the broken tanker. All night long she ground her bottom out so that by dawn she was no more than the semblance of ship above the waterline, while underneath the surface she had been reduced to twisted scrap.

No one, not even Featherstone, could understand why she did not break in half, for there was hardly any longitudinal strength left in her. The seas broke over her and she writhed and bent about the midships section; but still she held together. That she could not continue to do so for much longer was certain. The wind had gone into the north and a proper nor'easter was about to strike. *El Ciervo* had used up almost all her time.

On the morning of March 27 *Franklin* came back against all odds and managed to put two more compressors aboard the wreck. While she was about it, lifting and falling in the seas with the compressors swinging at the end of her boom like gigantic wrecking hammers, she was in as mortal danger as she had ever known. Again and again she struck the reef, but her iron plates gave, where steel would have cracked and broken.

Aboard *El Ciervo*, Buck Dassylva and his gang took charge of the compressors and eventually worked them into position and connected up the hoses to the airlines which had already been laid to the various tanks. Despite the breaking seas Buck managed to get every engine working. As high tide approached, the thunder of the compressors, muted by the roar of the surf, became a murmur of hope. Pound by pound the pressure mounted in the tanks as the water and oil was slowly driven down and out through the shattered plates of the wreck's bottom.

The salvage gang and the vessel's crew began to take up the slack on the ground tackle. *Banscot* and *Banshee* came in and gave their tow wires to *El Ciervo*, ready for the pull. *Franklin* stood by to take charge of the wreck if she could come off.

Dusk fell grey and ominous, and the hard wind howled out of the north. The sound of the laboring compressors was lost in the voice of the approaching storm. The ground tackle came bar taut and the two harbor tugs tucked their sterns down and pulled like ants straining to move the corpse of a gigantic beetle.

At 8 P.M., with the tide already falling and hope all but dead, there came a terrifying sound of ripping steel and *El Ciervo* began to move. No one cheered her. No one showed any overt sense of victory. The men aboard the ship and on the tugs were too overstrained, too tired to care.

Even as she came free into deep water they nearly lost her. She began to heel sharply until she was on her beam ends and only the automatic reactions of the compressor men, who ran to bleed the air from her high side, prevented a disaster. Almost regretfully she came back toward an even keel. It was her last resistance. After that she followed like a docile cow as *Franklin* took her in tow and edged her down the fairway to the safety of the port.

So Thrumcap was cheated of its due. That had not happened often in the past, for almost all the ships which had taken the ground there had become total losses and many of them—like the ill-fated *Bohemian*—had drowned their entire crews in Thrumcap's breakers.

Franklin had done her part in the rescue of *El Ciervo,* but she had a price to pay for it. She paid, not only in the damage to her fabric, but in the loss of Captain Pynn. The strain of the years that he had spent as mate and master of her had been too much even for the robust nature of that good seaman. *El Ciervo,* and the hours when *Franklin* lay inside the surf, had finished him. He gave up his command and left the sea forever. He was missed, for he had served the vessel well; but *Franklin* outlasted him as she had outlasted so many men, and as she was to outlast others yet to come.

John Pynn was succeeded by Captain Cecil Ormiston, who had been a tug-boat skipper on the harbor boats for many years. Chief Engineer John Sommers also went ashore, to be replaced by Charlie Read.

On Saturday, March 30, *Franklin* was lying alongside *El Ciervo* supplying steam for the pumps aboard the crippled ship, while Tom Nolan and diver Ozzie Isnor were down plugging her underwater fractures so that she could be kept afloat until the dry-dock was ready to receive her.

Franklin herself was due for an inspection and an overhaul on the Dartmouth slip on Monday morning. But at 8 P.M. that Saturday night Edward Woollcombe, who was then the General Manager of Foundation Maritime, was called to the telephone to receive a message from Naval Control. The navy reported that a large British freighter called the *King Edward* was in difficulties nine hundred miles east of Halifax and required a tow.

That distance put her outside *Franklin's* normal working range. In any case *Franklin* badly needed to be docked, and her new master deserved some time in which to get acquainted with his ship. Woollcombe remembered that the Dutch tug *Thames,* under command of the British Admiralty, was in St. John's—far handier to the casualty. He suggested that the *Thames* be sent to do the job. Naval Control replied that the *Thames* was out of action and that unless *Franklin* could reach her the *King Edward* would probably be lost, for she was in heavy weather and drifting rapidly eastward into the active submarine zone.

That settled the matter. Ormiston was called to the office, where he listened to the details of his first assignment. If he had any reservations they were not allowed to show—but it was different with his crew.

During the months since the war had begun there had been many changes in the crew. Some of the best men had left to join the Navy, and others, disgruntled by the low pay aboard the salvage tug, had gone to the far-better-paying merchant ships. Only a few of the old, tried men remained, and they too were distressed by the belief that they were being imposed upon, being asked to do too much for too little return while the company itself was waxing prosperous. *Franklin* was no longer a happy ship. Worse still, the rumor had gone about that she was no longer seaworthy.

When Ormiston passed the word that instead of being hauled out for repairs *Franklin* was setting out on a voyage that would probably take her a thousand miles to the east, without escort, and on a forlorn-hope job, there was hell to pay. Most of the newer members of the crew packed their gear and went ashore. A vital handful remained—but some of them were discontented men.

It was not easy for Read and Ormiston to find enough new firemen and sailors. The rumors had spread quickly, and the quality of men who *could* be persuaded to join the ship was therefore somewhat dubious.

Nevertheless *Franklin* put to sea at 11 P.M. that evening on a voyage that was ill-omened from the start.

Read and Ormiston discussed some of their problems before they were outside the harbor. Read had known and admired *Franklin* for a long time, but he was a realist.

"We may get out there, Cap," he said, "but unless we get easy steaming all the way—and no lost time—we'll never get that freighter back to port. Not on the coal we carry—and not with the black gang I've got below."

Ormiston was a realist too, but he could not afford to show his doubts.

"Just do your best, Chief," he replied shortly. "I'll do what I can to help you stretch your coal."

The first thing that had to be done was to avoid the great bulge of spring ice that was settling south from Newfoundland, for Ormiston knew that if *Franklin* got into the pack it would result in a crippling wastage of bunkers at the very outset of the voyage. But avoiding the ice was no easy matter. There were no accurate reports as to how far south it extended. Ormiston had to choose his course by instinct. He took a gamble and gave the steersman a heading which would leave Sable Island thirty miles on the port beam . . . a heading that *ought* to clear the pack, but one that added a hundred miles to the total distance they would have to go.

It was a good gamble. During the morning of April 2 they passed within five miles of the southern edge of the pack and were then able to alter into the north-east.

If Ormiston felt relief at this stroke of luck, it was premature. With the following dawn the sky began to cloud over and the wind began to rise out of the south-east. By noon it had built up a rough beam sea and *Franklin* was already laboring. By midnight on April 3 the wind had become a north-east gale and *Franklin* was making heavy weather of it. And at 2 A.M. the green hands in the stokehold lost steam pressure—the engine slowed and almost stopped, and *Franklin* began to fall off into the troughs. Read and Poirier together fired the boilers and brought her out of it, but the incident did nothing to make Ormiston feel easier in his mind.

To make matters worse there was no contact with the *King Edward*. Young Cyril Marryat, a quiet-spoken Newfoundlander who had only recently obtained his operator's papers, and who had replaced Lindsay McManus in the the radio shack, tried doggedly to raise the crippled ship. Time and time again he incurred the Navy's wrath by breaking radio silence, but his calls went unanswered.

The lack of contact made Orimston's job an almost hopeless one. *King Edward's* last given position was then four days old and quite useless. Ormiston knew that unless a new position could be obtained, and unless *Franklin* could run directly down on the casualty without losing so much as half a day's coal in searching for her, the tug could never get the cripple back to port.

In desperation he called Halifax, but there was no help there. The Navy had not obtained a new position either. The only information they could give did not reduce Ormiston's worries, for they had a delayed report to the effect that *King Edward* was thought to have been in collision and was believed to be seriously damaged and in a sinking condition.

Franklin drove onward toward a goal lost somewhere in an expanse of grey and storm-torn waters five or ten thousand square miles in extent. Her bunkers were dwindling fast.

Marryat worked his set at intervals, but now he was becoming chary with his calls, for these were submarine waters. For the most part he stayed on listening watch.

At dusk on April 5 Marryat stiffened in his chair. A call

was coming in—almost booming in. The call sign was that of an American weather ship. She reported that she was standing by the crippled *King Edward* but that she could not tow the big freighter. She was apologetic and long-winded about this, and it was some time before Marryat could get on the air with a succinct request for a position. The position came back in a few moments and then the chatty weather ship went on for an interminable time, filling the air with the amiable talk in which wireless operators like to indulge themselves in time of peace.

Franklin's people were immeasurably grateful to that weather ship—but within a few hours they had begun to hate her with an abiding passion. She would not keep quiet. She either did not realize, or did not care, that every German submarine in North Atlantic waters could hear her garrulous exchanges and could home on them. She was a good-hearted ship, but she was neutral—and secure. In her well-meaning efforts to assist the tug she began to transmit DF signals at intervals of an hour—on the hour. If she had lit a bonfire ten miles tall, she could not have issued a more obvious invitation to Doenitz's submarines.

As *Franklin* ran down the new position of the *King Edward,* the tension engendered by the fear of submarines rasped every man to nervous irritability. Aboard the casualty the tension must have been almost unendurable—for it was not until April 8 that the tug finally hove in sight.

Ormiston picked the cripple up on the horizon at 45.20 north, 38.53 west—one thousand forty miles east of Halifax, and only six hundred miles from the Azores.

Read could hardly bear to go on deck to take a look at her. "I was so damn sure," he remembers, "that I wouldn't be able to see her for the periscopes."

That his expectations were not realized was probably due to the weather, which had remained foul throughout the preceding four days. It was still blowing half a gale when the tug arrived, but no one cared to linger in that well-advertised locality waiting for better weather. *Franklin* came down on the cripple at full power, barely checked to windward of her, and shot a line aboard all in one motion. *King Edward's* crew made the wire fast with alacrity, and in half an hour the tow was under weigh. The weather ship, out of sight but still in the vicinity, sent a long and cheerful message of farewell, and she may have been somewhat hurt by the abruptness of Marryat's reply. It consisted of one word:

ACKNOWLEDGED

The wind had gone westerly by then and the obvious place to take the cripple was to the Azores. However, Ormiston felt that this course would be equally obvious to the U-boats, and so he decided to try to reach St. John's, six hundred and eighty miles away. In making this choice he was taking a severe risk that his fuel would give out before he reached port; but that was the lesser of two evils.

He offered up a prayer for decent weather and ordered Read to run his engine at its best speed consistent with economy.

Read was praying too. He had already burned a good deal more than half his bunkers. *King Edward* was a big ship—more than eight thousand tons dead weight—and she was in ballast so that she sat up high to catch the wind. Read wanted no head winds. And so for the next four days the wind blew steadily and strongly out of the west, and then north-west—a dead muzzler.

Franklin strained and quivered. She rolled abominably, for as her bunkers emptied she grew lighter in the water. The higher she rose, the less efficient she became as a towing agent—and the more coal she burned.

By April 15 Read was counting the lumps on the stokers' shovels, and that day, with St. John's almost within reach, the fog shut down and blinded them completely.

Ormiston dared not risk the narrow entry to the harbor in the fog, and most reluctantly concluded that they would have to stand off the shore all night. He called Read and told him of the decision.

"Why, that's just dandy, Cap," Read replied with the first touch of bitterness he had allowed himself to display. "And tomorrow we can burn the shovel handles and the toilet seats . . ."

As it happened, the toilet seats were spared, but only by a hair's breadth. When *Franklin* eased her charge into St. John's on the morning of April 16, there were three hundred pounds of coal dust in her bunkers.

The following day *Franklin* returned to Halifax, arriving there on April 20. She had been at sea for twenty days and had steamed more than twenty-six hundred miles. It was an endurance record that she never matched again—and never wanted to.

Franklin badly needed a breathing space. She had now been actively at work for ten years in Foundation's service, and since 1931 she had not been given a thorough refit. One had been due in 1939, but the outbreak of war had forced a postponement. Now she was dangerously overdue—so much so that within three hours of the time she arrived back in Halifax, Read had to take one boiler down to make emergency repairs. He had also felt obligated to notify Woollcombe that unless *Franklin* went to the shipyard at once, he could no loger guarantee the continued functioning of her machinery.

Woollcombe knew full well how matters stood, and he arranged for *Franklin* to go on the slip on April 24.

But on April 23, the Norwegian ship *Veni* broke her main shaft while still eight hundred miles south-east of Halifax. And all that night *Franklin's* crew and the ship-repairers worked frantically to put back the boiler mountings and restore the ship to service.

She sailed on April 24, but not to Dartmouth slip. On April 27 Marryat broke silence to get a fix on the *Veni*. He found her to be far to the east of her first position and drifting in the Gulf current at the rate of two knots. *Franklin* bore down steadily, for this time the weather remained moderately good, and late on April 28 the *Veni* hove in sight. She was then nine hundred miles out of Halifax.

The tow home began next morning, for it was too late that night to connect. *Veni* was in ballast and she rolled and charged "all about the shop." Nevertheless *Franklin* made good time and a submarine warning message received on May 2 lent her extra steam. Her pistons clanged and clattered, and her auxiliary gear, pumps and dynamos began to complain so noisily that Read was half beside himself attending to their troubles. This time he was not afraid of running out of coal. He was afraid of running out of engine; for not even the notoriously long-lived Scotch machinery could be expected to last forever under conditions such as *Franklin* had endured for ten years past.

The last two days of the voyage brought a failing wind, but they also brought fog of a thickness that was tangible. On May 5, *Franklin* smelled her way into Halifax on DF bearings and dead-reckoning alone, for Ormiston had not been able to see much past his nose for fifty-six long hours.

When *Veni* had been safely anchored and *Franklin* was again at her berth, Read went stumping up the dock to the office.

"*This* time," he said, "she goes under repair!"

The look Woollcombe gave him was apologetic. "Sure, Chief," he said soothingly. "We'll give the old girl her checkup right away—after one small matter is attended to. There's a vessel called the *Craig* up on Egg Island . . . now as soon as you have hauled *her* off . . ."

Read's reply was worthy of his long experience at sea. Nevertheless, he went back to his ship, ordered the stokers into the hold, and *Franklin* sailed. She had been at rest exactly two hours.

This time she sailed with a new skipper on her bridge. Ormiston had decided that he preferred the harbor tugs.

The *Craig* turned out to be a minor job. She was a small British freighter laden with lumber who had gone so hard ashore on Egg Island that, before *Franklin* could reach her, she had broken in two. *Franklin* connected to the stern section and radioed for the *Banscot* to come and take the bow. Kept afloat by the wood in the holds, the two parts of the *Craig* were ignominiously hauled into Halifax and beached.

This time Read took no chances. He blew both boilers down before going to see Woollcombe. Facing the boss with his hands shoved deep into his pockets and a glare upon his face that would have paralyzed a shark, he dared Woollcombe to order him to sea again.

Woollcombe knew when he was beaten. And, in any case, the *Aranmore* was then being commissioned and was to be ready for sea duty in a few more days. At long last *Franklin* could have her rest.

They hauled her up on the marine slip at Dartmouth. The steamship inspectors and marine engineers who examined her were shocked by her condition, and were adamant in their insistence that she could not again put to sea without a major and complete overhaul. So for the best part of that busy summer she lay out of her own element while gangs of shipwrights and fitters swarmed over her, inside and out. Her weaknesses were largely minor ones, for her hull was still as sound as the day it had been built, and her engine too had years of life ahead of it. Her trouble was a slow accumulation of small faults that, in ten years' time, had grown to dangerous proportions. The false economies practiced by most shipowners during the depression years had aged *Franklin* as no amount of hard sea-time could have done. The rejuvenation process was inordinately long and exceedingly expensive.

But when she again took the water she had renewed her youth. She was spanking clean with new paint and polish and had recovered much of her old jauntiness, while in her engine room the machinery gleamed and purred as smoothly as it had ever done.

She was once more ready for anything the war might bring.

The war was about to bring her seven months of idleness and lotus-living.

By the end of 1940 all Allied merchant shipping had come under direct control of the naval authorities, and even the Foundation salvage tugs—while they remained nominally independent under their own owners—were in fact subject to interference from the Navy. This state of affairs was to lead to increasing friction as the years advanced. Energetic and able as the Navy was, it never understood the sea the way the tug-boat skippers did. Nor could some of its officers easily tolerate the free and independent spirits of these sailors whose trade was as hard and dangerous in peacetime as the Navy's was in war.

Although the documents relating to the event are no longer available, there seems to be little doubt that *Franklin's* enforced rest during the winter of 1940-1941 resulted from a decision of the Navy.

Whoever made it, it was a decision of unparalleled foolishness. *Franklin* was ordered to proceed to Bermuda and to go on station there through the winter months. In theory she was to be available to give assistance to shipping which was following the southern tracks between United States ports and Europe. In practice, as everyone down to the meanest stoker on the meanest vessel in North Atlantic waters knew, independent sailings on the southern route had been reduced to the merest trickle. Only those Allied ships of sixteen knots or better were sailing independently by the southern routes. The rest—the overwhelming balance of all Allied shipping—were sailing out of Nova Scotian ports via the northern great circle tracks.

It was in the waters off Canada and Newfoundland, subjected to the full fury of North Atlantic winter weather, that salvage tugs were needed.

Franklin lay in Bermuda waters for seven months and she received one distress call, which, when she answered it, resolved itself into a minor breakdown which the disabled ship was able to repair herself.

During those same seven months *Foundation Aranmore* bore the brunt of salvage and rescue work in the northeastern approaches. She answered nineteen calls, and saved twelve vessels in that period.

In April of 1941 *Franklin* was at last recalled to Halifax. Her interim skipper left her for service in the Merchant Fleet, and she lay to her dock waiting for the beginning of the greatest year of her life.

19 ⚓ THE MAN FROM BURIN

THE OUTPORTS OF NEWFOUNDLAND cling to the broken coasts of that rock island in much the same way that the ancient maritime cities of Greece clung to their own inhospitable mainland. There are more than a thousand outports, some of them consisting of only a handful of families; but they are old settlements, many of them dating from the seventeenth century. During all the time of their existence they have been walled-off from one another by the almost impenetrable rock barrens of the interior. They have only known one road to human intercourse—the sea.

They have lived by and from and on the sea. Nothing of them has permanence except that which pertains to the sea: neither their neat frame houses, their straggling wharves, their canted flakes—nor yet their men. Through a dozen generations these men have sailed out to the Grand Banks and hand-lined for cod out of their little dories, with two hundred miles of searoom between them and the nearest land. They have sailed to Labrador and up that arctic coast as far as the cod would lead. And every summer their little ships put out, deep laden with salt fish, for Portugal and Spain and Italy.

The two- and three-masted schooners of Newfoundland (some of them not much larger than the Norse longboats) dared the Western Ocean in their hundreds for two centuries. They were good seaboats—it may be that there were none better—but they were built of poor timber and they were ill-found, for they were born of poverty. Many of them did not come back. Each year the flotsam on the coasts of Europe contained new fragments of Newfoundland jack pine and spruce.

The men of the island took to the sea young. There was no choice. At twelve some of them were hand-lining on the Banks, and by the time they had reached fourteen years only the sons of those feudal lords—the merchants—still remained ashore.

Mainlanders are sometimes heard to say—in envy and with discontent—that all Newfoundlanders are conceived in dories—standing up. If that was really so the people born on the Newfoundland coasts could not be better attuned to the environment in which they spend their lives than they are now. For they are truly of the sea.

It was these men, and there were scores of them across the years, who were the sinew and marrow of *Franklin's* crews. Not many of them remained with her over the years, for there was always the island calling them; but when one left the ship another came. It is not possible to speak of all of them by name or to tell their tales—but there was one amongst their numbers who is fit to represent them all.

In the town of Burin on Placentia Bay, a boy was born to the name of Harry Brushett in the year 1898. He grew to manhood; and at the age of twelve he went out to the Banks and learned to fish. He had five years of the dories before he became mate of one of the Burin schooners—a two-master called the *Vanessa*. At the age of eighteen Harry Brushett was master of the *Vanessa*, sailing to Alicante in Spain with cargoes of salt fish.

150

On his nineteenth birthday he was storm-taken in mid-Atlantic and, after thirty-six days of struggle, the *Vanessa* sank under the young skipper, leaving him and his crew of six adrift in a broken dory. Ten days later they were picked up by a Norwegian tramp steamer and so they returned by stages to their own home port.

Two days after his homecoming Harry Brushett put to sea again, this time as master of the schooner *Mary II.* Her destination—Alicante.

He sailed her until 1920, when he became skipper of the new three-master *George A. Wood* and, at the same time, bosun to a slight and lively Burin girl called Eva. Burin girls do not stay at home when the captain goes to sea, and so for the next five years Eva sailed in the *George Wood*, from Burin to Cadiz, Portugal, Jamaica, and Italy.

In 1925 the local company in Burin which owned the *Wood* went bankrupt and, with reluctance, Harry Brushett turned to steam. He spent the last years of the decade skippering coastal steamers running to every known port (and to some hardly known at all) along the Canadian and Newfoundland seaboards; and he grew intimate (but never foolishly familiar) with them.

The depression was the dark time. Newfoundland sank into an abyss of suffering that was medieval. Good skippers could be had for seaman's wages, and there were too few ships to go around. Harry, who had never bothered to take his examination for a foreign-going ticket, discovered that he was lucky to get a mate's birth in the ratty little steamers in the Newfoundland and Nova Scotian coastal trade.

He did not enjoy that life. It was a dull, bruising routine. Ship-owners are seldom generous men and in those days they were particularly penurious and grasping. The coastal steamers worked twenty-four hours a day; they were undermanned and their people grossly underpaid. It was a living —just.

In 1938 Brushett was on the beach in Halifax when there came a chance to join *Foundation Franklin,* on one trip to sea. It was no permanent job, and the pay was not even as good as on the coastal steamers; but that single voyage left an indelible imprint on Brushett. What he saw of salvage work was enough to convince him that here was a life well suited to his independent character. He went back to the coast tramps after that single voyage, but he kept his eyes on the salvage tugs thereafter.

When Woollcombe met him on the street one day in early 1941 and casually inquired whether Harry would care to take command of *Franklin,* there was no hesitation. So it was that in April of that year a most remarkable vessel and a most remarkable man became an entity.

In 1941 Brushett was forty-five years of age, and in that particular prime which relative youth and thirty years at sea alone can give. His face betrayed few indications of his character and kind, for it might well have been the face of a scholarly pedagogue in some small outport village. He was long and thin, "a tall, lean drink of water," as one of his men called him, using the word "water" quite advisedly, for Brushett never drank hard liquor. This abstinence (which was not a matter of principle but simply of distaste) made him somewhat incomprehensible to the salvage crews, most of whom tended to the other extreme. And Brushett's untouchability, his incisive quality of command, and his aura of almost Victorian rectitude also tended to set him apart from the men who served under him. In outward appearance and in casual conversation he seemed the antithesis of the roaring, hell-for-leather tug-boat man. But in his actions he was—by the admission of everyone who served with him—beyond compare. And, as they would learn, he *could* be roused—if there was good reason—to the kind of fearsomeness for which Newfoundland skippers have a wide renown.

When he took command of *Franklin*, Brushett also took command of a fine crowd of officers. There was an unpredictable genius named Neil McLeod as chief engineer, with steady, indomitable Reginald Poirier as second. On deck there was Tom Paisley as first officer and Emile Forgeron, one of a huge family of boys, most of whom were in the tug-boat business, as second. Marryat occupied the radio shack. Tom Nolan had been transferred to the *Aranmore*, but *Franklin* now had Bill Henderson, a man who had spent most of the preceding thirty years beneath the surface, and who was Tom Nolan's peer. And the man who ran the pumps and who was in fact foreman of the salvage gang was Buck Dassylva, of whom it is said that—had it been necessary—he could have refloated the *Queen Mary* single-handed.

Apart from a hard core of Newfoundlanders, the stokers, oilers and deck-hands who made up the balance of the twenty-four-man crew were a motley lot. The Navy and the Merchant Marine had taken the pick of those available, and the tugs were manned from what was left. Nevertheless the men who signed on for salvage work were often the most experienced seamen on the seaboard, even if they did have certain idiosyncrasies which made them appear undesirable aboard the merchant ships.

"The first day out," a chief engineer recalls, "my gang was useless. Then they'd begin to sober up. But before that awful moment of pure sobriety disabled them they would get into the vanilla extract. Then we'd have steam!"

Not all the hands were old shellbacks. A good many of them met the sea for the first time aboard the tugs. There was one poor Jewish lad, out of a clothing shop, who got into a small spot of trouble ashore and hurriedly shipped out on *Franklin*. He made a fine stoker once he had conquered his scruples against fat sowbelly. Then there was a six-foot Iroquois Indian, wanted by the police on a manslaughter charge, who turned to the seaman's life for reasons of health. There was also a poor fellow afflicted with hallucinations who had escaped a mental home. He would hold long conversations with *Franklin's* boilers, or with her bilge pumps, but he became an excellent oiler nonetheless. And there was an educated and highly imaginative Frenchman, who tried to abandon *Franklin* in mid-Atlantic when he discovered a small leak in a pipe and assumed with direct French logic that the ship inevitably must fill and sink.

They were not a dull crowd. To the last man they were individualists, from unorthodox molds. And they were probably the only kind of men who could have survived the years which lay ahead and, more than that, who could have accomplished the impossible with such monotonous regularity.

When *Franklin* put to sea under her new master, the shape of the war had changed. The early months of confusion were largely past. The Canadian Navy had shown a heartening growth, and just in time, for the U-boats had crossed the Atlantic in numbers and were about to begin a sustained assault upon the western end of the great convoy bridge. For months to come the Navy was to be outmatched and even outnumbered by its adversaries, and during this period scores of ships were to go down off the Canadian seaboard, while others floated with their bellies ripped by torpedo blast, waiting in hopes of rescue.

Halifax itself had changed out of all recognition. All ships (with the exception of vessels of sixteen knots or better) bound for Allied ports in Europe came first to Halifax. Here they were either assigned to the fast HX convoys, or they were sent on to Sydney to become part of the slow SC convoys.

Bedford Basin a day or so before a major convoy sailed was wonderful. On occasions more than a hundred freighters of every size and nationality lay so thickly clustered that from the heights of the old citadel they appeared as an unbroken expanse of spars and superstructures. Halifax had become the most important port in the Western world, for

153

through it passed more than three-quarters of the total tonnage which was sustaining Britain in her darkest hour.

This mighty concentration of ships, and the circumstances which surrounded them, continued to make for a steady increase in the number of maritime accidents. During 1941 Foundation's salvage vessels rescued twenty-seven ships, almost all of which would have been lost but for the efforts of the tugs.

Yet spectacular as this record is, it represented only a part of the salvage tugs' activities. When a ship was in distress a tug went out to her. When there were no SOS calls, the tugs worked even harder, at a myriad other tasks. *Franklin's* log for this period is a frenzied record, as the following sequence shows.

On April 11 Brushett took her to sea for the first time. Her destination was Boston, towing the freighter *Polar Chief,* which could not be repaired in Halifax because of the congestion in the shipyards there. On April 20 *Franklin* arrived back in Halifax, and on the twenty-first she sailed for Shelburne to assist in the launching of a big new schooner which had become stuck on the ways. Returning to Halifax, she sailed the following day for Argentia, Newfoundland, with two leaky wooden scows in tow. The scows filled up and almost sank off Canso, so Brushett had to put into Louisburg. While the scows were being repaired *Franklin* sailed for Janvrin Island to haul the freighter *Mana* off the rocks. When that job was completed she was diverted into the Bras d'Or Lakes to rescue the motor vessel *Dixie Sword,* which had also run aground. After releasing this ship, *Franklin* sailed for Inhabitants Bay to pick up the derrick-scow *Foundation Masson* and deliver it to Sydney. From Sydney she sailed for Halifax, where she had half a day in port before setting off to salvage the S.S. *Ceres,* which was ashore in Sea Coal Bay. That job was completed on the twenty-eighth of May, and on the twenty-ninth *Franklin* sailed for Rockland, Maine, towing the damaged freighter *Frances Dawson* . . . and so the record goes until the reader examining that log becomes incredulous, for surely, he tells himself, no ship and no men either could maintain such a pace month in, month out, year in, year out.

But a ship's log speaks nothing but the truth. From April 1941 till April 1942, *Foundation Franklin* steamed more than fifty thousand miles—a double circumnavigation of the globe. It was seldom that she was in any port for longer than it took to fill her bunkers, take on stores, and clear again. For her men life was an endless sequence of days and nights in stinking and miserable quarters on a small and most uncomfortable vessel. For her engineer officers it was an endless battle to keep the worn old machinery turning out a steady eleven knots. For the deck officers it was worst of all. As any merchant officer well knows, the hardest moments of a voyage are the beginning and the end, the departure and the ultimate landfall. Once well at sea, life settles into a routine that is only rarely disrupted by storms or accident. But the approach to land, in thick weather, at night, or even in the clear light of day, is always hard.

Franklin spent most of her time entering or leaving ports, or working close inshore upon those dangerous coasts. In blinding blizzards, in black fog, in every sort of weather, this was her fate: to be continually at the beginning or the end. And her officers had more to worry them than the safety of their ship alone, since more often than not they had an unwieldly tow, a dead ship, a derrick, a dredge, or a string of barges hanging on behind.

For Brushett, in those days, there was the added strain of learning a new and difficult trade—not from an instructor versed in its intricacies, but solely from experience and observation. As master he could not ask advice from his underlings, nor could he admit to knowing less than they. His method was to allow the salvage specialists, the men like Dassylva and Henderson, to carry on without any interference from the bridge while Brushett simply ran his ship—and watched. He watched to good effect. Before the summer ended he was as conversant with salvage techniques as many a man who had spent years in that complicated trade.

On July 8 *Franklin* sailed for Argentia with the two scows which had almost sunk during the first attempt in May. The scows continued to prove intractable and during a hard breeze on the night of July 10 the tow-lines broke and both scows went off on their own. Finding them in darkness and in a blow was an ugly business, but before dawn the wanderers had both been rounded up, volunteers had boarded them from a dory, and they were again safely tethered.

It was with considerable relief that Brushett delivered them to Argentia, and then set sail for Louisburg, where a derrick lay waiting to be towed to Halifax.

That derrick was destined to wait a long time.

Early on July 12 a fast HX convoy of nearly fifty ships had put out from Halifax bound for the British Isles. Escorted by three Canadian warships, the convoy made its way up the Nova Scotian coast past Scatari; its lines of merchantmen steaming close on one another's tails in unaccustomed and uneasy proximity—for no merchant skipper ever enjoyed the knowledge that *one* other ship, let alone fifty of them, lay within visual distance of his own.

That night, while the convoy was thirty miles due east of

Scatari and entering a bank of fog, one of the escorts got a submarine contact. The escorts swung back to drop depth charges while the commodore of the convoy gave the dispersal order.

Only those who have lived through it can comprehend the fearful confusion which results when fifty ponderous vessels, crowded into a square mile or so of ocean, suddenly proceed each its own separate way and at full speed. Blanket the sea with fog and total darkness, and the scene takes on the qualities of a gargantuan nightmare. On such occasions fate was kind when it allowed the majority of the ships to escape destruction at each other's hands.

On this occasion there were three collisons; but a single vessel took the brunt of them, for she was hit twice within three minutes.

She was the *Biafra,* a seven-thousand-tonner fully laden with war cargo. When the dispersal order was received, *Biafra* turned hard to starboard out of the middle line of the convoy and almost at once she was struck fair amidships by another vessel. The shock rolled her down until her port rails were under; but she staggered to her feet and while the water rushed into her engine room, she started to turn back to her original course. The turn was never completed, for she was struck again by a vessel from her own column which was turning hard to starboard.

There was panic aboard *Biafra.* The first collision had damaged her enough so that her chances of survival seemed remote; the second seemed to seal her doom. Her engine room, stokehold, and number three cargo hold filled up to sea level within a few minutes and she lay dead and helpless, with water pouring steadily into all her after-holds.

The confusion in the convoy was so great that no other vessel had time to spare for her. Half an hour later she lay quite alone, and sinking fast, while the rest of the convoy stampeded blindly off into the night like a herd of frightened steers.

She radioed a general SOS, despite the possibility that the submarine might also hear it. The submarine had now become the lesser of two dangers.

Marryat, on listening-watch at *Franklin's* radio, heard the call at 2 A.M., July 13 and moments later Brushett was giving a new course to the helmsman, while Neil McLeod was working *Franklin's* engine up to speed.

Franklin was then one hundred and twenty miles from the scene of the collision, or about ten hours steaming time. But when Marryat received the following message from *Biafra:* HURRY I AM TAKING WATER FAST, McLeod waved his magic wand and *Franklin* was soon logging almost fourteen knots; as fast as she had ever gone in all her life.

With a great foaming bone in her teeth and hot black clouds of smoke panting from both her funnels, she came bearing down through the fog. At 11 A.M. she raised *Biafra*. The lookout had a wary eye open for submarines, but everyone else was staring at the crippled ship which had loomed suddenly out of the murk ahead.

Listing fourteen degrees, and so far down by the stern that her after well-deck was almost awash, she seemed to be hanging on in complete defiance of the laws of buoyancy.

This was not a job where Brushett could stand aside and watch his salvage men do the work. This was *his* job and his alone. He acted with assurance and without a moment's hesitation.

He had immediately recognized that the only hope of saving the big vessel lay in getting a pump aboard. Simply putting a tow-line on her would have been so much waste effort, for she would have sunk before she was halfway to the nearest port. But swinging a three-ton pump out of the tug's hold and hoisting it up and onto the deck of a merchantman while there is a heavy beam sea running is no casual procedure. There were those aboard *Franklin* who thought it could not be done.

Brushett was not one of them. While he was still running down on *Biafra,* the hatch covers were coming off the afterholds, and the slings were being made fast to a gasoline-driven six-inch centrifugal. The two pumpmen, Buck Dassylva and his assistant Bob Cooper, were standing by. *Franklin* came sweeping in under *Biafra's* counter, rounded-to, and in a moment had a heaving line aboard. Within three minutes the heaving line had been replaced by a spring line and as soon as the two ships had been joined by this slender umbilicus, Brushett ordered the pump to be hoisted away. For a long minute it swung at the end of the *Franklin's* boom. The tug rose on a wave and at the crucial instant the boom swung inboard of *Biafra*; the pump dropped to her decks as lightly as a bird; the slings were cast off; and before *Franklin* had begun to slip away into the trough she had swung her boom into the clear again.

It was a masterful performance; but Dassylva and Cooper equaled it. At the instant when *Franklin's* boat-deck was level with *Biafra's* well-deck, both men had leaped across the intervening space. The fact that they were jumping to a sinking ship did not bother them. They, with their pump, would see to it that she did *not* sink.

Brushett would have liked to put a second pump on board, but this was out of the question for there were no more six-

157

inchers and it would have been impossible to swing one of the huge eight-inch pumps across the gap.

While this transfer had been taking place, another tug, almost unnoticed in the excitement, had come out of the murk on *Biafra's* bow and had quietly put a towing line aboard the ship. She was the *Cruizer* out of Sydney. For a while it looked as if she would take this salvage job right out from under Brushett's nose.

When he saw what had happened, the side of Brushett that his crew had not yet seen came to the fore.

He raised his megaphone and in a cold, controlled voice called to *Biafra's* skipper.

"I see you've taken *Cruizer's* wire. With half our power she has half our chances of getting you into port. You've two minutes to decide if you intend to keep her on before we leave."

Confronted by this ultimatum *Biafra's* skipper hurriedly bellowed an order to his crew, and the *Cruizer* soon found herself towing nothing more substantial than a hundred-fathom length of line. Discomfitted, she drew off, while *Franklin* put her own wire aboard *Biafra* and began to work up speed.

Meanwhile Cooper and Dassylva had already got a suction line done into *Biafra's* after-holds, and the pump was running. Seen from aboard the crippled ship, *Biafra's* plight looked even more desperate than it had done from *Franklin's* decks. Her already dangerous list was steadily increasing. She had no power of any sort and all of her own pumps were therefore out of action. She had been torn open amidships to a depth of eight feet, and the great V-shaped gash was twenty feet wide at the top and extended far down below the waterline. Apart from the completely flooded engine room, stokehold and numbers three, four, and five holds, the two remaining after-holds were better than half full. Dassylva and Cooper knew that at all costs they must hold the levels in these two, for if the water gained much more, the ship would go down by the stern. With only one pump, they engaged the sea in battle.

Franklin was now towing full out. Brushett signaled to *Biafra's* master that, considering the fog and the rising onshore wind, it would be advisable to make for Sydney rather than for Louisburg, which—though slightly closer—had a most difficult approach. *Biafra's* skipper did not agree. He did not think his ship would stay afloat even as far as Louisburg, and so Brushett deferred to his opinion—though unwillingly.

At 6:30 P.M. *Biafra's* master radioed *Franklin* to stop immediately. His ship was going down, he said, and he wanted to disembark his crew. Brushett stopped and most of *Biafra's* people quickly clambered into the lifeboats and rowed across to *Cruizer,* which was still standing by. *Biafra* was now abandoned except for her senior officers and the two pump men from the *Franklin.* These two did not share in the general alarm. They were almost holding their own against the water, and they believed that they could keep *Biafra* floating for another hour or two.

At 7:30 P.M. Brushett heard the outer bell buoy of Louisburg harbor ahead of him, and by taking sound bearings he fixed his position. His fears as to weather conditions here were more than justified. The fog was impenetrable and an onshore wind with a growing sea was making-up. Nevertheless he had no choice but to go in. *Franklin* almost ran down the pilot boat which had been summoned by radio, and which had come out most reluctantly. The pilots came on board, but they flatly refused to try to take either *Franklin* or *Biafra* through the narrow gut of the harbor entrance.

"Lie out here till dawn," they said, "and then we'll take you in."

Once again, the mild-mannered skipper of the *Franklin* showed his mettle. "That ship astern of me," Brushett said quietly, "is sinking. She will not last an hour more. She is going to be beached in Louisburg before that hour's up—if I have to pilot her inside myself."

Given no alternative the pilots finally agreed to help. By then it was almost pitch-dark, for the sun had gone and no light penetrated the enveloping fog.

With *Cruizer* on *Biafra's* stern to steer her, *Franklin* began nosing forward, smelling her way through the black shroud.

The little convoy safely passed through the outer arm and approached the abrupt turn in the channel which leads into the inner harbor. *Franklin* made the turn, but *Biafra* failed to follow. There was a muffled grating sound and she went up on Battery Shoal.

Biafra was temporarily safe, but not yet saved.

Franklin took in her wire and went alongside the casualty to swing five more pumps aboard. When these were all working, an unsuccessful attempt was made to haul the vessel off the shoal. Brushett was not disturbed; he had hoped to be able to take the ship to the foot of the inner harbor and place her on the mud bottom there, but since she preferred Battery Shoal, there she should stay until she had been repaired.

The patching took three days and was done largely by Henderson. He made a wooden patch for her gaping wound, building it plank by plank, while working at depths of twenty feet, in water that was too murky to give him any visibility.

He did the job entirely by touch. When he received a plank (weighted with iron to hold it down) he would jockey it into place, feel behind it for the curling edges of the shattered plates, then mark the spots on the plank where he wanted holes bored, and finally send it back to the surface together with an order for the appropriate "walking sticks."

These "walking sticks" were lengths of iron rod threaded on one end which was fitted with washers and a nut, while the other end was bent to order, on *Franklin's* forge, into a sort of shepherd's crook. They varied from three inches to three feet in length. When they were ready they would be sent down to Henderson together with the plank and he would fit the crooks of the bolts around the edges of the broken plates, then slide the plank over the bolts and draw it up tight. Before it was drawn right home he would insert a roll of canvas and packing, called a "pudding," between the outer end of the plank and the ship's side. Thus, when the plank was drawn up snug, the pudding was compressed, and a watertight joint was obtained despite the tortured curves and twists of the torn plates.

So the patch grew, plank by plank, until it was well above water level. Henderson then covered it from top to bottom with heavy canvas to seal the cracks between the planks—and the job was done.

Now Cooper and Dassylva took over. The rumble of their pumps and the roar of water pouring over *Biafra's* side echoed across the harbor for half a day until, at high tide, *Franklin* took a strain on the tow wire and the big ship slid off the shoal and idled contentedly along behind the tug to her berth beside a wharf.

There remained the task of making her seaworthy for the long tow to the nearest dry-dock, which was at Halifax. This took eight more days and consisted largely of the fitting of a "hard patch" of cement (as opposed to a "soft patch" of wood or canvas) inside *Biafra's* hull; and of the structural reinforcement of the vessel's weakened side by means of wooden and iron beams. During this period *Franklin* lay alongside, supplying steam to the damaged ship and, in the process, using up most of her bunkers. But when Brushett decided to cast off one morning and cross the harbor to bunker his ship, he ran foul of the agent representing *Biafra,* who had recently arrived upon the scene.

This man was a poor example of his kind. He knew little of the sea. When Brushett pointed out to him that it was imperative that *Franklin* be fully bunkered so that she could respond to any new distress call, he replied by ordering Brushett to remain alongside *Biafra* or forfeit his salvage rights. The fact that *Biafra* was now as safe as houses seemed to escape him utterly.

Brushett seldom accepted orders from landlubbers. Nor did he make a precedent this time. In very smart order *Biafra* found herself alone, with a ruffled agent pacing her decks, while *Franklin* steamed across the harbor to the coal docks.

Although she was back alongside within two hours, the agent refused to be placated. He accused Brushett of dereliction of duty, and was still at it when Marryat came into *Franklin's* wheelhouse with an SOS.

The message was from the Imperial Oil tanker *Icoma*, which had struck one of the coast rocks while in thick fog some twelve miles east of the port and had smashed her rudder. Her call was urgent. She was holding herself off a lee shore with her anchor alone, but the sea was heavy and she was beginning to drag. Her operator told Marryat that if help did not reach her within an hour or two she would be forced in over a series of exposed rock reefs and become a total loss.

Incredibly, *Biafra's* people tried to prevent *Franklin* from answering this call, by refusing to let go her mooring lines. Brushett simply abandoned the lines and was under weigh in fifteen minutes.

The fog was still impenetrable when *Franklin* got outside and Brushett took her down the coast by ear alone, listening first to the sound of the breakers on the reefs, and then to the mournful hoot of *Icoma's* whistle. The sea was running strongly and the same onshore wind which had caused trouble during the *Biafra* rescue was still blowing a hard breeze.

Brushett never saw *Icoma* until he was a ship's length from her. He had gone in by the leadline, between and around the same rocks that had smashed *Icoma's* rudder, but in a fog so dense that he could barely see the surface of the water from his bridge. *Icoma* was so close in by then that her starboard side was scraping up and down on the first ledge.

It took just seventeen minutes to connect up to her. Three hours later she was anchored safe in Louisburg. It had been as coldly daring a rescue attempt as *Franklin* ever made; but it had gone so smoothly, that it has long since been forgotten even by the men who helped her do the job.

DURING THE SUMMER OF 1941 *Franklin* was diverted from salvage work to assist in moving derrick boats, barges and other floating marine plant from Quebec and Montreal to the Nova Scotian ports, where they were to be used in expanding the ship-handling facilities. It was dull and exhausting work and *Franklin's* people returned to deep-sea rescue in October with considerable relief.

On October 16 the British vessel *Empire Razorbill* lost her rudder off Argentia only a few hours after she had received a warning message from the Navy to the effect that a submarine was believed to be in that area, and perhaps several.

Razorbill's master was considerably perturbed. Eight months earlier his vessel had been shelled by a submarine and left drifting and disabled until she was rescued by *Foundation Aranmore*. This new disablement again exposed him and his crew to the peculiarly unnerving experience of being adrift aboard a helpless vessel in dangerous waters and without an escort to protect him.

For the second time he found himself faced with the necessity of making a most difficult decision. The problem was to decide whether to maintain radio silence and trust to luck that a friendly ship would happen by and offer assistance; or whether to call for help—knowing that any U-boat in the vicinity could take a DF bearing on the radio signal. If a casualty chose not to call she might drift aimlessly for days and risk being driven ashore. If she *did* call, it might be a toss-up who reached her first—a rescue tug or a submarine.

In the end, most masters of disabled ships decided in favor of using their radios, but some sought to reduce the risks by means of subterfuge. For the most part these captains would limit themselves to one succinct SOS, and if they were particularly cautious men, they would not even divulge their positions. When the rescue ships insisted that they could do nothing unless they were given a position, the cripple might grudgingly furnish one that was purposely inaccurate. A very nervous master would sometimes indicate that he was a hundred miles from his actual position.

No one knows how effective this ruse was in deluding the Germans, but it is known with certainty that it was extremely effective in confusing the salvage tugs; so much so that on several occasions, it made it impossible for them to find the casualty at all.

In any event *Empire Razorbill* seemed to have believed that it was efficacious. She sent one message and gave one position; and then remained stubbornly silent for five days while *Franklin* steamed about the North Atlantic through a thick fog, becoming more and more baffled. There was no sign of the cripple within a radius of fifty miles of the position she had given. Time was wasting, and coal was running low. Eventually Brushett stopped chewing balefully on his pipe-stem long enough to give Marryat a message for transmission to the *Razorbill*.

"Tell her," he said icily, "that if she doesn't open up within ten minutes, we're off for home."

That woke the silent one. She came on the air hurriedly, pleading that—due to the fog—she did not *know* where she was. That may or may not have been true. In any event Marryat took a DF bearing on her as she made her apologies, and with this to guide him, Brushett ran down toward her.

Razorbill turned out to be a hundred miles away from her given position. The difference may have been due to drift but not, as Poirier was heard to say, "unless she had her engine running full ahead."

Nor was that intended as a joke. Many vessels which were crippled by the loss of a rudder, but which still had power, would keep steaming at full speed regardless of direction, in the hope that their aimless peregrinations would confuse any pursuing submarines.

It would not be fair to blame these merchant vessels for being so elusive. But neither would it be fair to blame the people on the salvage tugs for developing a virulent dislike for ships that caused them to steam many unnecessary hundreds of miles, and which forced them to use their radios with such abandon that only a submariner who was totally deaf could have avoided hearing some of the transmissions. A trifle bitterly the salvage men would point out that a deep-sea rescue tug was just as likely to attract torpedoes, or gunfire, as was a rusty old tramp steamer.

During the *Razorbill* rescue, one eager U-boat evidently *did* have her ears open. In any event, while *Franklin* and her charge were still sixty miles from Sydney—their objective—the Navy flashed a warning message to Brushett that a submarine was thought to have just arrived off the harbor entrance. The Navy reported that the sub was being hunted by a "patrol craft," but Brushett, who knew that this meant a converted pleasure launch armed with Lewis guns, was not comforted. *Franklin* came smartly about and ran for Louisburg while McLeod raised steam with such enthusiasm that the safety valves were soon wheezing and whistling like a calliope.

Having rid herself of the *Razorbill*, *Franklin* proceeded to

163

Pictou, a convenient base from which she could sail to the assistance of the belated vessels which were then hurriedly loading at Quebec and Montreal, hoping to get clear of the Gulf before the ice began to form.

One of these tardy ships was the Greek steamer *Chelatross*.

Through the years since steam has replaced sail, the most active competitors of the ship-breaking yards for the possession of ancient vessels whose days are done have been the small Greek shipping companies. The result of this competition is that countless aged ships have had their working days prolonged past all reasonable limits. The *Chelatross* was such a vessel. That she was still afloat in 1941 was a fact to make men marvel.

Nevertheless, when she left Quebec on November 2 bound for Sydney to join a slow SC convoy for England, she was worth rather more than a million dollars. The value was in her cargo. Her holds were crammed with six thousand tons of aluminum, copper and lead ingots; with army trucks; with artillery shells and with weapons. They were topped off, surprisingly, with cases of apples and rounds of good Ontario cheese.

She was in a hurry as she came down-river. Winter gales had already begun and *Chelatross* was too frail and ancient to argue with either gales or ice. She had already been alive on borrowed time for far too long.

Shortly before dawn on November 4, one of her officers hopefully plotted her position as being three miles north of Brion Island—the most northerly of the Magdalen group. The plot was made by dead-reckoning, for it was a dark night and there was fog besides. The officer had barely turned away from the chart table when the lookout raised a cry of alarm, and at almost the same instant there was a snarling crash of rusty steel on rock as *Chelatross* ground her way over a series of ledges and came to a shuddering halt on Brion's shore.

As the dawn broke it disclosed the red and grey sandstone cliffs of the island less than two hundred yards away, and rising a hundred feet out of the surf to a scant scalp of stunted spruce. There were no curious eyes to peer down at the stranded ship, for Brion was uninhabited.

A report of the stranding reached Featherstone through Naval Control at noon on November 4. The message gave little information concerning *Chelatross's* condition, but it mentioned the value of the cargo. Ten minutes after its receipt Featherstone was away on a cross-country dash to join *Franklin* at Pictou, and the following morning saw him landing aboard *Chelatross* from the tug's motorboat.

He had an odd reception. He had to fight his way from

the head of the Jacob's ladder to the bridge companion through a milling mob of curious sheep. A deck cargo of livestock was a standard fitting on Greek tramps in those days, and *Chelatross's* fifty ewes and lambs had taken advantage of the excitement to burst out of their pen.

At first glance the ship seemed beyond all help. She was flooded in every cargo hold as well as in the engine room and stokehold. However, when Henderson went down to make an underwater inspection he found a ray of hope. The hull was relatively undamaged, except in the area of the starboard bilge where the shell plates had been torn and crumpled like so much cardboard.

Featherstone weighed the chances. The ship herself was practically worthless except for scrap; but to lighter all the cargo out of her would be a protracted and risky business. He preferred to take most of the cargo off Brion's ledges in *Chelatross's* own bottom, and he concluded that, with luck, it might be done.

The obstacles in his way were formidable. *Chelatross* lacked three feet of draft to float, and the tidal range at Brion was so slight as to be almost useless as an aid in lifting her. The ship would therefore have to be lightened to give her those three extra feet of freeboard, and this in turn would mean the removal of fifteen hundred tons of cargo into lighters (for it was far too valuable to jettison). All holds would then have to be pumped dry and, finally, the bottom tanks would have to be emptied of water by blowing compressed air into them.

It was a big order—and time was short. At that season of the year five days without a northerly blow was the most one could expect—and the first blow from the north would smash *Chelatross* if she was still on Brion's ledges.

Having made his decision Featherstone radioed Woollcombe in Halifax for another tug, and for coastal vessels which could be used as lighters. Woollcombe responded by ordering the *Security* to sail at once with two barges in tow, while the *Aranmore* was instructed to follow as soon as temporary repairs to her engines could be effected.

Meanwhile Featherstone was getting on with it.

"Bring in the pumps," he signaled to the *Franklin*.

Although *Chelatross* was protected by the island from the sou'east breeze which was making-up that day, it remained a tricky business to back *Franklin* in over the shoals. Nevertheless Brushett had completed the transfer of the pumps by 2 P.M.

Putting the massive eight-inch and ten-inch pumps down into the engine room so that their suctions would reach to *Chelatross's* tank tops was a problem which Featherstone solved by having a huge hole burned in the engine room casing, through which the pumps were lowered until they could be bedded on the cylindertops of the engine itself. They were started up at 4 P.M. and slowly the water level in the engine room began to drop.

By dawn of the sixth the engine room was dry. The next step was to bleed the water from number three hold into the engine room. This roundabout method had to be adopted because as yet there was no way of getting the pumps down into the crowded cargo holds from deck level—nor could there be until the lighters arrived, or unless Featherstone chose to jettison the cargo. He did not choose to jettison. Instead he ordered his men to knock out half a hundred rivets from the bulkhead which separated the engine room from number three; and as the water spurted through these holes, the pumps took care of it.

The salvage gang, consisting of the pumpmen and divers, together with as many of *Franklin's* crew as could be spared (more than could be safely spared), had entered the *Chelatross* Stakes, as they called it, with their accustomed grumbling and with their accustomed capacity for endurance. There was no stopping them. Food was eaten on the run and sleep was a chimera. By evening of November 7 this indefatigable handful had managed to empty the stokehold and engine room, dry out the engines, start the fires and get steam to the ship's own pumps. They had also bled the shaft tunnel—risking their lives to do so as they cranked up the watertight doors against the pressure of the sea—and they had so far reduced the level in the cargo holds that the ship was showing signs of liveliness. Oddly enough their job had been made somewhat easier by the very antiquity of *Chelatross*, for the supposedly watertight bulkheads between her holds had proven themselves so porous that, for all intents and purposes, the holds were common, and the water in them could all be bled off into the engine room bilges and pumped out from there.

While the pumping had been going on, Henderson had plugged and patched the worst of the external underwater damage, so that the inflow had been cut to a trickle. *Franklin* had laid two sets of ground tackle and a strain had been taken on these to prevent the stranded ship from driving farther inshore.

At dusk on November 7 *Security* came puffing up with her two barges in tow, and a few minutes later the small chartered coaster M.V. *Bernardo* also arrived.

The salvors immediately began discharging cargo into *Bernardo* and the scows. Sling after sling of aluminum ingots came up, until number four hold stood empty. Then the cargo booms swung over number five. Number five was filled with bombs and artillery shells, and the accidental dumping of a load of bombs onto a scow's deck resulted in a somewhat more cautious and slower resumption of the work.

Nevertheless things were going famously when the wind, which was still from the sou'east, began to make up. By evening of November 8 it was blowing half a gale and both *Bernardo* and *Franklin* had been forced to leave the wreck and stand off shore, while *Security* shepherded her two scows to shelter at Grindstone Island.

Aboard *Chelatross* the salvors did not slow their pace. All night long the pumps thundered on, while in number four and number five holds men struggled in the darkness to brace the sagging bulkheads, and to pour cement patches over fractured bilge plates. At dawn the wind providentially dropped off and the tugs and lighters came back to the wreck.

By midafternoon of November 9, the battle had been almost won. Nearly sixteen hundred tons of cargo had been lightered off into the barges, into the *Bernardo*, and into the lake freighter *Donald Stewart* which had come down from Port Alfred. *Chelatross's* underwater damage had been patched, and the pumps had gained complete victory over the water in the hull. Air compressors, brought up from Halifax by *Foundation Aranmore* and Captain Power on the eighth, had been installed and connected to the pipes leading into the freighter's bottom tanks.

The five days were almost up, but the salvors had met the deadline fairly.

It had been an exhausting battle, relieved only by the sheep, which had attached themselves like limpets to the salvage men, who, unwilling to see the beasts suffer, had been feeding them on apples taken from the holds.

"It was kind of nice," one of the salvors, who had once been a farmer, remembers. "Kind of homey-like with all them sheep bunting and pushing at you, and the nice fresh smell of sheep-drops all around."

Preparations were now complete for the attempt to refloat the ship at high tide on November 10. At dawn on that date the *Donald Stewart* came alongside to take off a few more hundred tons of cargo. Then *Franklin* and *Security* put their tow-lines on the wreck. The air compressors were started. As the pressure mounted in the bottom tanks the water was slowly driven out. *Chelatross* began to roll a little as she came slowly back to life.

At 2:15 P.M., on the highest water of the day, the ground tackle was hove up taut. *Security* and *Franklin* began to strain on their wires and *Chelatross's* own engines were started and put full astern. The big freighter stirred and groaned and she was on the very point of moving when the two ground anchors began to drag. Inch by inch they were coming home and, with their purchase lost, *Chelatross* reluctantly settled back into her bed of rock.

The first attempt at refloating had miscarried, but with the anchors reset and with a few more tons out of her hold, it was obvious that *Chelatross* would come off. Unloading began again, feverishly, for everyone on the job had been apprehensively watching the weather that day, and as evening came down they noted an ominous drop in the wind. Then slowly it began to make again, and at the same time to haul into the north.

At midnight the wind was moderate from the nor'west, but the salvors hoped to be able to make their second attempt at refloating *Chelatross* with the early morning tide. Half an hour later they were wondering if they themselves would live to see that tide. Out of the north, full blown and savage, a gale of force 9 intensity had leaped upon them in that brief interval, and already the surface of the Gulf was white, while the seas were leaping over *Chelatross's* rails and reaching for her bridge.

The blow came up so suddenly that it caught the *Bernardo* and the *Donald Stewart* still lying alongside the wreck. *Bernardo* burst her moorings, and since she was lying with her head to sea, she managed to fight clear of the breaking reefs. The *Stewart* was not so lucky. Underpowered and awkward, and lying head to shore, she stood no chance of getting clear without assistance.

By 1 A.M. on November 11 *Chelatross* was being swept from end to end and had all but disappeared in a cascade of foam. The *Stewart* was beating against her so that the shell plates of both ships were being crushed. In the darkness and the flurry of spume and snow, *Franklin* began to edge in to try to save the *Stewart*.

It was tight, terrifying work. On the bridge of his ship Brushett could see nothing except an indistinct loom of spray that marked *Chelatross*. It had become wickedly cold, and ice was forming on *Franklin's* rigging. As the seas mounted, so did the tug plunge deeper into their troughs—and always closer to the rocks beneath. At any instant the men aboard expected to feel the impact as her forefoot struck. Still she came in until Brushett could see the lights aboard the wreck and aboard the battered *Stewart*. There was no question of going alongside and throwing a heaving line. At the outside range of the rocket pistol *Franklin* swung about, and as she did so her mate fired the gun. The rocket left an orange trail through the driven snow, and the line whipped

168

from its box. It was a long shot, but the gale became an ally in that moment and carried the spent rocket far enough so that it fell on *Stewart's* forepeak.

There was no time to haul the heavy towing wire across the rock-torn water. When the five-inch manila messenger line had spanned the gap, *Franklin* took up the strain.

"It was like trying to land a twenty-pound salmon on a piece of string," one of *Franklin's* crew remembers. "One good jerk and that manila would have parted, and then you could have said good-by to the lake boat."

The strain on the line was very nearly equaled by the strain on Harry Brushett as he eased his tug off shore. But the line held, and when she was two miles clear of the island and in the way of blowing to the east of it, the *Stewart* was cast off. She promptly hove-to to ride out the storm, while *Franklin* turned back to try to help the men aboard *Chelatross*.

She was too late. Neither *Franklin* nor *Aranmore* could now dare the storm-swept reefs, all of which were breaking white and showing their stone teeth to the night sky.

Things looked black enough to Brushett. To Power, with the memory of *Berwindlea* still strongly etched in his mind, it seemed clear that Featherstone had gambled once too often. *Chelatross* was doomed, and this time there was no *England Maru* to save the crew. Nor would it have mattered if a big ship had been near, for no lifeboat could have lived in that thundering expanse of surf.

An hour before dawn Power received the message he had been waiting for—and dreading. It was the last to come from the ill-fated Greek.

SHIP BREAKING UP NOW FEATHERSTONE SAYS YOU MUST GET US SOON OR NOT AT ALL

Power had already decided on a plan. What had failed once with the *Berwindlea* might succeed here. Telling Brushett to stand by the wreck, he took the *Aranmore* in behind the island, and this time he found a lee. Just as the dawn opened Brion's bleak silhouette, *Aranmore's* largest boat, with six men aboard, was launched. This time there was a powerful engine to help them through the surf, and the boat made a landing just before 6 A.M. Led by *Aranmore's* mate the rescuers climbed the sandstone cliffs, raced across the island and took station on the rocks above the broken ship. As the morning light strengthened through the haze of snow and spume, the mate signaled to Featherstone by flag that he should abandon the wreck. Meanwhile the rescuers had dropped half a dozen lines down the cliff face, and had anchored them securely at the top.

Chelatross had just two boats left. These were launched into the breakers on the wreck's lee side and the crew and salvors leaped aboard. The boats came in like flotsam driven in a spring torrent and both of them were swamped and smashed as they were flung against the rocks at the cliff's foot.

But the lines were ready. Half-drowned men reached up and caught the ropes and one by one they were drawn up the sheer face. From the top they looked back—some of them—and saw their vessel almost completely submerged beneath live water. The ship was gone—but not one man went with her.

When the last one was safe they were hurried across the island and taken off in the motorboat to *Aranmore*. But even that stout vessel was having trouble with the gale, and now she was forced to turn and run for shelter under the lee of Cape North. It was thirty hours before she could emerge and make for Sydney harbor to land the shipwrecked crew of the *Chelatross*.

Three days later the gale had moderated sufficiently to allow *Franklin* to get under weigh. She had been hove-to for the whole three days, and had blown halfway to Cape North herself. When she again raised Brion Island she found the *Chelatross* completely broken; her forward section submerged, her superstructure gone, and only the after deck protruding a few inches above the water.

The wreckage was heavily encased in ice, nevertheless *Franklin's* people made an attempt at further cargo salvage. *Aranmore* came back to lend a hand, but there was nothing to be done that season, for another northerly began to make up and the temperature dropped below the zero mark. On November 14 both ships turned for home.

Chelatross had been lost; but not her cargo. During the two years which followed, *Franklin* returned many times to the wreck and her divers succeeded in recovering a total of forty-six hundred tons of metal ingots, which were transshipped at Halifax and which eventually found their way to the war machines in England. So, in the end, the sea's victory had been a hollow one.

Some weeks later Featherstone was passing the salvage shed on the Halifax dock when he heard a familiar sound and smelled a familiar smell. Incredulous, he opened the shed door and was greeted by a loving bunt administered by a large ewe, by whose side a lamb was gamboling.

He called Tom Nolan.

"Well, sir," Tom explained, "we had some of them sheep on *Aranmore* when the *Chelatross* broke, and the skipper told me to butcher them and hang the carcasses in our refrigerator. But when I looked at that ewe and lamb, I didn't have the heart for it. So there she is. We signed her on the articles, and the lamb too."

Having listened stony-faced to this improbable yarn, Featherstone delivered himself of a ghastly pun.

"Good work, Tom," he said. "These days we need every salvage sheep we can lay our hands on."

It was a terrible joke, but the point was valid enough; for the existing vessels of the Foundation fleet were being worked to death, as the events of the next few days clearly demonstrated.

On November 15 *Franklin* was en route to examine a wreck on the island of St. Pierre, but before she had got halfway to her destination she was ordered to return to Halifax, where another major accident had taken place.

The ship involved this time was the *Empire Flamingo*, laden with eight thousand tons of explosives, steel billets, barbed wire and iron ingots which she had taken on at a United States port.

Flamingo was en route to Halifax to join a fast convoy when she was caught in a blinding fog just off the Nova Scotian coast. She must have been very badly confused as to her position, for when she turned inward to what she believed to be the entrance to Halifax harbor, she was in reality many miles south-west of that port.

In the early hours of November 16 she discovered her mistake, but not until she had run herself ashore.

The fog was then so thick that her officers were quite unable to decide where they were. They radioed for help, but this was to little purpose since they could not give the position of their ship.

When the SOS was received at Foundation's office, Woollcombe telephoned the naval authorities and through their co-operation managed to get two intersecting DF bearings on the *Flamingo* from the radio stations at Camperdown and Yarmouth. The plot of the intersection showed that the *Flamingo* was ashore in a fearsome maze of reefs near Mars Head, some seventeen miles from Halifax harbor.

Mars Head and Pennant Bay, which lies behind it, are among the most notorious ship-killers on that coast. Of the twenty or thirty vessels which have driven into that deadly cul-de-sac, not half a dozen have escaped; and the worst disaster in Canadian maritime history took place within a stone's throw of the spot where the *Flamingo* had gone aground. That was in 1875, when the crack White Star liner *Atlantic*, with eleven hundred passengers and crew aboard, drove up on those fatal ledges in the dawn of April 1 during a heavy fog. When news of the disaster belatedly reached Halifax, it was at first believed to be an April Fool's hoax and for precious hours nothing was done about it. By then a south-easterly gale had sprung up, and before nightfall the *Atlantic* was a battered wreck, with more than half of her people dead. Five hundred corpses were recovered from the sea, but at least another hundred people perished, and their bodies were pounded into fragments against the bold cliff face.

The tragedy of the *Atlantic* contains a mystery that has not been solved to this day. She was carrying five million pounds' worth of gold bullion in her strong room, but when the seas calmed down sufficiently to allow the authorities to board her, no trace of the gold could be found. It was believed that the crews of three American tugs which had been hovering about the scene a day or so after the disaster managed to board the wreck and to make off with the gold. If so, it must have been one of the largest hauls in modern history.

The *Empire Flamingo* was stranded upon the same ledge where the bones of the *Atlantic* lie. The weather was calm, but ominously so, for it was the calm that precedes a shift in wind—and the weather office had predicted that the shift would bring a heavy blow out of the south within two days.

Banscot and *Bansurf* were the only two tugs available when *Flamingo* called for help. Despite the entire lack of visibility these little harbor tugs nosed out through the murk, risking impalement themselves, until at last they found the casualty. But they could do nothing for her. Her momentum had carried her so far up the ledges that it was clear she would require the combined efforts of all the ships the company possessed if she was ever to be freed. Furthermore, her forepeak and number one hold were completely flooded, and her master was convinced that if she *was* pulled off she would immediately go down by the head.

Security was then working on a wreck in the Bay of Fundy, while *Aranmore* was occupied at Sydney. Only *Franklin* was immediately available but, though she was driving south at her best speed, she had a long way to go. Featherstone decided to use the interval before she arrived in attempting to remove some of *Flamingo's* cargo, and so *Banscot* went back to Halifax for barges and a gang of stevedores.

Franklin arrived at noon on the eighteenth and Brushett immediately began laying out ground tackle to prevent *Flamingo* from driving further on the reefs as she was lightened. Then he took his ship right up alongside *Flamingo's* bow (with no water under *Franklin's* stem at all) and transshipped several pumps. The fog remained so heavy all this day that *Franklin* had to maneuver solely by the lead, and by the sound of the long Atlantic swell roaring up on the reefs and ledges which lay about her.

By dawn of the following day the stevedores had removed a bargeload of barbed wire and pig iron. At high water in the morning *Franklin* connected her tow wire and tried a pull. *Flamingo* did not budge. Lightering went on at a frantic pace, for the weather office was reporting the implacable advance of a major area of low pressure—the sure sign of storm at sea.

The work continued all that night, and as the first puffs of a sou'east wind began to be felt during the following morning, Featherstone ordered jettisoning to begin, and billets of steel and iron began to plunge over the side. By midnight the wind had risen to a stiff breeze, and the sea was getting up.

Early the next morning, when *Security* arrived post haste to lend a hand, the wind had risen to force 7 and was sweeping the whole exposed shoreline so that the seas were breaking high over the *Flamingo*. By 3 P.M. the tugs and barges could no longer lie alongside, and *Banscot* had to run for shelter in Terrence Bay with a barge behind her. It was no longer possible for anyone to leave, or board the wreck.

Franklin's motorboat was launched and instructed to stand by in the wreck's lee, and to be prepared to tow *Flamingo's* boats out to sea and away from the murderous surf if she had to be abandoned. The stevedores were issued with life-belts and ordered to abandon ship into the lifeboats. To a man, they refused to leave her. It was not that they were brave. On the contrary, the sight of the turmoil on the reefs so unmanned them that they could not bring themselves to leave the illusory security of the *Flamingo*. Featherstone had no time to spare for them. "You've had your chance to get away," he said. "Now you'll stay with us to the end."

To anyone but Featherstone the end must have seemed near. But he had been marooned aboard so many wrecks that imagination no longer had the power to disturb him. He concentrated on the job in hand with such ferocious singleness of purpose that there was simply no room left for fear.

Darkness had fallen and the gale was howling savagely along the coast. The roar of breaking seas lifting high above *Flamingo's* decks drowned out the steady rattle of the pumps.

Featherstone contacted Brushett on the radio.

"We may come off," he said, "if a big sea lifts us just a little more. If we don't come off soon the ship is done. Can you come in and put your lines aboard?"

Never had Brushett been called upon to take a greater

173

risk. Nevertheless he backed his tug in over reefs that were breaking on both sides of him until a heaving line could be flung over *Flamingo's* counter. The messenger was made fast to it, and the wire followed while Brushett struggled to hold *Franklin* in position, and while she sheered and leaped like a startled horse. When the wire was secure *Franklin* began working out to sea, and once she was clear of the reefs, *Security* came bustling up and put a line upon her. Then the two tugs got down to it—their engines throbbing with an effort upon the success of which the lives of seventy-eight men aboard the stranded ship depended.

By this time the gale had reached its full intensity and was blowing force 9 to 10. Breaking seas were sweeping *Flamingo* end for end, and the salvors at the winches on her after deck were in danger of being swept overboard. The vessel's engines were run up to full speed astern. The seas were lifting higher under her, and she was striking harder on the rocks. The pumpmen were laboring over their gear, for the water was gaining in number one hold and was beginning to rise in number two as the underwater damage steadily increased.

Every man aboard, except perhaps the stevedores who were huddled in the accommodations, knew that she must come off within the next few minutes or stay on the ledge forever.

In that sounding and furious darkness the seas rose higher. At 8:45 P.M. a monster sea roared in, lifted the stricken vessel's stern, then passed under her to lift her bow as well.

She came off suddenly—so suddenly that the ground-tackle wire could not be cast off fast enough, with the result that her propeller fouled it and her engine came to a shuddering halt.

The two tugs, burying their noses in the seas, were now tethered to the shore by the ground tackle afoul of *Flamingo's* screw. They were barely holding her a few hundred feet away from the reefs. They could not hold her there for long, and as the wind and seas increased there was every likelihood that they too would be driven back upon the rocks.

Featherstone radioed urgently:

PULL FOR ALL YOUVE GOT YOU WILL HAVE TO BURST THE GROUND WIRE TO SET US FREE

Only the harassed engineers in *Franklin's* engine room will know where they found that extra margin of power, but find it they did. There was a neck-snapping jerk on the towline as the ground wire parted—and *Flamingo* was released.

But she was by no means safe. Brushett and Williamson (who was master of *Security*) held their course straight for the open sea, while behind them the half-sinking *Flamingo* wallowed along stern first, offering the gale and seas a wall to push against.

It took two interminable hours for the straining tugs to haul her a mile off shore, and at every instant, the men on board all three vessels expected the grossly overtaxed tow wire to snap.

Finally, with a scant mile of water between him and the land (and knowing that only a miracle had kept the tow wire intact so far), Featherstone ordered the line cast off while *Flamingo* dropped both anchors in an effort to keep herself from drifting back, until the tugs could take her by the bow.

Security used a rocket to re-establish the connection; but Brushett came in so close that a heaving line sufficed to close the gap. Then, with a tug pulling on each quarter, *Flamingo's* anchors were brought home and the tow continued—this time for Halifax.

At 1 A.M. *Franklin's* wire, strained beyond endurance by the initial tow, parted at her taffrail. While her crew broke out a new wire and put it on the winch, *Security* continued to tow to seaward in order to gain more offing from the land.

The gale blew harder, gusting up to eighty miles an hour. Snow, driven like bird-shot, whitened the straining ships. With part of her cargo gone and her trim ruined, *Flamingo* was rolling like a drunken pig. The pumps were laboring at full throttle to hold the levels in her holds—but slowly the water rose.

The old *Security* hung on. She was being swept time after time, and as seen from *Franklin's* bridge, she looked to be under water more often than on top. Brushett held his own ship under a tight rein, ready to heave-to at any moment either to pick up *Flamingo's* people, or to rescue *Security's* crew.

Featherstone had long since radioed Halifax for more help, but it was not until 7:30 the next morning that the little *Banscot* was able to put out through the wild sea in the harbor entrance; and even then she was not able to go beyond the lee of Chebucto Head. There she remained until the sinking freighter finally reached that imperfect shelter. It had taken ten hours for the tow to move eight miles.

The worst was over then. With *Franklin* made fast on one quarter and *Banscot* on the other, and with *Security* towing ahead, the flotilla cleared the narrow gap in the submarine nets and made its way up the harbor to anchor in final safety just at noon.

The sea had lost a round.

21 ❦ MAD GREEKS AND SABOTAGE

THERE WAS LITTLE ENOUGH RESPITE for *Franklin* and her crew during the memorable winter of 1941. Only two days after the *Empire Flamingo* rescue, *Franklin* again put to sea; this time in answer to the distress call of the Irish freighter *West Neris*, disabled by engine failure a hundred miles east of Newfoundland.

The gale which had almost killed the *Flamingo* was still blowing lustily when *Franklin* steamed out of Halifax, but it had shifted into the west. The beam seas were of such a size that Brushett was forced to reduce to less than half speed, for fear of driving *Franklin* under. It was frigid weather and the tiny steel cubicles which were the homes of officers and men alike were as clammy and chill as tombs. Only the black gang knew what it was to be warm—and they were fairly roasted.

As the little ship ran her easting down, the storm worsened. By the third day it had become so wild that Brushett was forced to heave-to. The anemometer mounted on the wheelhouse registered a wind speed of eighty-eight miles an hour, and then gave up and simply blew away. *Franklin* staggered under the weight of the seas, then rolled herself free and came up to face the next assault.

When she eventually raised the *West Neris*, the storm was still so intense that four hours were required to make the connection between the ships, and another three hours were needed to swing the unwieldy Irishman on course for St. John's.

Then the slogging match began. Hour after hour *Franklin's* boilers fed steam into the cylinders and the great pistons rose and fell with a mindless certainty, a hypnotic regularity that denied the reality of the untrammeled forces in control outside the vessel. The shaft turned imperturbably and sleekly in its bearings, while beyond, the throbbing and sibilant world of the machine, the big screw thrust against the fluid fury of the sea.

The gale was still from the west, and *Franklin* was driving straight into its eye. The antagonists were face to face, each equally determined that the other should be beaten down. The world had shrunk to a circumference of half a mile, as if in order to contain the struggle. Snow, mingling with the spume, froze on *Franklin's* upper-works, but could not last upon her decks, for it was pounded off by the hammer of the seas.

The isolation of these two vessels seemed absolute—but

it was not. Fifty miles away a big Dutch diesel tug of twice the *Franklin's* power was also laboring toward St. John's, with the disabled American freighter *Macbeth* in tow. *Macbeth* and *West Neris* were of the same tonnage and both were light, but considering the size and power of the newly-built Dutch tug the *Macbeth* should have seen St. John's long before *West Neris* did.

Macbeth never saw St. John's at all. After twelve days of struggle the Dutch tug ran low in fuel and had to abandon the American. When the tow was cast off, *Macbeth* was *four hundred miles farther east than she had been when the Dutchman picked her up*. Eventually it was a British tug out of Scotland which took the *Macbeth* in tow again, and delivered her to Greenoch on the Clyde.

Franklin's people knew nothing of this lost battle until long after they reached St. John's and anchored the *West Neris* in the harbor. They would not have been much interested in any case. They had long since concluded that there was no greater-hearted vessel on the Western Ocean than the one in which they served.

Franklin's people had some hopes of spending Christmas of 1942 ashore, but these hopes were soon dispelled. On December 19 she sailed for Bermuda towing a big suction dredge, and after a slow and difficult passage, she and her crew were allowed three hours to enjoy the sun and rum of the island before being ordered home.

When she arrived in Halifax on New Year's Day, there was no question of the men being granted shore leave. They simply took it. *Franklin* was an empty, silent vessel that evening when Naval Control contacted Woollcombe to deliver yet another SOS.

Brushett and McLeod spent most of the remainder of the night searching the shadier waterfront dives. By dawn a partial crew had been assembled, but most of the stokers were comatose. Having lugged them aboard, McLeod found he was too short-handed even to make steam, so Brushett cast off from the dock, allowed *Franklin* to drift a few hundred yards into the stream, and anchored there until the black gang had been restored to a minimum degree of sobriety.

No one thought of blaming the men. They were underpaid by any standards, despite a wartime bonus system. They received none of the benefits and none of the recognition that naval ratings expected as their due. And they worked and lived under conditions which even Nelson's seamen would have found hard to take.

Worse still, they worked alone and quite unarmed in

waters where death from enemy attack was becoming commonplace. During the first six months of 1942, not less than seventy-six ships were sunk by submarines in the coastal waters of Canada and Newfoundland, and though the staggering toll taken by the U-boats was carefully concealed from the general public, knowledge of it could not be hidden from the merchant seamen. The fear of sudden death in winter seas haunted every man who sailed out of the east coast ports that winter. Those who sailed out in convoy felt some measure of security; but the salvage tugs sailed independently, without benefit of naval escorts and without defense of any kind. Nor could their crews solace themselves with the belief that their vessels were too insignificant to merit attention from the submarines. The sinking of several British salvage ships, including the seagoing tug *Neptune,* had confirmed what the salvors—and the Germans—knew, that for every rescue vessel sunk there would be a score of crippled merchantmen who would never make safe port. Deep-sea tugs were a priority target; if not for torpedoes, then for surface gunfire, which was equally as deadly.

The days the salvors spent tethered to fat and crippled merchantmen, crawling along on a straight course at a speed of two or three knots like mechanical targets in a shooting gallery, were the kind of days that would drain the courage from the most heroic man alive. It was small wonder then that the crews occasionally "let fly all holts." It was a great wonder that they continued to go to sea at all.

With a sick and shaking gang of stokers shoveling coal, *Franklin* cleared Halifax at 9 A.M. on January 2 bound north-eastward five hundred miles to the assistance of the Greek vessel *Dimitrios Englessis* whose rudder had carried away. The winter weather was no worse than usual, and *Franklin* only had to reduce to half-speed on two occasions. By noon on the fourth of January, Cape Race was abeam, and shortly afterwards Marryat began to receive the *Englessis's* signals.

The casualty was clearly determined to prove herself the most loquacious vessel in Atlantic waters. During the succeeding twenty-four hours her master initiated an almost unbroken stream of plain language signals, mostly directed to Cape Race radio station, and containing passionate demands for tugs, destroyers, and cross-bearings. Occasionally he left Cape Race alone in order to dispatch insulting messages to the Navy, or to use the general broadcast frequencies to tell the world at large his troubles. If he expected sympathy, he was an optimist. The naval authorities ordered him off the air, and when he ignored the orders Cape Race was instructed not to acknowledge or reply to any of his messages.

Marryat was appalled by his garrulity.

"This time for sure, we'll find an escort waiting when we reach that ship," he told the chief engineer. "Only it'll be flying a swastika flag."

The Navy may have thought so too. Two destroyers were dispatched from St. John's in expectation that good hunting would be found in the vicinity of the vociferous Greek.

Finding the ship turned out to be a mad business. Not only was the *Englessis* transmitting false positions to her would-be rescuers, but she was steaming at full throttle in circles and aimless zigzags as the whim of wind and sea dictated.

"There she was bouncing about like a flea on a hotplate," Brushett remembers grimly, "and all the time screaming at us to hurry up and find her."

Continuous blizzard, banks of fog, and the usual gale weather made the pursuit no easier. Eventually, Brushett lost all patience, and ordered Marryat to break the seal applied to his transmitter by the Navy and to dispatch a message to the *Englessis*. It was phrased in typical Brushett style.

STOP ENGINES IMMEDIATELY AND TRANSMIT ACCURATE POSITION OR WE ABANDON SEARCH

The *Englessis* responded with a voluble assault on Cape Race and the other shore stations, demanding radio bearings —for she had by now got herself completely lost. The shore stations prudently refrained from complying, for if they had done so their powerful transmitters would have provided every submarine within several hundred miles with an accurate fix on the casualty.

When they continued to remain obstinately mum, the *Englessis* signaled *Franklin:*

TELL THOSE HELLIONS ASHORE TO HELP IN MY POSITION

The "hellions" stayed silent. They could not understand why the casualty's wireless had not already gone dead as the aftermath of a torpedo blast.

Since he could get no position, Brushett began a search pattern designed to bring him within DF range of the *Englessis*. This necessitated another ten hours of tension while *Franklin* steamed back and forth covering most of the possible approaches which any submarine that might have been stalking the Greek ship would have used.

It was not until late on January 5 that Marryat got a bearing. Brushett immediately sent *Franklin* roaring down it, and

at the same time ordered the *Englessis* to be prepared to iden-
tify herself by the exchange of an agreed series of whistle
blasts. Brushett intended to connect during full darkness, for
there were good and obvious reasons why he did not wish to
linger in that vicinity after the new day dawned.

Bucketing through the winter darkness at full power,
Franklin soon raised the loom of another vessel dead ahead.
Brushett blew the identification signal and the stranger
promptly responded with the correct reply. *Franklin* circled
to shoot a line aboard, but at the last moment the stranger
sheered off and vanished at high speed. Two hours later this
mystifying and frustrating experience was repeated.

One of the mates who was on the bridge described his captain's reaction with considerable awe.

"He had his pipe a-stickin' out of his mouth like he allus
did, awake or asleep. As each of them two vessels loomed up,
gave the right signal, and then went rushing off just as we
were circling to put a line aboard, that old pipe began to
shake like a fish pole in a high wind. And when neither of
them would even answer back to our lamp signals, I thought
sure he was goin' to give the order to come around and
ram. My! But he was just the maddest feller that I ever
see!"

Brushett was even wilder when, after his return to St.
John's, he learned that the strange ships had been the destroyer escort sent to guard the crippled freighter.

Because of the delays occasioned by the destroyers, and
because the *Englessis* had kept right on steaming in wide circles at full power, *Franklin* did not locate her until the middle of the following morning.

Even when *Franklin* came in sight the *Englessis* still refused
to stop. In reply to an order from Brushett to ready her
anchor cable for towing, she said that she would not take a
tow, but expected to be steered from astern. It was a good
thing for the *Englessis* that the tug's only armament was a
rifle and the rocket pistol. As it was, the heavy projectile
from the pistol only missed going through her wheelhouse
due to the fact that a heavy sea spoiled the aim of *Franklin's*
furious mate.

Englessis had some luck on her side.

She proved it when, as the wire was finally attached, a welcome fog came down to screen both vessels from any further threat of submarines. The fog lasted all the way into St.
John's, where the *Englessis* was delivered on January 8.

Never in his life had Brushett been so glad to see the last
of any ship. He *thought* he was seeing the last of her, at any
rate. Had he known that he would have the *Englessis* back on

his hands a few weeks later, he might have left the sea and bought a farm instead.

Franklin sailed from St. John's the following day to assist the motor vessel *Danae II,* which had blown ashore in Bay Bulls. While Brushett was out in the motorboat inspecting this wreck, he was hailed by Marryat, who had just received another SOS from sea. Twenty minutes later *Franklin* was under weigh.

According to Marryat's information, this new casualty, the *Apartheid* (which was not the ship's true name), had been in collision a few hours earlier when a submarine had attacked and dispersed her convoy near the Newfoundland coast.

Apartheid proved elusive too, but not quite so difficult to find as the *Englessis* had been. *Franklin* loacted her off Cape Race at dawn on January 12, drifting derelict and abandoned, while a Navy corvette stood by a mile to leeward. Running down to the corvette, Brushett found that she had the surviving officers and crew of the *Apartheid* aboard her. Brushett politely inquired whether the freighter's people would like to return to their ship, for unless they did so it would be extremely difficult to get a line aboard her. *Apartheid's* master replied that he would *like* to rejoin his vessel—but he made no effort to man the casualty's boats, which were still tied up alongside the corvette.

There was no time to lie around and wait for him to make up his mind. The seas were already running high enough to make connecting a difficult business, so *Franklin* kicked up the foam under her stern and ran on toward the casualty.

Three seamen and Charles Mosher, the second officer, volunteered to board her from a dory. They reached her safely, but found that she had been leaking bunker oil until her plates were coated with the stuff and her sides had become quite unclimbable. Mosher surmounted this difficulty by heaving a line attached to a grappling iron over the lee rails. Then the men swarmed up the rope and gained the deck. This was no mean feat, considering that when the vessel had been abandoned the previous evening during a much more moderate gale, and in far lower seas, eleven of her people had been drowned.

The boarding party now had to catch the rocket line, haul in the messenger, and then drag *Franklin's* heavy towing wire aboard by man power alone. This would have been an impossible task had not Brushett backed the tug in so close that her counter was actually under the flair of *Apartheid's* bows. He held her in this dangerous position for twenty minutes while the prow of the derelict, lifting and plunging in the heaving seas, threatened at every instant to strike the tug and split her open. Twenty minutes was none too long a time to allow the four men on *Apartheid's* forecastle to haul in and secure the twin bridles which were attached to a hundred-pound shackle and a length of towing wire which alone weighed three-quarters of a ton.

Before rejoining *Franklin* the boarding party made a quick inspection of the ship to see how seaworthy she was. They found some curious things. Although the vessel had a list and her engine room was partly flooded, she was otherwise quite sound and dry. Descending to the engine room grating, Mosher noticed that the telegraph there was pointing to full-ahead, while the telegraph on the bridge had been pointing to full-astern.

When he returned to *Franklin* he told Brushett what he had seen. As he considered the information about the telegraphs, and the abandonment of a ship that had sustained no vital damage, Brushett felt intimations of trouble ahead. He was a man who often played his hunches and so, as the tow was being shortened up to enter St. John's harbor, he ordered Mosher, Henderson, and two seamen to return to the *Apartheid* and to allow no one else aboard. In acting in this manner he was quite within his rights, for an abandoned ship remains in her rescuer's custody until the claims against her have been settled by the owners.

The flotilla had just entered the harbor when Brushett's anticipation of trouble was confirmed. A launch from the corvette came alongside the *Apartheid,* and under the leadership of a naval officer, the casualty's master and other officers came aboard and repossessed the vessel. Mosher had no choice but to submit to the Navy's will.

Brushett was flaming mad. As soon as *Franklin* docked he went ashore, rounded up the sheriff, and obtained a writ giving him full control of the *Apartheid* pending an investigation into the circumstances of her accident.

Armed with this he chased all of *Apartheid's* people off the ship, with the exception of two of her officers who were allowed to remain aboard so long as they did not interfere with anything. Then Brushett began repair work. The engine room was pumped out easily with a single four-inch pump and the salvors found that the collision damage had been limited to a superficial gash which stopped short above the water line. The consequent mystery of why the ship had flooded at all was soon solved when Henderson discovered that a threaded steel plug in a circulating pump had been removed, allowing the engine room to fill.

This was curiouser and curiouser. Taking no chances, Brushett ordered a twenty-four hour guard to be mounted. At 2 A.M. the next night one of the men on guard hurried aboard *Franklin* to report that someone had shut off the steam which was being pumped across to the casualty from *Franklin*, and had opened all *Apartheid's* engine room skylights. The temperature was then fifteen degrees below zero. Had not the skylights been promptly closed, and steam restored, the casualty's pipes would have suffered frost damage which would have taken weeks to repair.

The ship was cleared of her own people after this, and there was no more trouble then. However, later on a protracted legal battle in United States courts grew up out of the *Apartheid* affair, and Brushett was accused of something akin to piracy. When this approach failed to intimidate him the charge was withdrawn and he was asked to modify the evidence which he had given and which pointed to sabotage. But asking Brushett to change his evidence was rather like asking Newfoundland to move a little further out to sea; and presently the matter was quietly buried—at least as far as Foundation Maritime was concerned.

There was never any mystery about the matter as far as *Franklin's* people were concerned.

"That ship was bound for Murmansk with a cargo of stuff for the Ruskies," one of them explained. "And the winter run up north was bad business. Wouldn't have wanted to make the trip myself. Somebody must have figured that the collision was a godsend, and maybe they were disappointed that it wasn't worse."

In any event, *Apartheid* missed the voyage and thereby probably saved her life, for the convoy of which she had been a part was later decimated by a combination of U-boats, aircraft, and surface raiders.

Franklin lay alongside her until February 3, keeping an eye on things. Then, to his unutterable disgust, Brushett was ordered to take the *Dimitrios Englessis* in tow for Halifax.

What followed was a nightmare, pure and simple.

As *Franklin* came up to connect the wire, Brushett found that every order he issued was being promptly countermanded by *Englessis's* skipper. The resultant chaos drove Brushett close to mayhem. He took the deck himself to get things straightened out and then suddenly, and incredulously, he became aware that his adversary was still issuing orders, but right at his elbow, and on Brushett's own vessel. With monkeylike agility the Greek captain had slid down the line connecting the two ships, the better to prosecute his battle with the tug-boat master.

There was a moment of horrible suspense as *Franklin's* crew waited to see murder done before their eyes. But Brushett fooled them. He simply grabbed a boathook and chased the Greek captain right back up the rope, hastening his progress by judicious thrusts with the sharp end of the pole.

It was an inauspicious beginning. Things got worse as soon as the two vessels had cleared St. John's. *Englessis's* master decided to shorten the voyage by spasmodically running his engine up to full power. Whenever he did this his ship would charge off until she was right abeam of *Franklin,* and sometimes even ahead of her. The strain on the half mile of wire, pulling at right angles to the course she was trying to maintain, would put the tug in irons and leave her helpless. Each time this happened an hour was wasted getting things straightened out. And it happened seven times in the first ten hours. After the eighth time Brushett flashed a lamp signal to the *Englessis.*

DO THAT ONCE MORE AND WILL CUT THE WIRE AND DAMNED WELL LEAVE YOU HERE

This had a chastening, if temporary, influence upon the impatient Greek. She kept station—more or less—until they came abeam of Louisburg and met the edge of a vast field of ice. The sight of the ice evidently distressed the *Englessis,* for it sent her off on another berserk dash. She came foaming up under full power and dragged some fourteen hundred feet of wire right under the pack. The wire promptly burst.

It was a lovely winter night—moonlit and calm; but it did not get the admiration it deserved, for the two vessels were lying directly over one of the ambush positions favored by U-boats waiting to attack the coastal shipping bound for Sydney.

Franklin came whooshing down on the *Englessis,* her funnels smoking like twin dragons, for Brushett was understandably anxious to get a temporary line aboard the cripple and make tracks for somewhere else.

To the everlasting astonishment of *Franklin's* crew, the Greek chose this of all moments to have a fit of sulks. *Englessis's* people absolutely refused to assist in making the new connection.

It was at this point that Brushett's maltreated pipestem finally snapped. "Mosher!" he bellowed in a voice that Captain Kidd might well have envied. "Stand by to board that ship! We'll put the wire on her ourselves."

They did it too; but it was an agonizing task, for the manila spring was so heavy coated in ice that its diameter had increased by several inches. Trying to handle this rock-hard line at a temperature of twelve degrees below zero was enough to try the patience of a Newfoundlander; but the boarding party persevered and finally made it fast by dint of tying an immense bowline in the rope, then slipping it over the *Englessis's* forward bollards.

So ferocious had been the attitude of *Franklin's* people

during this contretemps, that the *Englessis* crew stayed cowed until the voyage was ended. Nevertheless the very name of that ill-natured vessel is still enough to make Captain Brushett turn blue about the gills.

Scarcely had the *Englessis* been disposed of than *Franklin* was off again, this time to take part in a prolonged effort (one that eventually required the services of most of Foundation's fleet) to salve a six-million-dollar war cargo from the American vessel *West Jaffrey* which had been holed, and which later sank, near the south-east tip of Nova Scotia.

Diving and grappling from mid-February through to August, Foundation salvors recovered three-quarters of *West Jaffrey's* cargo in usable condition; including twenty-eight medium tanks which were restored to service and trans-shipped at Halifax for North Africa. *Franklin* assisted in this work whenever she was free of other commitments, but it was really that old hoodoo, the *Foundation Jupiter*, to whom most of the credit for this phenomenally successful operation was due.

Towards the end of February *Franklin* was ordered back to Halifax and told to report to the Naval Gun Wharf. Enemy submarine activity had become so intense in home waters by this time that the naval authorities had at last been prevailed upon to arm *Franklin* and *Aranmore*. *Franklin* received a six-pounder upon whose breech the date 1909 was stamped. She also received two naval gunners (ex-merchant seamen, both) who quickly convinced all on board that it would be less dangerous to be torpedoed than to risk firing this museum relic. Brushett, whose saturnine sense of humor was not always appreciated by his crew, did not agree with this pessimistic attitude.

"Must be a good gun," he pointed out. "Otherwise it wouldn't have lasted this long."

All the same he never put it to the test.

Armed with this weapon *Franklin* was ordered to proceed from St. John's on March 12 in search of the *Empire Celt*, whose bow had been blown off by a torpedo one hundred miles southeast of Newfoundland. She had been abandoned and her crew had been brought in by a corvette; but someone thought that she might have remained afloat and so *Franklin* was dispatched.

She did not go willingly. Gun or no gun, her firemen decided that they would sail no more without an escort; and so they went ashore and stayed there. Brushett's best efforts failed to locate them all, and he finally gave the order to cast off with three men still missing from the black gang. McLeod blew up. It was normal for each man of his gang to have to do two men's work but, he announced, he was damned if he would force each of them to do the work of three. He and Brushett snarled at each other inconclusively for a while, but the impasse was complete until Brushett signaled for one of the harbor tugs, threw a line on it, then had the tug tow him into mid-harbor and cast off. McLeod, who had gone below, came running up the engine-room ladder when he felt the motion, and he met Brushett on the after deck.

"Now then, mister," Brushett said briskly, "what about a little steam?"

The alternative was mutiny at sea. He got his steam, and *Franklin* sailed, albeit in no happy frame of mind.

She never found the *Celt*. In ten days she made three attempts and steamed a thousand miles, unescorted, through waters that were getting stiff with submarines. But the *Empire Celt* was never seen again.

22 ◈ A NAVAL ENGAGEMENT

WHILE THE BOOTLESS SEARCH FOR *Empire Celt* was in progress, the March gales had been working up toward their annual paroxysm. The worst time of the year for shipping in the North Atlantic had come again; but in the spring of 1942 the assaults of gales and seas were becoming secondary to the murderous activities of men.

Doenitz had convinced Hitler that the place to cut the arteries of the Western Allies lay at their beginnings in the coastal waters off the American continent. And so in the early spring the U-boats sailed westward—not in ones and twos, but in massive packs, until there were as many as twenty of them operating in Canadian coastal waters at one time.

Convoy after convoy, inbound or outbound, was attacked. In St. John's and Halifax, merchant seamen who had survived the unheralded explosions and the perishing waters of the winter sea appeared in pathetic little groups at Seamen's Homes and in the hospitals. They were few in numbers, but they represented many ships.

Franklin's people saw them and heard their tales, and the fear which no seaman can escape grew in their hearts. They knew that a single torpedo in *Franklin's* belly would send her to the bottom so swiftly that there would be no time to launch a boat. There would be only time to die.

They began to be filled with a hatred of the ocean that the worst of the winter gales had not been able to instill in them, for fear and hatred walk hand in hand. It was inevitable that some of this futile rage should be deflected upon those who were entrusted with the protection of the ships at sea.

The consequent hostility towards the Navy was not without justification. Some of the naval escort vessels put into port after convoy voyages and lay at dock for days on end, recovering from their ordeals; while the salvage and rescue tugs suffered the same grievous treatment under gale and sea, and knew no rest at all. The salvage crews watched green hands and green officers in spanking naval uniforms do foolish things that jeopardized not only the escort vessels, but the merchantmen they were supposed to guard. They lived in the shadow of the Navy's overweening pride, and of its condescending attitude toward the dirty, disreputable vessels of the salvage fleet and their ill-assorted and undisciplined men.

"Maybe we had no business to feel the way we did. But every time I came ashore in Halifax and saw the papers, I'd read that the Navy had the war at sea damn near won. And I'd wonder about the ten or a dozen distress calls that Sparks had picked up during our last voyage—calls from ships that went down before anyone could reach them. I'd see the merchant seamen in Halifax being treated like something not quite human, with nowhere to go but the cat houses and the dirtiest dives. The streets would be full of the Navy, strutting about as if they owned the place. Maybe it was wrong for us to feel resentful. We knew most of them were only kids, come from farms a thousand miles inland, as like as not. They were the amateurs, and we were the professionals, and that would have been bad enough, but it got worse when they were taught to think of themselves as a bunch of little tin gods. They could be taught *that* all right. But nobody could teach them how to know the sea.

"Probably we'd have taken it all with just the usual amount of bitching except for one other thing. When we went to sea, the Navy wasn't there. Maybe they had too much to do and too few ships, to spare any for us. But we used to see the escorts lying in St. John's and Halifax so thick you couldn't have sculled a dory in between them—while we were going out alone to try and haul in some torpedoed merchantman.

"The Navy must have had its reasons for the way it acted, and maybe they were good reasons too. We never heard them. They wouldn't bother to explain things to chaps like us. So we had to go by appearances, and the appearances were bad."

Right or wrong, this was the way the men who sailed the tugs had come to feel—and it was an unhealthy state of mind. One of the results was that it became increasingly difficult to obtain hands to man the ships, and almost impossible to keep them for more than one or two voyages. The consequences of this were that the officers, and in particular the masters and the chief engineers, were forced to shoulder yet

187

another heavy worry on top of those which they already carried. It was a situation that could not go on, and it was Harry Brushett who put a stop to it.

On Sunday, March 22, *Franklin* was lying at St. John's when Brushett received an order from the Navy telling him to proceed to the assistance of the torpedoed British tanker *Athelviscount* at a point six hundred miles south-east of Newfoundland.

Brushett immediately countered with an ultimatum. Unless an escort was forthcoming, he said, the tug would lie at Bowering's wharf until doomsday.

It is doubtful if any other merchant skipper could have made that ultimatum stick—but Brushett did. Two hours later a corvette came dashing out toward the harbor mouth and signaled for *Franklin* to fall in astern.

The weather outside was thick. Snow squalls and fog patches whipped across the Banks in the grip of a rising westerly that was blowing the disabled tanker farther eastward with every hour. She was already at *Franklin's* extreme range, and Brushett was driving his ship hard in an effort to reach the casualty quickly—but *Franklin's* best was only about twelve knots. That must have seemed like a tedious crawl to the commander of the corvette. Or perhaps he was annoyed at having been sent to sea for such a trivial matter. At any rate the escort made no attempt to stay close to its charge, but went haring away at full speed in a series of gigantic circles.

Brushett watched this performance with a jaundiced eye until just before dusk when the corvette happened to come in sight again. Then he ordered Marryat to send an Aldis signal:

SUGGEST YOU SLOW DOWN AND SAVE FUEL BY HOLDING STATION ON ME WE HAVE A LONG WAY TO GO

The corvette did not even deign to reply, but went whooping off into the murk again and vanished.

That night the weather thickened even more, and by midnight the storm, the snow squalls, and the scud had reduced visibility to the point where *Franklin's* people were only able to catch occasional glimpses of the corvette as she cut in across their bows at more and more infrequent intervals. Finally at 2 A.M. on March 22 they glimpsed her for the last time, heeling hard over in a turn. They did not see her again until four days had passed.

The weather cleared the next morning, but the gale continued unabated until March 26, when *Franklin* arrived at the pinpoint in grey nothingness where the *Athelviscount* should have been. The tanker was not there, and nothing in the heaving expanse of foam-flecked sea gave any clue to her whereabouts. As usual *Franklin's* transmitter had been sealed by the Navy before the voyage began, and this time Brushett let it remain sealed. Marryat stayed on listening watch while *Franklin* began a search pattern along the *Athelviscount's* presumed line of drift.

She was still searching some hours later when a United States destroyer came on the air to announce that she was standing by the torpedoed tanker. Marryat hastily took a DF bearing on this transmission, and *Franklin* began to run it down. The sea was singularly violent and it was not until dusk that the lookout raised a smudge of smoke on the horizon.

The smudge soon resolved itself into the lean profile of a destroyer, and the American knifed down on *Franklin*, saluted, then turned to lead the way.

As they closed with the ten-thousand-ton *Athelviscount*, she loomed up out of the turmoil of the sea like a waterborne Gibraltar. She had been westbound in ballast when an acoustic torpedo took her in the stern and now her bows were thrust up to the dark skies in a ponderous wedge of steel, while her counter lay almost at a level with the sea.

Brushett's attention was so intently fixed on her that he hardly noticed a third ship standing by. It was the escort corvette, which, having lost *Franklin* during the first night out, had come straight on to the casualty, getting new positions as she came, but not bothering to relay these to the rescue tug. As *Franklin* turned toward the tanker, the corvette shot out to meet her—her lamp blinking briskly as she came. This time it was her turn to be ignored. Brushett was far too busy to even waste a glance on her.

A thunder squall struck out of the north-west just at this moment, and during the flurry of its passage *Franklin's* people were wrestling with the heavy towing gear on the spray-swept after deck. The day was already old, and it was vital that a line be put aboard the casualty before the darkness came, but the seas were so immense, and the tanker's bows reared up so high, that not even Brushett could get close enough to put a heaving-line aboard. Coming up to windward of her he signaled that he would fire a rocket, but as the tube flamed over the big ship he saw with concern that only a handful of men were running forward to take the line. There were not nearly enough of them to take the place of *Athelviscount's* useless winches, so Brushett was forced to ease his tug in to such close quarters that her destruction beneath the plunging forefoot of the tanker seemed almost certain. Nevertheless he somehow managed to keep *Franklin*

189

out from under until the twin bridles had been hauled up the steel cliff, and the wire was secured.

Under other circumstances (and with most other masters) the tug would have lain off until dawn before trying to connect. Brushett felt that another twelve hours' drift toward the east might well spell the difference between success or failure in his attempts to save the ship. So he had accepted the risk, and at 8 P.M. of a black winter night the manila spring took up the strain and the tow began.

It was only then that there was time for communication with the casualty. As the *Athelviscount's* lamp flickered through the darkness, Brushett learned why he had seen so few men upon her decks.

When the torpedo struck—full in the engine room—almost the entire engineer staff together with some of the deckhands had been working amongst the machinery on an emergency repair. The blast had killed every man inside the engine room and had wounded most of those in the accommodations aft. The entire stern section of the ship had flooded until only the empty cargo tanks forward were left to hold her up. When *Franklin* took her in tow she was drawing forty feet of water aft, and was literally floating on her midship bulkheads.

Athelviscount's master had prudently sent most of his surviving crew over to the American destroyer before the weather became too violent for lifeboats to live. He and a handful of his officers and men had remained aboard their vessel with the faint hope that she might still be saved.

The message to the tug concluded with these words:

WE LIKE YOUR LOOKS AND THINK YOU WILL GET US IN

It was signed, as if a confirmation of a hopeful omen: Captain Franklin.

As the tow got under weigh the American destroyer foamed up alongside and her lamp began to wink:

GOOD LUCK TO YOU HAVE TO GO BUT LEAVE YOU IN GOOD HANDS

By "good hands" she presumably meant the corvette. If so, she meant well, but she was not very accurate. Hardly had she passed out of sight when the corvette again began to signal to the *Franklin:*

AM RUNNING SHORT OF FUEL, she said abruptly, NOW RETURNING TO ST. JOHNS

And five minutes later she was gone.

So *Franklin* and the tanker were left alone seven hundred and fifty miles from the nearest land, in a force 8 gale and in submarine waters, to sink or swim as best they could.

All the same they were not as much alone as they might have liked. During the next few days Marryat received three U-boat plots along the route which *Franklin* would have had to follow to reach Halifax. In addition he intercepted four SOS calls from ships which had been attacked between *Franklin* and the shore. The sea looked empty, but it was not.

When the Homeric struggle began *Franklin* was almost equidistant from St. John's and Halifax. Before sailing Brushett had been instructed to make for Halifax; but the Western Ocean was bent on seeing to it that *Franklin* did not go either to Halifax or to St. John's. An excerpt from the ship's log sets the tone of battle.

"March 27. *Day commences with west-south-west wind rapidly increasing to gale force with rough sea.* 6:56 A.M. *Tow-line parts due to chafing across casualty's bows. Too rough to reconnect. Standing by for moderating weather. . . .*"

Franklin's log gives no more than an intimation of the kind of weather which was being brewed that day; but any man who knew Harry Brushett would also know that a storm which could prevent his even putting a rocket line aboard the casualty must have been fearsome indeed.

During that morning the two ships drifted at such a pace that by noon they were twenty-five miles farther east than they had been at dawn. Plotting the drift, Brushett saw failure facing him and he could not stand the prospect. He rang down for half-speed on the engine, eased around out of the tremendous head-seas, and then blew—rather than ran—down on the tanker like a Mother Carey's chicken.

Reversing the usual order of things he shot up under the *Athelviscount's* lee (a position to be avoided because a big ship, with more surface to the wind, always drifts off faster than a small one and may well overrun a little vessel which is to leeward of her) and fire the rocket pistol. The line blew out almost parallel to the tanker, dragging the rocket off its course; but before it was quite lost, the projectile snagged in the tanker's foremast rigging.

Desperate hands grasped for and seized it, and at once the messenger line began to pay out. Handling the telegraph with the precision of an organist Brushett meanwhile kept his little vessel from being overrun by the massive bulk of the tanker until the wire had gone across the narrow gap. This time it was shackled directly to one of *Athelviscount's* anchor chains so that there would be no further danger of its chafing on her bows.

Franklin once more forged ahead and took the strain. After two hours she succeeded in bringing *Athelviscount* head into the wind again, but more than this she could not do. Although laboring valiantly she was unable to make progress, or even to hold her own. More slowly now, but just as implacably, the tug and tow were still being blown to the east.

Struggling like a beast upon a treadmill, *Franklin* kept at her task as if unconscious of the uselessness of her attempt to defeat the imponderable forces of the sea. The wind howled somberly in her rigging. The grey seas flung their spume and water-smoke high over her mast-heads. And she lay down to it and pulled with a strangely insistent stubbornness that is the property of life itself.

Through the four days which followed, there was no improvement. Those days bore no relation to time as we know it. They were, rather, a cessation in time—an absence of it. Nothing changed, except that men and ships grew four aeons older.

On the morning of the fifth day Brushett looked at the dead-reckoning position on his chart (it had been six days since he had been able to get a fix from the heavens) and then he turned to his mate.

"Grandy," he said, "We'll give it another twenty-four hours, and if the storm hasn't fallen light by then we'll turn around and run for Ireland."

He meant it too; but in any event they did not have to make that passage. Toward evening on the fifth day the wind began to fall off. Although *Franklin's* churning screw never changed its beat, the tow began almost imperceptibly to make some westing. By daybreak on the sixth day *Franklin* had regained the distance she had lost in the preceding five. She was back where she had started when the tow began.

As the wind dropped out *Franklin* was able to lay a course. Halifax was now out of the question as a destination, because of the depleted condition of *Franklin's* bunkers, and the prevailing westerly winds, so Brushett chose St. John's.

The new course put the two ships into a gigantic beam-sea and they both proceeded to try to roll themselves to death. The tanker, huge and heavy in the water, was rolling viciously enough—but *Franklin* was rolling like a barrel on a demented teeter-totter. Early in the morning of April 1 she took a sea that laid her over until her starboard rails went under. That roll caught able-seaman Walter Wilson in the act of descending a companion ladder, and *Franklin's* recovery was so violent that he was jerked off the ladder with such force that his right arm was sprung out of its socket. It flailed limply from his shoulder like a length of rope-end.

Brushett and Grandy tried to slip the bone back into place, but the tissues had been so badly torn and the deformation was so acute that they could do nothing with it. Brushett told Marryat to call the *Athelviscount* on the lamp, to see if by chance she had a doctor aboard. The tanker's reply came winking back:

MY STEWARD KNOWS FIRST AID BUT NO ONE CAN LAUNCH A BOAT IN SUCH A SEA

To which Brushett replied:

WILL YOU TAKE A CHANCE IF WE COME AND FETCH YOU

YES, came the instant answer, IF YOU CAN CHANCE IT SO CAN WE

Franklin eased down to dead-slow while Grandy and three Newfoundland seamen went aft and cast the lashings off the dory. Waiting their moment they threw the dory over the taffrail and leaped aboard, all in one motion; then they were rowing to get clear as *Franklin's* stern heaved up and came crashing down again.

What Captain Franklin's thoughts were as he beheld that trivial little cockleshell bouncing toward him over the great swells, he never would reveal. But he was a brave man and he kept his word. He and his steward hung down from *Athelviscount's* lee side on a Jacob's ladder that swung out, then in against the ship like a pendulum; and as the dory lifted beneath them, they jumped for it.

Captain Franklin was the kind of seaman the salvage crew could understand. As he crouched in the bottom of the fragile bit of flotsam to which he had committed his life, his glance was caught by a wooden plug shoved rather haphazardly into a hole in the floorboards. Pointing to it, he raised his voice and yelled a question over the skirling wind.

"Is that the plug we pull out to drain her—when she sinks?"

The Newfoundlanders grinned and rowed a little harder.

Captain Franklin and his steward were heaved aboard the tug by the boat's crew, then they descended with Brushett into the forepeak where Wilson had been lashed down in his bunk. For the next three hours they worked over him with slings, with purchases, with every aid their knowledge and ingenuity could command; and they had no success. They had no anesthetics either; but Wilson, a man of fifty-six years of age, did not utter one cry of pain. The three sweating men, all of whom had had decades of sea service behind them, were violently seasick. They were not ashamed of it.

"The motion in that fo'castle would have made a stone god lose his biscuits," was Captain Franklin's comment.

They had done their best, but in the end they were forced to leave Wilson lashed to his bunk, his arm still dislocated, to endure until the voyage was ended.

Franklin had now been at sea for ten days and nothing had been heard of her ashore since the departure of the corvette. Woollcombe and Featherstone were equally worried, and the Navy grew increasingly pessimistic as the days slid by.

The Navy broadcast several messages instructing Brushett to break radio silence, but Brushett ordered Marryat to keep the transmitter sealed.

"The only hope we've got is silence," he said. "If we open up we can count on a sub finding us—but we cannot count on anyone else."

Marryat remained on listening watch. The days dragged on.

By April 4 *Franklin's* bunkers were so nearly empty that, in the terrible roll and heave of the sea, her propeller was being constantly thrust out of water. Either Poirier or McLeod had to stand by the throttle every instant. As the propeller lifted and began to race, they cut off the steam; as it buried itself again they gave the steam back to the cylinders.

Exhaustion had passed the point where it was apparent to those whom it had engulfed. The stokers—the men the shore people referred to as dead-beats and bums—shoveled coal, hauled ashes, and did not know it.

Brushett himself was at the limits of his endurance, for he had hardly been off his bridge since the voyage began. He would not rest. "There were seventeen men aboard that casualty," he said. "There was the ship herself. And there was *Franklin* and her crew. I wasn't tired."

By April 5 the Navy had concluded that *Franklin* and her tow had probably gone down. The U.S. Air Force was asked to send a plane out of Argentia to search for wreckage, and a big amphibious aircraft was dispatched at noon.

At 5 P.M. that day, Woollcombe received a message from St. John's.

AIRCRAFT REPORTS BRIEF SIGHTING TWIN STACK TUG
TOWING WHAT APPEARS TO BE SINKING SHIP 100 MILES
S.E. ST. JOHNS

In Halifax there was jubilation and in St. John's there was a great bustle. An escort vessel was ordered to prepare for sea while more aircraft were sent out immediately. The first of these planes located *Franklin* at 10 A.M. on April 6. At 9:50 A.M. Brushett had sighted the land mass of Cape Race.

The wind that morning was moderate but showing signs of shifting to sou'east. *Franklin* had been towing for ten days, and had been at sea fourteen. She had less than a day's bunkers left. Brushett knew that if her fuel failed, or if the wind went into the sou'east, both she and *Athelviscount* would probably drive ashore. As a safety measure then, he signaled to Captain Franklin suggesting that he and his remaining crew come aboard the tug. If the worst came to the worst *Franklin* could then slip the tow and claw off the lee shore before her fuel ran out.

Both ships were stopped while the survivors from the tanker came aboard the *Franklin*. As they got under weigh again the two masters stood on *Franklin's* bridge together and watched the sky with eyes in which perpetual strain would leave a mark which would be there when both lay dying.

They watched the sky. Down in the engine room McLeod and Poirier watched the steam gauges. There was nothing in the bunkers now but dust.

Night came down. The glass began to drop. The wind was rising and shifting slowly, but it had not yet begun to really blow. It seemed to prolong its indecision from hour to hour with a cruelty that was almost human. Then at dawn, for no good reason and contrary to all precedent, it simply dropped away leaving a calm and a great settling bank of fog across the entrance to St. John's.

Out of that fog came a corvette, steaming as if the hounds of hell were on her tail. She circled *Franklin* and the tow, jauntily kicked her heels and signaled: FOLLOW ME.

Franklin did not follow. *Athelviscount* was now drawing forty-one feet of water and there was only forty-two feet over the entrance to the harbor at low tide. *Franklin* stopped her engines and waited for the rise. It came at last, but with it came the wind, and a blinding snow squall. Brushett could not wait for visibility to clear. Inching her way silently (she could not waste steam making fog signals), *Franklin* came blind into the narrow entrance and there she was greeted by three harbor tugs who quickly put their lines aboard the *Athelviscount* and guided her the last few hundred yards towards an anchorage.

The story should have ended there, but it did not.

Once in the harbor *Athelviscount* was boarded by a party of naval officers who took over command of the last few minutes of the tow. One of them stationed himself on the tanker's bridge and, having signaled for the three harbor tugs to pull ahead, he turned to watch something happening astern and forgot about the tugs. They pulled. The mooring wire which *Franklin* had already made fast to a buoy snapped like a string and the *Athelviscount* went charging across the harbor and fetched up hard against the opposite side.

Burning a mixture of coal dust and berserk rage, *Franklin* came bursting up alongside the tanker and Brushett stepped to the wing of the bridge. For a pregnant moment he stared up at the gold-braided officers above him, and then he bellowed in a voice that all St. John's could hear:

"Why in the hell don't you brass monkeys stay up in the trees where you belong?"

The brass monkeys hurriedly vanished from his sight.

Having released the *Athelviscount* and re-anchored her, *Franklin* made fast to Bowering's dock, with just enough coal left, as McLeod put it, "to cook a pot of beans."

Almost before the lines were fast a messenger stepped aboard. Captain Brushett was ordered to report at once to the senior naval officer.

"Now what?" asked Brushett, and the messenger replied stiffly. "There have been alleged infringements of regulations by your vessel."

Captain Franklin was standing close enough to overhear.

"Mind if I come with you, Cap?" he asked—and grinned.

Brushett grinned in reply—but the grin was thin and wolfish. They went off together.

Fortunately the senior naval officer in St. John's had been a seaman once himself. Therefore he did not order either Brushett or Captain Franklin to be clapped in jail at the conclusion of that memorable interview, as a lesser man might well have done. But when the masters had left his office, the admiral wiped his brow and turned to his chief of staff.

"The last time I got a strip torn off me as wide as that," he said nostalgically, "was when I was a middie with the China Fleet. You'd better see that *Franklin* gets an escort from now on!"

23 ❦ THE SEA TAKES THREE

THE ADMIRAL IN COMMAND at St. John's was as good as his word. From this date onward, whenever *Franklin* sailed from that port she had an escort if one was available. Often enough none was—but that was not the admiral's fault.

Through the rest of April *Franklin* was busy towing ships (which she had previously rescued from the high seas) to United States ports; but on May 4, while she was returning to Halifax from Boston, Marryat intercepted an SOS from the *Empire Story*, a new, war-built merchantman laden with three million dollars' worth of army trucks and tanks, which had sailed from St. John, New Brunswick, on May 3 to make a convoy rendezvous at Halifax.

The tides in the Bay of Fundy (they are the highest in the world) had combined with an obliterating fog to set the *Story* far off her course, and on May 4 she struck the land near Briar Island. Her damage was so severe and her condition appeared to be so desperate that her crew and officers abandoned ship as soon as the SOS had been dispatched.

Franklin was less than a hundred miles away at the time of the accident, and she came on at forced draft into the bay. There the fog shut down about her too, but Brushett felt his way along until he was off Digby Neck. Here he almost collided with a government fisheries vessel which had been at the scene of the accident. The master of the fishery vessel called through his megaphone to say that the *Story* had refloated herself at high tide (the tidal range at this point was about thirty feet) and had then drifted off into the murk, derelict and abandoned.

Brushett began a hurried search, for he knew that the abandoned ship would be taking water and that she might not stay afloat for long. *Franklin's* whistle boomed eerily in the fog as she zigzagged back and forth following the current of the inflowing tide, until eventually the sixth sense that only seamen have, led Brushett to the drifting vessel.

Dead silent, and ghastly in her grey camouflage, she lay so low in the slick and swirling water that *Franklin's* people at first thought she was no ship at all, but a half-submerged reef. Only when they had eased in to within a few hundred feet could they make out the details of her superstructure through the enveloping murk.

The tow wire was put aboard direct from *Franklin's* after deck, for there was obviously no time to spare, even to land a boarding party, if the vessel was to be saved. *Franklin's* engines were worked up to full speed and Brushett laid a course for Digby—the nearest port into which he would have a chance of bringing the half-sunken vessel for a safe beaching.

Those of *Franklin's* people who were off duty watched the ghostly shape behind them with straining eyes. They were fully aware that at any instant she might take the plunge.

They towed for an hour. Although no man could see it, Brushett knew that the entrance to Digby Gut was not more than a few miles ahead. He stepped out on the bridge wing to see how the *Story* was coming, and at that instant she began to lift her bows.

Brushett's warning shout reached the watchers on the tug's after deck and sent them scrambling for shelter; for the

Story was going down stern first and *Franklin's* wire was lifting high out of the water and coming under an intolerable strain as the whole weight of the dying vessel surged back upon it.

She reared up slowly until her bows were pointing almost perpendicular toward the unseen sky. For a moment she hung there on her bulkheads; then with a gargantuan sigh, as of a thousand harpooned whales in mortal agony, she began to slide back into the depths. The trapped air, rushing to escape, blasted off her fore-hatches and whistled shrilly through her ventilators. Then there was only a great yeasty bubble on Fundy's brown and turgid water.

The *Story* had tried hard to take the *Franklin* with her. As the doomed ship began to rear, Brushett had rung for full speed astern in order to ease the strain upon the wire; but *Franklin's* forward momentum could not be halted in time and the tow wire burst. Three hundred yards of one-and-three-quarter-inch steel cable came whipping back toward the tug with an ear-splitting scream.

A loop of it hit her after ventilators and sliced them off as cleanly as a cutting torch could have done; and it was only by the grace of God that the bulk of that flailing cable passed to starboard and smashed harmlessly into the sea. It could easily have taken *Franklin's* funnels and perhaps her bridge as well.

A piece of the Manila spring also came back on the end of that gigantic whip, and this was flicked in under *Franklin's* stern, where it wound itself about the tug's propeller.

Poirier, on watch below, was quick to feel the drag, and he instantly cut off the steam. His quick response probably saved *Franklin*, for if the propeller had made a few more revolutions it would have become hopelessly ensnarled—and *Franklin* was then only a few miles off the Fundy shore and in the grip of the swift inward setting of the tide.

For half an hour—and it was as tense a thirty minutes as any man aboard remembered—Poirier and McLeod worked to free the propeller by gently starting, and then reversing the engine so that the shaft turned only a revolution or two in each direction.

They could smell the land by the time the propeller began to turn freely again and *Franklin* was able to claw away from that waiting shore.

The loss of the *Story* gave rise to some gloom aboard the tug, for sailors have their superstitions and they believe that ill-luck, like big seas, comes in cycles built around the magic number three.

After taking a tow to New York on July 27, *Franklin* was

dispatched to help the freighter *Broompark,* which had been torpedoed just east of St. John's, and which was then being towed by an American naval tug which could not handle the big ship alone.

Franklin arrived on the scene on August 1 after three days of hard steaming, to find the Navy tug laboring mightily against the inertia of a seven-thousand-ton ship which had sunk almost to her decks. The dying *Broompark* refused to stay astern of the Navy tug and insisted on swinging out abeam so that the tug was in irons most of the time.

Franklin's arrival was greeted with relief by the Americans, who asked Brushett to take a stern line from *Broompark* in order to hold her on course for St. John's. Brushett complied at once and the sinking vessel reluctantly straightened out and began to move toward the land.

She was not destined to reach it. When the little convoy was only fifteen miles out of St. John's the *Broompark* lowered her head and took the plunge.

Brushett got his steering line off just in time. Had he been a few moments later the sinking vessel's rearing stern would probably have dragged *Franklin* right in under her.

While Franklin sheered off at speed, Brushett turned to watch the death throes of the ship. She was a brand-new vessel, only a few weeks out of the yards, and she had been fitted with the latest device for defense against torpedoes— steel nets which had been hung from booms along both sides. Unfortunately the nets had not been made continuous around her bows, and a U-boat had slipped a torpedo in from dead ahead.

"Someone had left his coat on one of the hatches," Brushett remembers, "and when the air in her after-holds blew out it sent that coat a hundred feet into the air, so that it came tumbling slowly down waving its arms and coattails like a live thing. It would have seemed funny anywhere else; but when you are watching a ship dying, everything you see is horrible."

Franklin returned to St. John's for bunkers, then on August 3 she set sail for Halifax in convoy. She had barely put to sea when she was ordered to the assistance of the torpedoed *Belgian Soldier* at a position only fifty miles ahead.

Franklin fell out of convoy and laid course for the sinking ship—not without some trepidation, for Marryat was now intercepting an almost continuous series of SOS calls and submarine reports from the convoy to which the *Soldier* had belonged, and which was being attacked by three or four U-boats.

No escort was detached for *Franklin,* and she steamed straight for the battleground with her two naval ratings sitting by the six-pounder and praying that they would not have to fire it.

The scene when *Franklin* arrived off Cape Race was one of utter chaos. More than sixty merchantmen were lumbering off to every point of the compass, while in the distance the escort vessels sought the submarines. *Franklin* weaved and twisted to avoid the mad rushes of the frightened giants. Locating the *Soldier* had to be done "by guess and by God," for there was not a hope of getting a message to or from her, in the babble that was filling the ether.

Brushett did his best, but he had still not found the cripple when a naval message came booming through to inform him that the *Soldier* had gone down, and that *Franklin* was to divert immediately to the *Empire Ocean*, which had driven ashore on Cape Race in her efforts to escape the submarines.

Franklin reached the *Empire Ocean* two hours later. As Brushett looked at her from his bridge he prayed that she would not be so badly damaged as to need pumps—for he had none aboard. All *Franklin's* salvage pumps had previously been removed for use upon another ship aground in Nova Scotia.

At first glance the *Ocean* did not seem to be in very serious trouble. She had driven onto a steep shore so that only her bow was on the rocks while her stern was in such deep water that Brushett was able to back *Franklin* in close enough to make fast to her.

While Brushett climbed aboard to check the damage and to speak to the wreck's skipper, the salvage crew connected the tow-line to the casualty's stern so that it would be ready when it came time to pull her off. They were standing by, waiting for orders, when the *Ocean* crunched a little and then of her own free will slid off the rocks.

There was a moment of wild confusion. As Brushett ran to gain *Franklin's* deck he heard the casualty's bosun yelling from forward that the ship was filling by the head, and filling fast. Both vessels were swinging broadside to the rocks and there was no time for anything except to get *Franklin* under weigh, still connected to the *Empire Ocean's* stern, and then to claw off from that bold headland.

Fifteen minutes later they were clear. Then *Empire Ocean's* master bawled through a megaphone that the whole forward part of his vessel had flooded and that she was threatening to go down. His own pumps could not begin to cope with the leakage, he said, and he was preparing to abandon ship.

Brushett's dilemma was a dreadful one. He knew that if he stopped towing in order to put his wire on her bow, the water pressure on *Empire Ocean's* midship's bulkheads might well increase sufficiently to rupture them and so to send the vessel down at once; but on the other hand if he continued towing her astern he could only make the slowest progress, and she would probably sink before he could reach St. John's. He concluded that his only hope of saving the ship was to continue towing stern first until he found a place where he could get the cripple into shallow water where she would not sink beneath the surface. Raising and repairing her could then be undertaken with the proper gear, and at a later date.

The only trouble with this plan was that there were not more than two or three places along that forbidding shoreline where he could hope to beach the *Ocean*. The nearest one was the indentation in the cliffs at Aquaforte Harbor, which lies between two massive headlands separated from each other by only three cablelengths. In daylight it might possibly have been entered by a tug with such a tow—but by this time it was already night.

Nevertheless Brushett laid his course for Aquaforte. He arrived off it in pitch darkness, with a fog haze to make things worse, and discovered (as he had anticipated) that the navigation and range lights had been removed as a wartime security measure. He decided to take a supreme risk and try to get in between the headlands using his searchlight to guide him, but when the mate went to switch it on, it was found to be broken beyond repair.

Empire Ocean had now settled until her foredeck was awash, but she did not seem to be taking any more water. Her midship's bulkheads were still holding and might do so for a little longer if the suction induced by the vessel's sternway could keep the full pressure of the sea away from them. Nevertheless her crew prudently abandoned her, some of them to come aboard *Franklin*, and the rest to lie alongside in lifeboats.

Without slackening pace Brushett swung *Franklin's* head away from the black line of cliffs and laid a new course for Ferryland Harbor, a few miles farther north.

Despite the best her engineers could do *Franklin* was now barely able to keep weigh on the sinking hulk, and it was five interminable hours later before the loom of the headlands told Brushett he was approaching his goal. It began to look then as if he might succeed. He headed his vessel in toward the narrow entrance.

As he closed the land it was imperative that he shorten up the tow-line, else *Franklin* herself would have run aground before the *Ocean* was in shallow water. The second mate, Cecil Bellfountain, ran aft to the towing winch and began to take in the wire as *Franklin* slowed. But inevitably some of the weigh came off the *Ocean,* and as it did so her midship's bulkheads began to sag.

Brushett sensed what was happening and yelled to Bellfountain, "Get out of it! She's going to go."

The mate just had time to scurry for cover in the alleyway as the freighter's stern began to lift. Up and up it went until the vessel was standing straight up and down. Then with a hollow roar the rest of her bulkheads burst and she drove down into thirty fathoms taking with her two naval gunners who had remained aboard when she was abandoned.

Once again the broken tow wire flashed back at *Franklin,* and this time it took a human toll. It wrapped itself around the waist of a deck-hand and flipped him overboard still tightly held within its coil. Inexorably the wire dragged the seaman down—but slowly enough so that his voice could be heard clearly for some seconds pleading for someone to release him.

He was the first man *Franklin* had lost in all her years of saving life.

Fortunately there was no time for men's thoughts to linger over the series of disasters which had culminated in the sinking of the *Empire Ocean.* Hardly had *Franklin* bunkered in St. John's than she was dispatched to the scene of a new stranding on the southern tip of Nova Scotia.

The vessel concerned this time was one of the new United States Liberty ships, laden with fifteen hundred tons of high explosives and an additional eight thousand tons of war cargo, including eighty-five army trucks. Her name was the *William Maclay,* and she had driven on Elbow Reef almost twenty miles off the mainland coast of Nova Scotia, and in a complex of reefs and rocks from which no large vessel had ever been refloated. Her position was near the wreck of the *West Jaffrey,* but ten miles farther off shore and completely exposed to every wind that blew.

The salvage of this vessel was one of the most nightmarish operations in which *Franklin* took a part. It required thirteen days to free the ship, and during that time there was only one period (and it was of less than two hours' duration) when the scene was not completely blanketed by fog. So impenetrable was the murk that for the first four days of the operation *Maclay* was believed to be on Zetland Shoal, a mile from her true position. During this time *Franklin* was maneuvering absolutely blind over water she believed to be sufficiently deep for her; but which in reality was studded with rocks, any one of which could have ripped her bottom out. The area of the stranding would have been formidable enough in clear weather—in fog it was a frightful place into which not even the local fishermen in their light motorboats would willingly penetrate. To further complicate matters the Fundy tide came across these reefs at speeds of up to five knots both on the ebb and on the flow.

Yet to a certain extent these were routine risks. What could not be considered routine were the problems involved in handling the *Maclay's* cargo. Featherstone had estimated that two thousand tons would have to be lightered off before she could be freed, and this figure was to include seven hundred and fifty two-ton blockbuster bombs. These had to be swung out over the side and dropped into barges which *Banscot* had brought down from Halifax. The perpetual swell over the reef kept the barges bouncing up and down like bobbins, and the men handling the winches were amateurs —being fishermen who had been hired locally. Time after time a sling of bombs would be dropped too fast and would meet the barge rising on the swell. The sling would burst, and the huge bombs would go trundling over the barge's deck while the salvage gang leaped out of the way. On one occasion a winch operator lost complete control and ran a bomb right up to the end of the cargo boom, where it whirled around and around three or four times before it came crashing down fifty feet into the hold of a small steel cargo vessel which was being used as a lighter. As it hit, the bomb was deflected by a balk of timber and shot off sideways, thundering through piles of small-arms ammunition and crates of gelignite, until it fetched up with a mighty crash against the ship's forward bulkhead.

There was a deathly silence after it had come to rest. Featherstone, standing on the *Maclay's* bridge, had watched the incident with the detachment of a man who knows that this is the finale. Apparently everyone felt the same way and it took them some time to realize that they were due to go on living.

"For three days afterwards," Featherstone remembers, "I couldn't get the taste of gunpowder out of my mouth."

It was shortly after this incident that Foundation Maritime received a memorandum from the War Shipping Authorities which read, in part:

William Maclay, Cargo Precautions

You will *not* repeat *not* handle Bombs, Two-ton, Mark III, without observing the following precautions:

1. All personnel will wear crepe-soled shoes and will be clad in overalls which have no metallic buttons.
2. These bombs are filled with a cast explosive which is subject to crystallization and self-detonation. Under

NO circumstances should they be jarred, or subjected to shock of any kind.

Woollcombe, who received this document in Halifax, put it thoughtfully away under the blotter on Featherstone's desk. He felt that Featherstone might be interested in reading it *after* the job was done.

Captain Turner on the *Banscot* had to haul the bomb-laden barges off to Pubnico. He was not fond of his charges. "Big green horrors," he said feelingly to his mate. "Gives me the creeps to look at them."

The mate, who was a reading man, replied: "Did you know, Cap, those are the same kind of bombs they're dropping on Berlin, and there's as many of them in the *Maclay* as has ever been dropped on any city yet?"

"That made me feel much better," Turner remembers. "Made it easier to imagine what would happen if she blew."

She did not blow, and after thirteen days of groping their way about like blind mice in a featherbed, the salvors refloated the *Maclay*. Despite the fact that every bottom tank was holed, that three of her cargo holds were tidal, and that she had almost completely broken in two amidships, they got her into Pubnico and beached her there.

Temporary repairs to make her seaworthy enough to tow to Boston took another ten days, and during this time diver Bill Henderson discovered a new peril of his trade.

There was a great gap leading into one of the *Maclay's* holds amidships where she had torn her side plates open. This hold was partly filled with hundred-pound sacks of flour, and loose sacks kept drifting out through the aperture into Pubnico harbor, where a mob of fishermen waited to pounce upon them. After a while these unofficial salvors decided to help the forces of tide and waves a little, and so several of them began to hook sacks out of the hole with boathooks. After several successful hauls one of them snagged what seemed to be a particularly fat and heavy sack, and he yelled for assistance. Two of his comrades jumped to help him and together the three men hauled out their catch.

It was Bill Henderson, with the sharp end of a boathook securely caught in the seat of his diving dress.

24 ❖ A SHIP AFLAME

THE *Maclay* EPISODE brought an end to *Franklin's* hard-luck streak. On September 3 the United States Troopship *Wakefield* (formerly the passenger liner *Manhattan*) had sailed from New York, bound for Belfast with eight hundred construction workers aboard. These men were being shipped overseas to build a naval and air base, and they were considered to be as valuable to the war effort as an equal number of trained soldiers. Their value was clearly recognized by the enemy.

On the morning of September 4, when the *Wakefield* was two hundred miles east of Halifax, several mysterious fires broke out simultaneously aboard her. The cause of these fires was never officially explained and, indeed, the entire incident was kept from the press; but they were almost certainly due to sabotage. There had already been a good many similar cases of incendiarism aboard vessels which had put out from U.S. ports bound for Europe.

In any case the fires aboard the *Wakefield* were soon out of control. Her naval escort closed in quickly, and despite a moderately heavy sea and wind, life-saving operations were soon successfully under weigh. By noon *Wakefield* lay abandoned and stopped with great coils of smoke rolling out of her to testify to her distress.

Wakefield was an American vessel and under U.S. escort. Word of the disaster was therefore first radioed to the American authorities and four U.S. naval tugs were ordered out from Boston and New York. Fortunately for the *Wakefield*, the message concerning her was also relayed to Halifax. It was doubly fortunate that *Foundation Franklin* lay at her dock ready to sail on that grey morning.

The *Wakefield* was within the area which Washington had agreed should be the bailiwick of Foundation Martime, therefore although *Franklin's* services had not been specifically requested, she put to sea. Brushett knew only that a naval vessel was in serious trouble some two hundred miles to the east.

Franklin steamed hard, and as dawn broke on the fifth, an American destroyer came boiling down upon her out of the murk of a bleak morning. Presumably acting on the assumption that *Franklin* was one of the expected U.S. tugs, the destroyer came hardaport, cut across *Franklin's* bow at thirty knots and imperiously signaled the tub to follow after. *Franklin* opened up to the magnificent speed of thirteen knots, and an hour later came in sight of the *Wakefield*.

She was an appalling spectacle. A grey behemoth aflame, she lay ringed by three prowling destroyers, each of which vanished at intervals into the acrid smoke to leeward of her, where the rising westerly wind drove it down upon the sea.

Wakefield was a twenty-thousand-ton vessel, and dead in the water. *Franklin* was only six hundred tons, but as vital as the sea itself. Neither she nor her people hesitated for an instant at the magnitude of the task before them. Brushett never slackened down, nor did he waste time circling. *Franklin* came at the flaming ship like a determined terrier, and when she was so close that the heat was blistering her own paint, she came smartly about with her stern six feet from the giant's side.

Second Officer Cecil Bellfountain and three seamen made the leap from *Franklin's* bulwarks to the scrambling nets which still hung over *Wakefield's* side as they had been left when she was abandoned.

They went up the nets with considerable alacrity, for the steel plates were hot enough to scorch the ropes. Once on deck they raced forward to take a heaving line thrown up from *Franklin's* stern. The smoke swirled about them so that they appeared to Brushett like midges in a campfire smudge as they hauled in the messenger line, passed it around a bollard, and threw the free end down again to *Franklin's* deck.

Franklin's capstan began to clank and foot by foot the heavy wire towing pendant crawled up to *Wakefield's* foredeck as the messenger was brought in on the capstan-head.

There was no time—and those were no conditions—to try and free an end of *Wakefield's* massive anchor chain to act as a spring. But a spring was needed, so Brushett used the old method of shackling a one-hundred-fathom length of fifteen-inch manila line between the wire pendant and the towing wire.

Bellfountain and his gang came down the nets less than twenty minutes after they had mounted them. Half blinded and with seared hands, they made the leap to *Franklin's* heaving stern. As they landed, her propeller began to churn urgently and she began to draw away.

The wire paid out and the strain came on it, but for half an hour *Franklin* might as well have been trying to get Bell Island into motion. At last, and almost imperceptibly, the choking plumes of smoke pouring out abeam of the *Wakefield* began to change direction, angling off astern. *Wakefield* was under weigh.

Franklin labored as she never had before. The sleek destroyers, useless in this emergency despite their thousands of horsepower, circled the two antagonists—the flea before the whale—with manifest impatience. Her engines thudding with the pulse beat of a terrible exertion *Franklin* worked up to her full power—and was towing at two knots.

At noon the next day the four U.S. naval tugs came scampering down on the *Wakefield*, and *Franklin* was all but lost in the subsequent melee. The Navy took over. Three of the four tugs shackled their wires directly onto the *Wakefield* while the fourth placed hers on *Franklin's* bow. Then with a great tootling of whistles the Navy prepared to hustle *Wakefield* in to Halifax in proper style. They did not actually ask

Franklin to cast off and go and hide herself, but a commander bellowed through a megaphone to Brushett, as his big diesel tug swung in ahead of the tow:

"Keep that hay-burning barge out of my way—we've got a job to do."

Brushett said nothing—but he seethed. An intransigent mortal at the best of times, he never did take kindly to orders issued by the temporary sailors of the wartime Navy.

Two hours later he was no longer silent. It had begun to blow hard out of the nor'west, and as the seas mounted and the beam wind took the tugs, the naval vessels began to get into the most unholy snarl. Although they were able and powerful enough, they had been designed according to American mercantile experience, which, while admirably suited for barge towing in sheltered waters, was not adequate to conditions in the North Atlantic. The U.S. tugs had their towing winches situated so far aft (almost over the counter) that if they were set off course by wind or sea they simply could not get back on course again. The strain upon the wire would not let them come up, and consequently they went into irons and were in danger of capsizing if they tried to pull at any acute angle to the line of their tow wires.

The tug on *Franklin's* bow was the first to get into irons, and since she could not get out again she began to veer off to port and to haul *Franklin* after her.

"That might not have been so terrible," one of *Franklin's* mates said afterwards. "We could have gone to Bermuda on that course. The trouble was that the other three tugs were heading for St. John's, Greenland, and Ireland respectively. We just couldn't go to all those places at the same time."

In any case the terrible-tempered Harry Brushett was going to Halifax. He ordered the tow-line of the tug ahead of him to be cut free, and then by the hair-raising expedient of turning back toward the *Wakefield* and then steaming in a circle over his own tow wire, he regained his correct course.

Wakefield was amost stopped by then, and the remaining three tugs were trying desperately to get straightened away. One of them almost made it, but at the crucial moment parted her towline—for she had not been using a spring. The other two were in such a helpless state that they were forced to cast off voluntarily.

The wind had now risen to force 7, a heavy blow, but nothing much for *Franklin*. Nevertheless it was too strong and the seas were too high to allow the naval tugs to reconnect. Disconsolately they grouped themselves in a flustered little convey off to leeward as *Franklin* continued single-handed with her tow for Halifax.

The American tugs had been chastened. But their people

were made of good stuff. When *Franklin* hauled the *Wakefield* through the submarine nets the next afternoon and beached the still flaming hulk at McNab's Island, the assembled U.S. tugs and destroyers saluted her with a great blowing of sirens and whistles in honest recognition of a job well done.

"They were good chaps," Brushett recalls magnanimously. "Would have been good seamen too—if they had our advantages."

The *Wakefield* story was not yet finished. Featherstone had taken command as soon as the liner approached the harbor. He had brusquely vetoed naval orders that she be brought alongside a dock, for he was fully aware that any attempt to flood out the fire while she was afloat would probably result in another capsizement such as the one which had sunk the *Normandie*. So *Wakefield* went on the beach and for a week U.S. and Canadian naval and civilian fireboats fought the blaze. They beat it in the end, and they saved the ship. Her damage was extensive, but her hull had remained sound enough so that the American Navy decided to take her back to Boston and convert her into a light aircraft carrier.

She sailed in mid-September—with *Franklin* towing on the starboard bow while a U.S. naval tug towed on the port. And the skipper of the naval tug took his orders from Brushett without complaint. He knew a ship when he saw one—even if she *was* disguised as a "hay-burning barge"—and he knew a seaman when he saw one too.

Wakefield was saved to fight again and *Franklin* went back to Halifax with a certain jauntiness about her bearing.

Franklin was an iron ship and her people almost matched her strength; but no human flesh could endure what she endured without attrition. So it was with Harry Brushett. He docked *Franklin* at Halifax on October 5 and three days later he was in hospital suffering from complete exhaustion and from a consequent disability of the legs which amounted almost to paralysis. The doctors told him that he would be ashore for months, and that he probably would never sail again, for there was some question of his heart having been overstrained as well. But the sea, and the men of the sea, have not yet learned to worship the oracles of science; and Brushett was a man of the sea. He listened to what the doctors said—and kept his council.

One month later he appeared at Foundation's office and quietly announced that he was about to resume command of *Franklin*. Woollcombe was dubious, but he was also mightily relieved, for *Franklin* without Brushett was only half a ship. Eventually he agreed to let Brushett have his way; but, with unconscious hypocrisy, ordered him to take things easy for a while.

Three days later he dispatched *Franklin* to refloat the collier *Aun* from the rocks at Port au Port in a bitter winter blizzard.

That job took three days and was successful. Then Brushett was sent to sea to hunt for a number of barges that had been lost by U.S. tugs en route to Newfoundland in the same gale. *Franklin* did not find those barges, for after three days she was diverted, first to look for the *Balsam Lake*, then, within two hours, to look for the *Lady Hemlock*, which, together with their tugs, had gone missing in the incessant gales of that period. Almost before she had got squared away on course she was diverted yet again to assist a minesweeper ashore at St. Peter's canal. She had almost reached the canal when she was again diverted. This time to Cape Egmont to assist the tug *L. T. Porter*, which had just blown ashore there. *Franklin* was within ten miles of the *Porter* when she was diverted to help the tug *Sorel* ashore at Port aux Basque. Finally on December 15 she was sent back to the *Porter*, and this time was actually allowed to complete her voyage.

It was too late by then to save the *Porter* which had been so badly damaged by the unbroken period of storm that she had become a total loss. And it was almost too late to save Brushett too. His physical resources had been completely exhausted by eight days of winter blizzards during which he had hardly slept for two consecutive hours. The slim gains he had made in the hospital had been forfeited for nothing, and he was barely able to stand when, on December 16, he was ordered to abandon the *Porter* and sail for Sydney to take a vessel called the *Llancarvon* in tow for Halifax.

That was a particularly dreadful tow. The wind was nor'-west and at gale force during the entire voyage. *Llancarvon* was one of those misbegotten vessels that all seamen hate, "a proper bitch." From the moment the wire was put aboard her on December 16 she did her level best to kill the tug that towed her.

She refused to stay behind, but would come charging up directly abeam of *Franklin*, then swing off to lie in the troughs at right angles to the tug with her bows pointing dead at *Franklin's* bridge. Brushett would then have to bring his tug around while being swept by the beam sea, and after two or three hours he would manage to get himself and the tow back on course. At that moment *Llancarvon* would charge out abeam on the other side, and Brushett would have it all to do again.

From Sydney to Halifax, a distance of about two hundred

miles, took ninety-eight hours. Brushett was off the bridge for seven of these.

On December 22 he was carried off the ship and returned to the hospital, where the doctors clucked their tongues and admonished him for having doubted their infallibility.

"This time," they said, "we hope that you'll be sensible. Perhaps a year from now you may be able to leave your bed and settle down in some nice quiet job ashore."

It is debatable how closely Brushett would have adhered to their instructions in any case; but when *his* ship, *his Franklin*, went to sea a few weeks later under another skipper and made such a shambles of a job that she actually abandoned a tow and fled for shelter—Brushett became a man whom no hospital could hold.

He resumed command on February 15, 1943, after a two weeks' "holiday" which he spent—typically—as a relief skipper for Captain Power on the *Aranmore* during a cruise to St. John's towing a sinking hulk of a dredge.

25 ❧ TWO KINDS OF RECOGNITION

THE WINTER OF 1943-1944 brought with it a renewed outburst of U-boat activity off the Canadian seaboard and again convoys were being heavily attacked, with the resultant inevitable confusion and an increasing number of collisions. There were times when the merchant skippers complained rather bitterly that more ships were being lost or disabled as a result of the restrictions imposed by convoy discipline than were being sunk by the enemy. There was some truth in their complaints. During December and January, Foundation tugs brought in six ships that had been seriously damaged in collisions; and several other such vessels were never brought to port, but died where they had been struck.

Only one of the collisions made the newspapers.

An Eastern Canadian Port, March 30 (Canadian Press)
   The minesweeper HMCS Guysborough *recently left a Christmas dinner in port to spend three days and nights towing a disabled American Liberty ship to safety.*

   The rescue of the Liberty ship laden with $1,000,000 of war cargo was carried out in heavy seas and stormy weather. The Navy said tonight that HMCS Guysborough *was in port after convoy duties when she was sent to pick up the American ship badly damaged in a collision at sea.*

   "On arrival at the scene," said one of her officers, "we found the engine room flooded and the steering

210

*gear out of action. It took us a couple of hours to get
a towing cable shackled to her. All went well for the
first three hours, then the cable broke."*

Guysborough's *crew repaired the cable and towed the
ship for another hour, then the cable broke a second and
a third time.*

*Next day the tow was resumed, but the lines broke
time and time again because the heavy freighter drifted
all over the ocean and the strain was too much for the
towing cables.*

*The work had to be carried out under extremely dan-
gerous conditions.* Guysborough *finally managed to tow
the ship to safety. On the final lap of the trip she had
some help from a tug.*

It was a good report, as newspaper reports go—but they
seldom go far enough, or in the right direction. *Guysborough*
had had her troubles true enough, and her crew deserved
recognition for their efforts. And if by this and a few other
well-chosen press releases, the public was given the impres-
sion that Atlantic salvage during the war was strictly a naval
operation, then that was probably a good thing as far as re-
cruiting and naval prestige were concerned. But now that
the war is long since over it can do no harm to tell the
truth.

On Christmas Day of 1943, *Franklin* was setting a precedent. This was the first Christmas in four years that she
had been in port. Her people were celebrating, but warily,
and none of them was surprised when at 2:30 P.M. the long
wail of *Franklin's* whistle rang out over Halifax and Dartmouth. Resignedly her people put down their glasses, their
after-dinner cigars, or their lady friends from off their laps,
and made hurriedly for the docks.

A distress message from a vessel called the *Robert Peary*
had just been passed to Foundation from the Navy, together
with instructions that *Franklin* was to sail at once. The information was meager, consisting of a dubious location and
the fact that a naval vessel was reported to be standing by the
casualty.

The *Peary's* position was given as about two hundred miles
off shore, south-east of Halifax. Brushett laid out his course
and *Franklin* steamed past Chebucto into a head sea and a
gale of wind. But it was only an ordinary gale and the tug
drove on at a good pace.

It was midnight on the twenty-fifth before Sparks got in
touch with *Guysborough*, who was standing by the stricken
freighter. She reported to Marryat that she had given up all
attempts to tow the *Peary* and was in fact quite unable to

put a line aboard her due to the fierceness of the storm. She also gave a position for herself and for the casualty.

By then the gale had chopped into the nor'west and was blowing about force 8, forcing *Franklin* to reduce speed. Nevertheless she reached the position given by *Guysborough,* at 9.50 A. M. the next day. There was no sign of the *Peary* or of her escort. For the balance of the day Brushett searched the wrinkled face of the grey sea and found nothing. It proved impossible to regain contact with *Guysborough,* who would not, or could not, acknowledge Marryat's repeated calls. Eventually Marryat contacted Halifax and received a new position from the naval shore control.

This one also turned out to be inaccurate, and it was not until dusk on December 28 that *Franklin* finally raised the crippled ship.

The minesweeper was hove-to head to wind, but the *Peary* was in the trough and far down by the stern as a result of the collision damage she had sustained. She was being swept by every heavy sea that passed and, seen through the curtain of blowing snow, she was a spectral shape.

Despite the advent of darkness *Franklin* came directly down upon her and a connection was made using the heaving line. By 8:40 P.M. the tow was under weigh for Halifax, which then bore one hundred and eighty miles to the west-north-west.

In thickening snow and falling temperatures, and with a steadily rising wind, they made little enough progress that night. At dawn *Peary's* master signaled to Brushett that his after bulkhead, which alone was keeping the ship afloat, was being badly strained and had begun to leak seriously. He was afraid that it might let go at any instant.

Franklin gave of her best. A hundred and sixty miles of head sea and head wind still lay before her, and the ship astern was sheering from side to side with depraved abandon. *Guysborough* was finding it hard even to keep contact with the little convoy, for the seas were now so heavy that she could hardly drive into them. *Franklin* was working. She was making good three knots.

There was no moderation in the gale that day. At dusk on the following night the cripple took a violent sheer until she rode out almost abeam of *Franklin* and then, with pure brute ugliness, she turned hard away, bringing such a strain on the tow-line that it rose out of the water for five hundred yards.

The wire itself withstood that savage lunge, but the strain of it was too much for *Franklin's* steering gear and the rudder chain was ripped from the quadrant, leaving her as helpless as her charge.

Bellfountain went aft at once, and returned to tell Brushett that men could not live, let alone work, under the quadrant grating while the tow wire was still fast, for the *Peary* was hauling *Franklin's* stern so far down that every sea was breaking on the after deck. Nor was this the worst of it. The constant jerking on the wire was sending the rudder crazy, and the quadrant arm was banging back and forth with a violence that could have decapitated a man with ease.

Brushett had two courses open to him. Either he could cast off the wire in order to ease the strain so that his men would have a chance to repair the steering gear; or he could remain fast to the *Peary,* and hope for some moderation in the weather before the casualty was overwhelmed. He deliberately chose the latter course; for he was aware that if he cast off he might not find her again in time to save her or her crew.

The two ships lay at the mercy of the storm for six hours. The blizzard screamed about them, while on Monkey's Island the first mate, soaked and freezing, played *Franklin's* searchlight on the casualty so that there would be some warning if the two ships began to drive together. Meanwhile Bellfountain worked with the engineers to devise a tackle which could control the quadrant arm. They rigged one too, but did not dare to use it then, for if the rudder had been subdued and lashed securely to one side, it would have acted either to bring the breaking seas full abeam of *Franklin* or to head her off with the seas quartering astern. Either course might well have proven fatal to the little ship.

So they waited through those six hours of winter darkness. Then the wind began to haul a little, and in the confused sea which followed the shift Brushett saw his chance. He gave the order. The arresting tackle was set up taut; the rudder was firmly held, and two men crawled aft under the grating to struggle with the chain amidst the freezing slush.

By midnight *Franklin* and her charge were under weigh.

There is not much to tell about the remainder of that voyage. The *Peary* was brought through the submarine nets on December 31 and safely anchored in Bedford Basin, with *Franklin's* pumps aboard to hold her leaks in check.

Franklin did not remain to greet the newspaper reporters or the naval press relations officer. At dawn of the following day she was at sea again, answering another SOS.

Nevertheless, the *Peary* episode was one of the few times during the war when *Franklin* made the newspapers at all. For it was she who had "assisted *Guysborough* on the final lap."

January brought two further rescue missions for *Franklin;* but they were both routine jobs, and not worth more than half a line in Brushett's private log. However, in early February there *was* a job that struck the skipper's fancy. He and the *Franklin* were called upon to sort out the mess resulting from the collision of a big steamship—and a railroad train.

It happened during a filthy February night when a howling blizzard swept over Halifax and left snowdrifts five feet high in the city streets. It caught half a hundred ships anchored in Bedford Basin, and it handled them with such ferocity that several broke adrift. One of these was a United States naval transport. When her cables parted she drove straight for shore, and as if with deliberate malice, she managed to point her prow at the Rockingham Railway yards. Her eight thousand tons carried her up over the shallows, and when she stopped she had made a satisfying wreck out of a train of fourteen railroad cars.

She could not be left to gloat. At dawn Brushett was called at his home, and he set out to find his tug. That was not so easy. No traffic was moving in the city, and after a futile struggle to scale the drifts in his front yard on foot, he showed his mettle by going back for a pair of snowshoes. He was still wearing them, so they say, when he came flopping aboard the *Franklin*. *Franklin* herself lay so deeply mantled in snow that it took two hours of hard shoveling to free her sufficiently so that she could go to work.

By the use of ground tackle the errant naval transport was refloated and taken back to her anchorage, where she could lord it over her sisters and brag of the blow she had struck in the long battle between the two great rival users of steam engines.

It was a good time for a moment of light relief. There was little enough to make men smile in the job that was waiting for the *Franklin* and her people less than a week away.

At this stage of the war the mass-produced United States Liberty ships were becoming numerous in the North Atlantic. Their contribution to the winning of the battle of supply was increasingly important, and it may well have been that without them the war might have dragged on for a longer period. However they were by no means perfect ships. They were the largest all-welded vessels ever built until that time, and their builders had not yet mastered the technique of plate welding for ocean-going vessels. As a result the early Libertys had a distressing tendency to break apart when they encountered heavy weather, and the number of them which were lost at sea due to this cause alone, was staggering. Most, but not all, of those which broke went down. One of the few to survive was the *Joel E. Poinsett*.

The *Poinsett*, proud bearer of one of the triple-barreled names which were in vogue in the American Merchant

Marines during the war, was outbound for Europe in convoy in late February. At the turn of the month the convoy ran into a period of heavy weather and hard gales and, on the night of March 1 at a point four hundred miles south-east of St. John's, the *Poinsett* succumbed to the buffeting of the long seas and began to break. Her deck plates tore right across just forward of her bridge, and the jagged rent moved quickly down her flanks. Girders bent and snapped and stanchions bowed. The scream of breaking metal fought with the wind for precedence and in those terrible few minutes it won out.

There was very little time in which to abandon ship. The crew was mustered to boat stations and the boats went over into the darkness laden with half-clothed men who carried with them not much more than their lives. They were fortunate. A corvette was close at hand and she steamed down to give them a lee, while another merchant vessel rounded-to and picked the *Poinsett's* crew out of the black waste of waters. Then the rescue ships rejoined the convoy and steamed on. The dismembered and abandoned *Poinsett* drifted into the gale spume and disappeared.

It was to be assumed that the two sections of the casualty would sink within a few hours; but due to a freakish bit of luck she had broken between the two cargo holds, and the bulkheads fore and aft had both held firm. With the next dawn a long-range Coastal Command aircraft making its lonely swing into the western sea spotted the stern half of the broken Liberty and radioed naval headquarters in Halifax.

Naval Operations called Foundation. It seemed a long-odds chance to send a tug four hundred miles into that gale-lashed sea to try and save the stern of the Liberty. But it was a chance worth taking, for once more the U-boats had come back to gain the upper hand, and once again Allied shipping losses were rising to appalling figures. Half a ship, with her engines undamaged, could sail again with a new forward section welded on.

Woollcombe agreed to take the gamble. He went down to the docks, where he found Brushett aboard *Franklin,* writing up the report of his last operation.

"We've got a tough one for you, Cap," he said. "The stern half of a Liberty, four hundred miles to the east. You know what the weather's like. The planes have spotted her twice now, but only through rifts in the overcast, and they never got a position you could use. You'll have to look for her blind."

Franklin put to sea within the hour and despite foul weather, driving snow squalls and the usual heavy seas, by

March 3 she had reached the approximate position where the *Poinsett* had last been seen. There was nothing to see now, and no way to see it in any case. The snow squalls had become so nearly continuous that a lookout was lucky to get one glimpse through a "hole" for each hour spent staring into the white nothingness.

The search seemed hopeless. It was doubtful if the hulk was still afloat, for the gales had gone north-west and the seas were big enough to belabor a whole ship into submission. It required little enough imagination to visualize what they would do to the thin bulkhead of a half-ship. Nevertheless, Brushett set up a search pattern and began steaming in twenty-mile legs from north to south along the *Poinsett's* probable line of drift.

For *Franklin's* people what followed was frigid monotony, combined with the usual fatigue of life at sea during a winter storm. Once a day, if they were lucky, they got a hot mug of tea from the galley. Usually they ate hard tack and canned stuff. The fug and stench continued to build up in the tightly closed accommodations until men who had been to sea for thirty years were sick unto exhaustion. The seas beat down upon the old iron decks with a steady, insistent clangor. In the stokeholds the black gang shoveled coal and hauled out ashes, and the engineers watched the steam gauges with bloodshot eyes.

They searched—and every time they thought that there was no more hope, an aircraft radioed a report that the *Poinsett* was still afloat. Seventeen times Brushett laid a course for the rough positions given by the planes. Seventeen times he found only snow-blurred, empty ocean.

The search continued for eight interminable days. When *Franklin's* people wanted change and execise they emerged from the alleyways, roped in pairs, and fought the accumulating ice with picks and axes until the cold penetrated their wet clothes and drove them in again.

On the evening of the eighth day, a Royal Navy armed trawler bore down upon them and flashed a signal:

HAVE FOUND YOUR GIRL JUST FOLLOW ME

Franklin swung up into the wind and followed avidly. But not quite believing. And then, very suddenly, the high grey hulk of half a ship loomed up ahead.

"She was a terror to behold," Brushett recalls. "Seeing her suddenly and close up like that, after days of staring at empty sea, she looked as big as the whole of Newfoundland. We had no time to stare at her, though. I figured we had to get a line on her that very hour or we would lose her in the night. Grandy and Bellfountain, my deck officers, came to the bridge and we planned the thing.

"Grandy and three men were to take a dory and board her somehow, while I brought *Franklin* in so the two ships were stern to stern and close enough so the boarding crew could hoist the pendant and shackles aboard by man power alone. There was no time for anything else that night. We knew it was pretty risky, but with the *Franklin* under us nobody worried very much."

Brushett's assessment of the situation varies in only one detail from that of his men. As Innes, the new chief engineer put it. "With *Brushett* on the bridge, nobody worried very much."

Brushett was worried, all the same. He always hated to see any of his men leave *Franklin* during bad weather, even in that paragon of virtues, a Newfoundland dory; and he sweated until they were safely back aboard again. This evening, in darkness that was already so heavy that the searchlight had to be switched on, he watched Grandy, Bo'sun Harry Strickland, and Able Seamen Stanley Young, Clifford Boudreau and Angus Chiasson jump into the dory as it lay heaving wildly at *Franklin's* rail. He watched as the four men took their stroke and the pumpkin seed flipped high on the crests of waves that were running twenty to thirty feet in height, and then slid away again toward the towering bulk of the *Poinsett*. He waited until he saw them against the side of that steel cliff; and then he began to handle his ship.

Words can tell little of what it means to back a vessel to within spitting distance of the stern of a derelict that is looming mountainous above your transom, and to do it in a full gale, at night, in the depths of the winter ocean. Words cannot say how it is done, either. Only the hands of men— of the helmsman at the wheel, of the skipper on the telegraph handle, of the engineer officer at the throttle—can *show* how it is done.

When the maneuvering was over, *Franklin's* stern lay eight feet from the massive blades of *Poinsett's* propeller as these rose clear of the water, hung ten feet in the air, and then crashed down to vanish in white foam again.

In order to con his ship, Brushett was forced to take a position on the tiller grating in the extreme after part of the tug. From this precarious vantage point he directed things by means of men posted at the head of the engine room companion and at the foot of the bridge, who relayed his shouted orders to the chief engineer and to the helmsman.

As the *Poinsett* began each ponderous lift, and her cruiser stern began to rise full fifty feet above the pygmies who would try to save her, Brushett edged *Franklin* in. Then as that four-thousand-ton pile-driver of grey steel began to fall, *Franklin* inched out to let it clear her by the span of a man's arms.

Meanwhile the boat's crew had gone aboard—but not as easily as that. Grandy and his gang had come alongside and had tried to seize the dangling boat falls and shinny up them, but the dory was lifting and falling so steeply that this proved impossible. Grandy had thought it might be so, and so he had come prepared with a coil of light line attached to a small grapnel. Waiting until a wave brought them up within twenty feet of the *Poinsett's* rail, he threw his iron, and it caught. As the dory fell away he paid out line, but already Stanley Young was halfway up to the deck far above. Three of them went up that way, shinnying up a single thin rope that was already coated in freezing slush.

Their job then was to catch a heaving line from *Franklin's* stern and without bothering to use a messenger, to haul in the ends of two one-hundred-and-fifty-foot wire pendants and make them fast on the port and starboard after bollards.

Each pendant was a leg of the bridle which would take the towing wire. Each pendant, with its shackles, thimbles, and its share of the common swivel, weighed six hundred pounds. Three men had to take each pendant up by the strength of their arms alone.

They did it; but only because Brushett held *Franklin* in, through the thirty minutes of that struggle, with such unbelievable skill that she never once swung out to drag the shackles overboard and thereby tear the pendants from the hands of the three straining men above.

When they had one pendant fast to the *Poinsett,* things became even touchier aboard the tug. She could no longer get away even if she wanted to. Her movements became those of a terrier on a close tether. The *Poinsett* rose and fell, and just as the second pendant was made fast, she fell too soon.

Brushett describes that moment perfectly:

"I looked up at her," he said, "and I could see she was going to come down square in my lap. But she was one woman who wasn't welcome to sit there."

Brushett got clear, but the *Poinsett* came down on *Franklin* with such irresistible force that she squashed the bulwarks flat and drove *Franklin's* stern three feet under water. That she did not smash the steering gear was one of those little miracles which sometimes occur so that seamen can live their lives to a full conclusion.

Franklin's propeller was already turning frenziedly as her stern came up again, and she scooted out from under like a puppy whose tail has just been stepped upon. The winch began to hiss and chatter as the towing wire paid out, and the men of little faith who had closed their eyes at the moment of impact opened them again with a memorable relief.

The dory crew came back in darkness, and although they were not completely exhausted, nevertheless it took strong hands to haul them over the rail to safety. Then, and then only, Brushett could relax and take the hard-bitten, empty pipe out of his teeth, and fill it with a steady hand.

"We thought, y'know," he remembers with a half smile, "that the worst was over. Sailors always think like that— perhaps they have to. But we might have known . . . she turned out to be the most terrible thing to tow that I have ever seen! She simply would not come. She would do everything but somersault on the end of the wire. Two or three times an hour she would turn right end for end, and we'd be staring back right into her open wound. She should have sunk herself, but it looked like she wanted to sink us first."

Grimly *Franklin* hung on to the incubus astern. Stubbornly her engines labored and at their best managed to turn up enough revolutions to give the tow three knots. At the worst *Franklin* stood still.

"The only hope we had of moving that abomination, and of keeping her under some kind of control, was to tow dead into wind," Innes remembers, "and by the grace of God we had a nor'east gale most of the way home. It didn't quite last out though, and on the last day we had to heave-to and wait forty-eight hours for the wind to veer back into the east."

It was probably the first and last time in *Franklin's* history that any of her people looked with real affection on a nor'east gale.

The tow home took a week. While they were still four days out of port *Franklin* ran short of grub and the ubiquitous Grandy and his crew took to their dory and fetched a barrel of butter, a case of canned meat, and ten pounds of tea from the hulk. And for this act of piracy they were later severely castigated by the War Shipping Administration in Halifax. That castigation was the closest thing to recognition for the services they rendered to the bureaucrats who ran the war at sea.

They did not care. They got their recognition elsewhere, and it was of the kind that counts.

As they neared the coast the murk lifted a little and Brushett found to his horror that he and his recalcitrant floating anchor were heading fair and square into the middle of an outbound convoy of a hundred ships.

It was a dreadful moment. *Franklin* had not a hope of hauling clear and Brushett did not wish to break radio silence and thereby jeopardize the convoy by asking its commodore for instructions. He gripped his pipe a little more fiercely, and waited for events.

The armada bore down irresistibly. "A whole damned ocean full of ships," Innes recalls with awe. And at the moment when it seemed that *Franklin* must be overwhelmed, a signal string showed from the commodore's ship. It said:

> *All vessels will alter port and starboard to clear the tug and tow. And to the* Franklin: *Steer your course and best of luck good friend.*

And so they did as they were told and steered their course. Right down the middle of that phalanx *Franklin* steered, her funnels belching black and her crew all out upon the deck. And as they passed through the vast convoy, each merchant ship in turn saluted with her whistle; and the outbound crews lined the rails and cheered the little one who had saved one of their sisters from the northern seas.

That was the kind of recognition that had meaning for the salvage men. It was the only kind they ever cared about.

26 ❦ TO FRANCE AND BACK

THE LAST FULL YEAR of war in the North Atlantic had now begun, and it was as busy a time for the salvage tugs as any which preceded it. During the twelve months from May of 1944 until May of 1945, Foundation's tugs rescued twenty-two ships from sea and shore. Five of these were torpedo victims, for the U-boats remained active along the Canadian and Newfoundland coasts well into the spring of 1945.

Foundation itself had never been more muscular. Its salvage fleet consisted not only of the *Aranmore, Franklin, Security,* and *Ocean Eagle,* but in addition it now owned the *Lord Strathcona* and the *Traverse,* for in late 1944 it bought up its last major rival in home waters, the Quebec Wrecking and Salvage Company. The harbor tugs now numbered fourteen vessels and the ancillary equipment, consisting of lighters, derrick boats, water boats and barges, had become truly a formidable fleet.

Chadwick's navy had become a reality; but despite its size the heart and soul of it remained with two vessels and their crews: *Franklin* and *Aranmore.* Between them they continued to do the lion's share of the work.

During this final year of war *Franklin* rescued the *Empire Ortolan, Nellie Dixon, Burin, Samlistar, Trevince, Esso Pittsburgh,* and *Pontiac.* She assisted in further salvage on *Chelatross.* She took more than thirty tows of warships, dredges and dead ships from ports as far north as St. John's, to ports as far south as Baltimore. She was a busy ship—as usual.

And being busy, her people took their work as casual routine; they did their jobs, and quickly forgot about them. In all that period only a handful of isolated memories stand out.

The *Pontiac* is one. She was a U.S. naval supply and repair vessel of seven thousand tons with three hundred men aboard, outbound from Halifax in the spring of 1944. Ten miles off Chebucto Head she was holed in a most unusual manner when one of her paravanes (which were used to sweep for moored enemy mines left by submarines) suddenly went out of control, turned inward and struck the vessel with such force that it drove clean through her side. *Pontiac* began to take water faster than her pumps could handle it, and the SOS she flashed to Halifax was laden with urgency. The seas were bad that day, and the wind was strong enough to endanger any lifeboat. *Pontiac's* master gave his vessel only two or three hours at most to stay afloat.

There was no delay in Halifax. *Franklin* received the message direct through the eager ears of Marryat. There was steam up in both boilers, and within ten minutes *Franklin* was away.

She reached the *Pontiac* in an hour and thirty minutes from the time the distress signal was received, and she had a line on the sinking ship in twelve minutes more. *Pontiac's* bows were then only four feet above the seas and her stern was lifting ominously.

Brushett threw caution to the winds and worked his tug up to full speed with reckless disregard for the strain upon the wire. If the wire broke, the ship was lost. But, he reasoned, if *Franklin* failed to get her into port within another hour she was lost in any case.

Seldom in her history had *Franklin's* boilers carried such a head of steam. The safety valves hissed constantly, and the old engine drove the shaft at the maximum number of revolutions it would take. Chebucto Head came abeam and a pilot boat stood out but was waved off. There was no time for frills. *Pontiac's* bows were now at water level and her foredeck was awash.

They came through the submarine nets at full speed, disregarding the strict naval orders to slow down; and the gateships barely managed to get the nets open in time to save them from *Franklin's* headlong rush. Once through the net *Franklin* turned to starboard for Meagher's Beach, still at full speed. Abruptly she turned away again and at the same moment ordered *Pontiac* to slip the line. The big transport drove sluggishly forward until her bows grated and she came

221

to rest in shallow water with her decks above the surface, and without the loss of a single man.

"Fifteen minutes longer, and we would have lost her," her master told Brushett later that day. It was a slim margin of success, but adequate.

One of the other memorable events of that period had to do with the freighter *Moira*, which radioed for help while forty miles off Louisburg. *Franklin* went out to her from Port Hawksbury and found the distressed ship sound in limb and body, but short of fuel, Brushett offered his tow-line, but *Moira* refused it. Apparently the presence of the tug gave her master sufficient new courage to attempt that last forty miles to port on his own resources.

Somewhat disgruntled, Brushett turned *Franklin* for shore and ran into Louisburg; but he had barely put his lines on the dock before Marryat brought him a new call for help from the *Moira*. This one unequivocal. It said:

NO FUEL ENGINES STOPPING REQUIRE TOW AT ONCE

Three hours later *Franklin* was again at *Moira's* side with the towing pendant and the messenger laid out ready for use.

"We'll shoot a line over your fo'castle," Brushett bellowed through his megaphone to *Moira's* master.

"Never mind," came back the reply. "We are burning the cabin furniture and woodwork, and have steam again."

Brushett's pipestem took a terrible strain. *Franklin* turned back for Louisburg with a burst of speed that helped relieve her master's feelings. She had not yet reached the port when *Moira* again whined for help.

"I ignored her," Brushett said. It was the only safe thing to do. If *Franklin* had gone back out and been rebuffed for a third time, *Moira* would very likely have found herself with a collision hole amidships, and in proper trouble. Brushett was not the nursemaid type.

His famous pipe was again in serious danger, but for quite another reason, early in 1945 when *Franklin* was returning from St. John's to Sydney after delivering a dredge.

The ice was bad that year and as twilight fell one evening, Brushett found his ship beset. For an hour he worked her along leads in the pack, but as darkness became complete he gave up the attempt to reach freedom and decided to spend the hours till dawn in the sanctuary of a little open lake, surrounded on all sides by shores of ice.

It was really quite a pleasant place to lie, for there was no sea running in the protection of the ice, and *Franklin* was able to make fast to the edge of the pack, stop her engines, and relax.

The third mate was on watch until midnight and he made

himself comfortable on the bridge. This snug harbor reminded him of certain cosy little ports he had known along the Labrador coast during his fishing days, and the flicker of the northern lights across the mile-wide expanse of black water aided the illusion. He was admiring the lights when his reverie was brought to an abrupt end by the realization that he was looking at something which had no business to be where it was. He snatched the night-glasses from their hook, stared for a moment, and then in a horrified voice muttered down the voice pipe to Brushett's cabin.

"Cap," he said. "You'd best get up here quick!"

Brushett was awake, which was fortunate, for otherwise he would never have heard his subordinate's subdued call to action. He pulled on his boots, went out on deck and climbed the bridge ladder.

The mate handed him the glasses and wordlessly pointed to the northern shore of the lake.

Brushett stared.

There could be little doubt of what he saw. The outline of a submarine's conning tower and periscope on a still night, silhouetted against white ice and against the swishing yellow of the northern lights, was not something about which a man could be easily mistaken.

Brushett and his mate looked into each other's eyes, and when they spoke it was—by unspoken agreement—in the most muted of whispers. "Go below," Brushett said, "and tell the men that if any of them so much as clears his throat or scratches a match I'll have his hide—if the fish don't get it first."

It was an awful night—and endless. There were some aboard the *Franklin* who later claimed that they did not even breathe until the dawn—but that is probably an exaggeration. Not even a Newfoundlander can go that long without oxygen.

It was not a dead calm night—dead calms happen in the North Atlantic only once or twice in a man's life—and the wind was strong enough so that no one was ever quite certain whether or not he had been able to hear the beat of the submarine's diesels as she lay charging her batteries. In any case it was difficult to relegate the beat of a man's own heart into the background long enough to hear much else.

"It may all have been an illusion, I suppose," Brushett says as he recalls the incident. "But none of us was going to find out. It *looked* like a submarine and it *sounded* like one. *We* tried to sound and look like a small black piece of darkness, and we must have succeeded—or maybe he saw us all right but thought we were a little fishing trawler and didn't want to give away his position by wasting a shell on anything so insignificant. Anyhow he submerged an hour before dawn and we never saw hide nor hair of him again."

The end of the war, when it came on May 7, 1945, made very little difference to *Franklin* or her people. They were at sea when the war ended, and two days later they were again at sea to assist a tanker which was breaking up during a late spring gale. One enemy had withdrawn, but the other —the old familiar one, and the most tenacious and terrible of all—remained. The struggle against the Western Ocean continued unabated.

The first summer of the peace saw *Franklin* busy with the aftermath of war. When Japan collapsed, the vast armada of warships which had been massed during the time of need became a useless encumbrance. The Navy was rapidly being disbanded and there were neither men to sail the warships, nor ports to sail them to. And so it came about that the proud frigates, corvettes, and destroyers which had so often shown their disdainful heels to the salvage tugs now found themselves being ignominiously towed from their one-time bases to the laying-up yards at Sydney and Louisburg.

Day after day, trip after trip, *Franklin* bulled her way up the coasts with one, two, and even three of the doomed and silent ships of war behind her.

"It was kind of sad," one of her people recollected. "They looked so useless and so dead. For pretty near five years they bossed us about like we was a bunch of sea-lice, and then here we were, towing them to the graveyard behind the old *Franklin*—and she still going strong."

Franklin, being a proper lady, was never one to harbor old resentments, but Poirier remembers that during the year and a half when these tows were being made he never saw the old girl work so well. Her engines never faltered and she seemed to find the strength of youth in her ancient machinery, and to take a gay delight in hauling a brace of corvettes through half a gale at a good five knots.

The summer of 1945 brought her another job that grew out of the war, and this was one to set a feather in her cap. In early August she was ordered to take bucket dredge *Number 17* from Rimouski to Bordeaux, France.

Number 17 was one of a series of war-built dredges which had served their purpose in keeping the western ports functioning, but which were now urgently required to reopen the blocked ports of Europe. *Number 17* was a mammoth. She consisted in effect of two pontoons, between which the machinery of the endless bucket apparatus was suspended. In appearance she looked vaguely ship-like for she had a bow and a stern; but in fact she was more of an aquatic city block. She was four hundred and sixty feet long—nearly three times *Franklin's* length—and she bulked almost ten times as large. She had been built for work in protected harbors and her designers had never envisaged her making a trip to sea, let alone making a trans-Atlantic passage.

But the French needed dredges, and so Foundation was asked if the company could deliver such a tow.

The job came at an awkward time for Reg Poirier, who was now *Franklin's* chief engineer. The tug had been laid up for annual overhaul in late July and her crew had been paid off. When Reg came to hire a new black gang he found that the sudden rise in wages due to the efforts of the recently formed seamen's unions, had put Foundation's wage scale even farther behind the times than usual. Consequently he had great difficulty getting any stokers at all, particularly when they were told that their first job would be a trans-Atlantic tow.

The upshot was that when *Franklin* sailed from Rimouski with the lumbering dredge behind her, the black gang included—as one of the engineers inelegantly phrased it—"some of the worst damn scruff I ever see."

Poirier was not happy. A cautious man by experience and nature, he held a gloomy view of the chances of completing the crossing without a mutiny—or, from his point of view far worse—without running out of coal in mid-ocean.

Keeping in mind *Franklin's* range and the immense bulk and weight of the tow, Brushett laid out his course to touch as many ports as possible. Consequently the first leg of the voyage was to Sydney—for bunkers—then to St. John's—for bunkers.

Bunkers, bunkers, bunkers—it became the theme song of the trip, and haunted every hour of Poirier's time.

From St. John's they steered for Fayal in the Azores, and when they reached that port there were three and a half tons of coal left aboard the *Franklin*. Poirier looked to the next, and much the longest, leg, up the Portuguese coast and down the Bay of Biscay, with pessimistic forebodings. He communicated his distress to Brushett, and that good seaman went against his own convictions and not only had *Franklin's* salvage holds filled with coal, but even sanctioned the addition of forty tons, in bags, on the fore and after decks.

They sailed from the Azores with the decks almost in the water and for the first forty-eight hours, until they had used up the deck load, they were a pious lot.

"I doubt if anybody actually prayed, you know," one of the mates said, "but a good missionary could have worked us over if we'd had one aboard. And right then when a puff from a bagpipe would have sunk us, some bloody fool in the black gang comes on deck and starts to whistle for a wind!"

Coal was not the only problem on that voyage. Twenty-six men shut up in the narrow confines of the *Franklin* was a tight squeeze at the best of times. When many of these were hard-case types, and when the voyage lasted for forty days of which thirty were spent at sea, tensions were bound to mount to the explosion point. Poirier kept his deer rifle loaded and a revolver underneath his pillow, and when one of his firemen got drunk on lemon extract and threatened to throw a vital engine part overboard, Poirier went for the revolver—and he would have used it too, if the fellow had not suddenly sobered up a bit.

Brushett, who bore the total strain, also carried the responsibility for a twelve-man crew riding the dredge. He had but little faith in the seaworthiness of the tow and he suspected that one bad blow would sink it.

That no such blow overtook them was partly luck, but was as much due to Brushett's intuition, which kept him in the ports at which they called until he felt that it was safe to sail.

They were several days at Fayal, and during this time most of the crew went ashore on a glorious spree. They had little enough money, since most of the black gang had been logged so many times for disobedience and laziness that their pay was insignificant. Some of them solved this problem by selling their clothes—right down to their underpants —and then investing in local wines. One of them was brought back aboard with a badly lacerated arm. It seemed like a minor wound at the time, but it was to prove itself deadly serious.

When they sailed from Fayal the black gang was so far gone that three or four of them were deathly sick at once, and Poirier and his second had to turn-to and stoke the fires in order to keep steam up. Then, eight days out of the Azores, the stoker with the damaged arm developed gangrene. It spread with frightful rapidity up to his shoulder. There were no ships with doctors within reach, and the land still lay a week away.

Brushett did his best with the tug's first-aid kit, but it was hopelessly inadequate, and on September 16 the stoker died.

They buried him at sea.

When they reached the mouth of the Loire on September 18 the officers were filled with an almost incredulous relief— but it was to be short-lived.

The Loire had been heavily mined by the Germans and mine sweeping operations were by no means complete. Only a narrow and inadequately buoyed channel was known to be free of mines, and navigation of this channel required an expert pilot.

There was none available for *Franklin* and her tow.

Brushett could not lie off that dangerous shore and wait for he had insufficient coal, and if a bad blow came on—of the kind for which Biscay is infamous—he would be in serious trouble. He decided to risk the channel by attempting to follow in the wake of a freighter which had pre-empted the only available pilot.

The freighter proceeded at ten knots while the best *Franklin* could manage was a little over six. After an hour the freighter was out of sight and *Franklin* was alone.

It was impossible to turn back, so Brushett continued upstream against an increasing current which soon began to make the dredge unmanageable. Once it swerved far outside the channel buoy, rounding in three hundred yards on the wrong side. Both the dredge crew and the tug crew held their breaths, but nothing happened.

After fifteen miles of this nonsense they reached the ship anchorage in the river, and dropped their hook. Then, and then only, a pilot condescended to join them.

They got rid of the dredge two days later, and on the twenty-third of September they sailed for home. Alone and unhindered *Franklin* made a good passage, arriving in Halifax on October 5. The trials and worries of the outbound journey were forgotten, and there remained only the ever-present sense of pride in *Franklin* for another job well done.

27 ❦ DEATH OF A CAPTAIN

Franklin ARRIVED BACK FROM FRANCE upon a note of sadness. Her old companion, the *Aranmore*, was gone. It had been decided that there was no longer a place for a vessel of *Aranmore's* antiquity in Foundation Maritime. The fact that she was still as sound and as capable as ever did not weigh sufficiently in her favor. She was old. She had to go.

They sold her foreign, and she went to a Cuban company engaged in the banana trade—and in March of 1948 her new owners killed her on a reef off Haiti.

Something of the shape of things to come should have been apparent to *Franklin's* people after that, but they did not worry overmuch. None of them, and in particular not Harry Brushett, could envisage the day when *Foundation Franklin* might be deemed dispensable. Captain Power was not so optimistic. He and Brushett loved *Franklin* with an equal ardor, and one day he spoke of his misgivings.

"Times are changing, Harry," he said. "One of these days

some bright young engineer is going to look at *Franklin* and decide she belongs with the ark. Watch out for her."

The warning seemed pointless in the late days of 1945. There was more work for *Franklin* than there had ever been, and she continued to do that work almost faultlessly.

The rescue of the *Empire Abbey* was a case in point, for it demonstrated as nothing else could have done the enduring qualities of the little salvage ship.

The *Abbey* was a new vessel of five thousand tons, built in 1944 for wartime use, and converted to the trades of peace. Her task was to assist in feeding the starving people of Europe, and on January 15, she sailed from Bristol bound for St. John, New Brunswick, to take on a cargo of frozen meat.

Still clad in her wartime paint, and with her paravane "A" frame still rigged over her bows, she put to sea. A day later she cleared the offshore banks of Sole and had the deeps beneath her.

The skies had been overcast and threatening for a week past, but there was no real indication of the weather those dark skies were breeding until January 17, when the *Abbey* was smitten by the full fury of a nor'east gale that came upon her with such suddenness that she was laid over almost on her beam ends by the first onslaught.

She was in ballast, and therefore high and light. Nevertheless she righted herself and her helmsman brought her back on course. And so she began what was to be a twenty-six-day struggle for survival against the grey seas under.

Her master was a mariner of many years experience upon the North Atlantic. Captain Harry Dunning had brought a dozen different vessels through the winter storms of the Western Ocean; but on this occasion he admitted by radio to his owners that the issue was in doubt almost from the first day out of port. Never before had he encountered such sustained ferocity on the part of seas and winds. There was no respite, no momentary lull to let a man catch his breath, or to let a weary ship lie easy.

For sixteen days the gales from the north and west did not abate, and for sixteen days the *Abbey* rolled and heaved her way westward at a snail's pace while her officers and crew grew red-eyed and silent. Alternately the propeller labored deep beneath the white seas, then was thrust clear to race wildly in the foam-filled air—day after day, day after day, until metal could no longer stand the strain. On January 31 the shaft snapped clean across, and the propeller fell away into a thousand fathoms depth.

It was shortly after midnight that *Abbey's* SOS was picked up by the Naval Control station at Halifax and relayed to the Foundation Company. Having bunkered and stored, *Franklin* cast off her lines four hours later and headed out to sea.

The *Abbey* then lay about five hundred miles east of Halifax, but the endless days of black skies had prevented her officers from getting accurate sights. Consequently, they had been forced to give a dead-reckoning position which turned out to be over a hundred miles too far to the south. Nor had Dunning and his navigator been able to estimate the truly incredible eastward drift that wind and sea had brought about. They thought their vessel was drifting east at half a knot. She was actually making almost five times that much. Later it was estimated that she drifted one hundred and twenty miles eastward in the forty-eight hours which followed on the loss of her propeller.

Enclosed in a hemisphere of snow and storm scud not two hundred yards in diameter, *Franklin* drove out into the winter ocean in search of the *Abbey*, with no more certain guide than Brushett's knowledge and his intuition.

With Poirier pushing her to her limits, *Franklin* was a hundred miles beyond Sable by dawn on February 2 and Brushett had seen enough to guess that *Abbey's* given position could not be accurate. With difficulty Marryat established radio communications with the crippled vessel, and after an exchange of messages between the two masters the presumed location of the *Abbey* was shifted one hundred and thirty miles to the north-east.

It was still a blind search. The DF equipment was not functioning properly, and proved useless at its usual range. Brushett therefore laid out an interception course based almost solely on his feeling for the sea and weather. For twenty minutes he had stared at his chart, with an occasional glance through the wheelhouse window at the sounding fury of the winter storm.

At last he put the point of his pencil on the blank expanse of paper. "Mate," he said quietly to Grandy, "she ought to lay right here."

Marryat sent off a message to the *Abbey*.

WE WILL CLOSE WITH YOU ABOUT 11 PM AT THAT TIME
PLEASE FIRE A RED ROCKET AND REPEAT ON DEMAND

At 11:05 P.M. *Franklin's* lookout reported seeing a rocket bearing three degrees to port. By midnight *Franklin* was stopped beside the casualty.

As *Franklin* had been closing with the *Abbey*, the wind had dropped out a little and the sky had cleared; although the seas were still running like unchained giants, and the forecasts were for renewed gale winds from the south-east.

The interval of relative calm was evidently to be short-lived. Therefore, and despite the risks involved, Brushett decided to put his towing wire aboard the *Abbey* immediately. He brought *Franklin* in so close that as she lifted on the seas to the level of *Abbey's* deck, he could make out the haggard features of her crew. Grandy fired the rocket over *Abbey's* forecastle and the exhausted men aboard the cripple hauled in the messenger and the towing pendant, and made it fast with the alacrity of desperation.

Before 1:30 on the morning of February 3 the wire was taut and *Franklin* was towing hard for Halifax.

They made the best of the brief respite granted to them by the sea, but by noon the promised south-east gale had come upon them. It blew like the Bull of Barney. When it had reached a velocity of sixty miles an hour and had very nearly stopped *Franklin* in her tracks, it suddenly shifted to south-west.

Within two hours it had overmastered the two vessels, and was blowing them both back toward the mid-Atlantic.

The high sides of the empty *Abbey* gave the wind ample substance to push against, and the wickedly confused cross-sea that followed on the wind shifts was throwing *Franklin* about so violently that her screw was in the air as often as it was in the water. Poirier and Burns, the two engineers, never left the steam valve for an instant, and their hands and wrists grew numb from spinning the brass steam-wheel back and forth as the propeller raced, then labored deep again.

All through that day and night the struggle continued, and through those hours the wind gradually increased its power and swung further to the west. *Franklin*, straining her guts out, was still not even able to hold her own, and slowly but implacably the distance from Halifax increased.

It was at this juncture that the cable parted.

The chafing strain on the pendant where it passed through the *Abbey's* bow chock had been too much for anything that her people could do to counteract it, and at 9 A.M. on the fourth the wire broke.

There was no hope at all of reconnecting until the storm had abated somewhat. Both ships began to blow off to the eastward at three knots.

They drifted for twenty-four hours, until at 9 A.M. on the fifth the *Abbey* was fifty miles farther east than she had been when *Franklin* first brought her in sight.

The wind had now gone into the north-west, and although it was still at gale force, Brushett decided he would wait no longer. Once more *Franklin* came in upon the casualty as she lay lifting and rolling like a child's toy in a millrace; and once more Grandy put the rocket line aboard with his first shot. The risk to both ships, as they lay so close together in the heaving sea, was obvious; and the exhausted sailors on *Abbey's* deck were galvanized into a display of energy which resulted in the connection being completed in less than twenty minutes. *Franklin* literally leaped away at the signal, and the behemoth behind her pounded harmlessly down into the empty sea.

During the afternoon the wind moderated in direction, if not in force, and came around into the north-east. But to show that the weather was not relenting toward the two vessels, the sky darkened and all that night snow squalls drove down in blinding gusts.

All through the sixth *Franklin* towed hard and made good progress, and it began to look as if the worst was past. The morning of the seventh dawned clear and fair with a moderate north-west wind. Only three hundred miles now separated the ships from Halifax, and aboard both vessels men showed the relaxation of the strain by falling into that deep slumber which is close to coma.

The masters knew no such relief. Both were uneasy about the weather, and worried about the towing arrangements. Twice Brushett had begged the *Abbey's* master to free his anchor chain and to attach it to the towing pendant so that the wire would not come aboard the casualty at all, and therefore would be freed from chafing on her chocks. Twice Dunning's men had tried to obey the suggestion, but had lacked the strength to carry it out.

The fears about the weather were well founded. During the morning of December 7 the skies darkened once more and the wind came back—this time out of the south-west. The seas gathered themselves and the battle began anew. By noon *Franklin* was stopped in her tracks, and the storm was still gaining in intensity.

At noon the pendant parted.

Once again they drifted east. They drifted for the balance of that day and through the night, and it was not until dawn on the eighth that the wire was reconnected. *This* time it was done as Brushett had desired.

By noon on the ninth the two vessels were abeam of Sable, but the indomitable tenacity of the tug was still being challenged by the resisting sea.

All through the next day *Franklin* struggled to the west, making almost no progress in the face of the new gale. The night came down, and with the succeeding dawn there was yet no certainty that this nightmare voyage would ever end. Aboard the *Abbey* in this, the twenty-fourth day of her ordeal, the endurance of men had reached its uttermost limits.

At midnight, through the harsh clatter of storm static, Marryat received a message from the *Empire Abbey*.

OUR CAPTAIN HAS JUST DIED HE HAD NOT SLEPT FOR THIRTEEN DAYS

Brushett was still standing with the message flimsy in his hand when he became aware of something which, after the long days of roaring sound, was almost silence. He raised his head, stepped to the wheelhouse door and opened it.

The wind was gone.

There was nothing except the muted fury of the water, and a faint echo of the gale in the soft rustle of a dying wind playing through the rigging of the tug.

The sky was clear. Stars clustered coldly in the night, and as Brushett looked ahead he saw a far, faint loom, and knew it for the searching beam of Sambro Light.

28 ❦ SABLE SANDS AND ST. PIERRE

THE RESCUE OF *Empire Abbey* was followed by an unusual assignment when Brushett was ordered to Bermuda, there to pick up the twelve-hundred-ton Rockefeller yacht *Corsair*, and tow her to New York.

Before the tow began Brushett decided that two of his men should ride the luxurious vessel. Competition for the honor was fierce. Buck Dassylva, by virtue of his seniority, was picked as one, and to accompany him went a young New-foundlander whose total experience with luxury in the past had been limited to the appointments and fittings of *Foundation Franklin*.

On April 10 *Franklin* put out from Bermuda. Dassylva and his companion were ensconced aboard *Corsair* in almost regal splendor, and they prepared to enjoy themselves as even a Rockefeller probably never had. They took over the owner's private apartments. They dined from Limoges china, and drank their draughts from magnificent crystal goblets. And when they felt wearied by all this dissipation, they reclined at ease on expensive lounges in the soft Gulf Stream breeze.

It was a fine life indeed for toilers of the seas.

On the second day, as they crossed the Stream, they encountered wind—not a full gale, but still a good hard blow. And it was at this point that the *Corsair* decided she would not willingly continue to suffer the indignity of being towed by a dirty little tug and of being manned by a couple of scallawags.

She was a lovely ship, a wind ship originally, and her spars were tall and graceful. As she began her attempts to shake

232

loose from the tug she laid her spars right over until their gilded tops were close enough to the seas to catch the ocean spray. When that failed to free her, she took charge, spun her wheel ferociously, and went surging off for Greenland.

The tow wire brought her up with a heartless jerk, whereupon she spun on her heel and headed south for Trinidad until the wire brought her up again.

"She was a thoroughbred," Brushett remembers. "She never gave up trying. For seven days she gave us one of the hardest tows we ever had. She came across the Gulf Stream broadside-on, and she pitched and rolled and plunged until we were sure the sticks would go out of her or she would drive straight down to Davy Jones. She hated us, and showed it. What she did to those poor chaps aboard her could only have been done by an angry woman."

There was no communication between the tug and the tow, but once in a long while someone aboard *Franklin* would catch a glimpse of a small, bowed figure creeping to *Corsair's* rail, and hanging over it . . . once in a long while. For the rest, the two prisoners in a palace were too sick and desperate even to bother crawling to the rail. By the time the voyage was over the young Newfoundlander was ready to head straight back to Fortune Bay and a diet of salt cod and honest hardship. When they took him, white-faced and shaking, from *Corsair's* decks in New York harbor, he was heard to mutter:

"Lordy, b'ys! I be too weak a feller to be a millionaire!"

Franklin bade farewell to the *Corsair*—without regrets—and sailed for Halifax. She was less than halfway home when Marryat intercepted an urgent SOS from a Greek freighter, the five-thousand-ton *Alfios*, who was hard aground on Sable Island's sands.

Of all the menaces to shipping on the unfriendly coasts of Canada's eastern seaboard, there is none with such a murderous reputation as Sable Island, for through the years since records have been kept, some three hundred vessels have been engulfed by those shifting sands.

Alfios drove ashore on Sable during the night of April 23. She went on during a dense fog. Since she possessed no DF or radar equipment, her first indication of Sable's proximity came when the ship—traveling at nine knots—shuddered her way across the first of two offshore bars.

Before the weigh came off her she had crossed both bars and had thrust her bows almost into the dunes along the shore.

The Sable Island life-saving crew, riding their half-wild ponies along the shore from West Light, arrived quickly on the scene. The perpetual Atlantic swell breaking along the sands made even the launching of a surf-boat quite impossible; but a breeches buoy was put aboard the *Alfios* with a rocket-gun, and the life-savers signaled for the ship to be abandoned.

Their signals were ignored. After several hours of vain attempts to convince the *Alfio's* master of the dangers of the situation, only one person had been sent ashore—a young woman passenger.

The captain and his crew remained aboard, for the Greek skipper was convinced that he could save his ship.

His was a brave attitude, but a foolhardy one. As he should have been aware, the first onslaught of a northerly gale would not only doom the ship, but her people with her. And as for the hope that she might be refloated, it was so tenuous as to be a fantasy.

Brushett's description of the rescue attempt can hardly be improved upon.

"By the time we arrived off the wreck she had swung broadside to the shore and I knew we had no real hope of taking her off. The only chance, with Sable, is to catch the ship when she goes on first, before the tides and the cross-current sets her broadside. Then there may be a chance—a little one. But once the currents get to work, they trap her. The sands of Sable are alive. They flow about a ship until they build a wall between her and the open sea. She may be afloat inside that wall, but she is finished just the same.

"It was like that with the *Alfios*. She was afloat when we got there, but in a little basin that was getting smaller with every sea that broke. It was just a matter of time until the basin vanished. Then the sands would suck her down.

"There was still heavy fog as we approached, and we had no radar. But a United States naval tug out of Argentia was standing by four miles off shore, and her skipper offered to take us in using his radar set. Depth sounders are no good near Sable. The sand shifts too much and too fast, and there are so many wrecks lifting up and sinking down into the bottom sands.

"The Navy tug did a fine job. She guided us in within a mile of shore and that put us inside the fog bank so we could see again. We felt our way in a bit further, using the lead, but twelve hundred yards was the closest we could go. The seas were lifting and falling about eight feet then, and every now and again *Franklin's* bottom would hit sand.

"Our big problem was to get our line ashore. It was too far for the Schermuly rocket-gun, and no boat's crew could have lived through the surf. The U.S. tug tried floating a line in on a rubber raft, but the currents just whipped it sideways up the coast. Then the life-saving crew tried to shoot a line out with their heavy gun, but the wind was onshore and blew the rocket back.

"There was just one way I could see to do it. I ordered our sea-dory slung out aft, and we rigged her with a mast and a small square-sail. We filled her with a great big coil of light manila, laid down so it would run out free and not foul the dory. Then we launched her, trimmed the sail to suit the wind, and sent her in.

"She ran lovely. She went in over the first line of breakers and never took a drop aboard. Going over the second line she half-filled, but stayed on course. The third line hit her so hard it knocked the water out of her again, and she kept going. The last line was too much for any boat. It swamped her, knocked the mast overside, and left her pretty well broke-up. But by then she had carried inside the surf. Two of the life-saving crew stripped off and went for her. They got her, and hauled her in to shore.

"So then we had a line to land. We connected up a bigger messenger while the life-savers were carrying their end of the light line to *Alfios* and putting it aboard of her. Then *Alfios* started winching in our messenger with our towing wire attached.

"Although I had been pretty gloomy up till then, it began to look like we might have a chance. *Alfios* was still afloat, and with both tugs pulling on the wire there was just a glimmer of a hope that we might work her out.

"When *Alfios's* people got their end of the wire aboard, and had made it fast, they signaled us and we began to pull. Old *Franklin* tucked her stern down until the screw was churning up sand as thick as soup. The wire came taut, but then we saw that it was slanting out to starboard—not running true toward the *Alfios* at all.

"We pulled for all we knew, but I could see it was no good. I guessed at what had happened. When we had been paying out our wire—as slow as we could too—the people on the *Alfios* hadn't been taking in the messenger fast enough, and a big bight had formed in it. The current had grabbed that bight and carried it away off to starboard, and when we took a strain, it caught up on a wreck.

"There are so many wrecks in that sand that it was pretty near bound to catch. We knew that even if we worked it free of one, another would probably grab hold. All the same we hauled as hard as ever *Franklin* could. The wire just stuck tighter.

"We tried everything. We worked *Franklin* back and forth like a fish on the end of a line. She was bumping so badly by then, that you could hardly tell if we were ashore or afloat ourselves. But nothing worked.

"It was coming on to blow and dark was falling, and we daren't stay much longer. As the big seas began to roll in they let us down harder and harder on the sand, and it was just a matter of time before the sand took hold of us. So just after dark we had to cut the wire at our stern and let the whole thing go. Sable got three-quarters of a mile of our best wire.

"We lay offshore that night and it blew pretty hard. By dawn, when we came to work in again, we could see it was all over. *Alfios* was in the sand and it was taking her. She had a list of fifteen or twenty degrees and was going down almost as you watched. But right until the end her master wouldn't quit. When the life-savers finally did get him and his crew to leave, they had cut it so fine that another half-hour's delay would have done for them."

It is strange the way ships come and go in Sable's sands. The *Alfios* vanished completely within a few days of her abandonment; but in the summer of 1955, after a hard nor'-easter, the beach patrol riding their lonely rounds came upon a big freighter standing almost clear of the sands. It was the *Alfios,* risen from the dead. She stayed in sight for six months and then her grave closed over her again, as it has closed over so many others of her kind.

For the rest of the spring, and through that summer, *Franklin* was employed mainly in towing destroyers from Sydney upriver to Quebec. This was routine labor, but not dull. Towing dead destroyers through the narrow and congested shipping lanes was taut and exhausting work, but, as Brushett remarked: "It was what the old ship was designed and built to do some thirty years ago."

That was true enough, for as H.M.S. *Frisky, Franklin* had been originally destined for just this kind of task. The wheel had come full cycle.

Her people were restive and uneasy all that summer, for they had heard faint rumors of the outcome of a conference which had been held to determine the future of their ship. Like most business conferences, it was devoid of any emotions which could not be evoked by facts and figures. In a warm and airless room far from the sea, *Franklin* and all that she had been, and was, became no more than words upon a page of typescript.

They weighed her up—and found her wanting.

"The day of the coal-burners is gone," they said. "She costs too much to run. Burns too much fuel keeping steam up at her dock. A diesel burns nothing when it isn't actually at work."

"Too old," another added. "She's an antique now. Have to

do everything the hard way on her. We need the kind of tug where everything is done mechanically."

There was only one voice raised in her defense. It belonged to Captain Irwin Power, and though he was not present at the conference (being without influence in an age which had already doomed his kind), nevertheless his words still carried a little weight.

"Give her a chance," he pleaded. "She's sound yet. As sound as any ship afloat, and she *is* able. Convert her to oil and she'll give you another ten years as good as the ten just past."

Some of those to whom he spoke barely paused to listen, and when he was out of earshot they were heard to mutter: "Sentimental old fellow; doesn't understand about business." But there were a few who listened. They were those who remembered that *Foundation Franklin* had made the company. They were those who remembered the names of some of the hundred vessels which had been saved from the grey seas by this single ship.

These few came to her defense and the upshot was that orders were given to draw up plans, and to obtain cost estimates for her conversion from coal to oil. A stay of execution had been granted.

If *Franklin* knew that she was infirm and antiquated, she did not show it during the balance of that year. In the months of July, August, and September, she took ten major tows a distance of fifteen thousand miles, and was not delayed an hour by any weakness in her structure or any defects in her machinery. Indeed she set a record then which was not to be equaled even by the magnificent new diesel tugs which were still in the future of the company. She may well have been old, but as Power had said of her, she remained an able ship.

The essence of her ability, and of the ability of her master, was to be displayed during the last days of August when a vessel called the *Fort Boise* went ashore amongst the multitudinous rocks and ledges off St. Pierre Island.

The *Boise* was a seventy-one-hundred-ton Britisher, built in 1943. She had loaded a part cargo of five thousand tons of zinc concentrate at Botwood, and she was inbound for the Gulf on the night of August 22.

Her course should have carried her well south of the treacherous waters near the St. Pierre and Miquelon group, but someone erred and the error was compounded by a dense fog. Shortly before midnight the *Fort Boise* drove in amongst the reefs of the Great Bank, past the doleful beat of the surf on the Lost Children Shoal, and took the rocks beyond.

Foundation Maritime first heard of the disaster at dawn

on August 23, when a radio message was received from a shipping agent on St. Pierre. According to his report the *Boise* was not seriously damaged. The weather was good, and salvage prospects seemed excellent.

Franklin was at that time undergoing her annual inspection and refit, but Woollcombe was able to persuade the steamship inspectors to let her sail immediately under a temporary permit. Hurriedly she was put in order; bunkers were taken in and her salvage gear was loaded. At noon on the twenty-third Brushett took her out past Chebucto Head.

She arrived off the casualty during mid-morning of August 25 and Brushett dropped his anchor half a mile outside the shoals while Tom Nolan, acting as salvage foreman, took a dory to inspect the wreck. Nolan found the vessel hard aground from her bridge forward, and surrounded by such a nest of rocks and reefs that even his dory had to wiggle like a fish to make its way through them.

These sunkers lie scattered off St. Pierre in such profusion that it is as if the contents of a celestial stone-boat had been dumped into the shallow sea. A prevalence of heavy fogs, of sharp squalls and onshore gales does nothing to make the place more attractive. There is also a very swift but unpredictable current which sets at four knots in among the sunkers. In the background there is the brooding loom of the almost barren cliffs of St. Pierre itself. Of the many unprepossessing places on the coasts of the eastern seaboard, not many can hold a candle to St. Pierre. The island remains a French possession—the only one in North America—largely because no one else ever wanted it.

Nolan's report on the condition of the *Fort Boise* was not optimistic. The ship was completely flooded in her number two and number three holds, while number one was filling fast. Her cargo of zinc concentrate had turned into a kind of glutinous mud which boded ill for the pumps. Her main structure had been badly strained and there were signs that she was already beginning to break apart below the water line.

Nevertheless Brushett and Nolan concluded that, given fair weather, they stood a chance of saving her.

Work began at once. *Franklin* eased in between the sunkers, sometimes with only half a dozen feet between her sides and the black rocks; but she kept coming until finally she lay alongside the wreck. Her boom was swung out and pumps and self-closing clam buckets were hoisted aboard *Fort Boise*. With almost all of *Franklin's* crew to help him Nolan set about installing the pumps in the flooded holds, while the ship's crew rigged the clam buckets to their own derricks and began jettisoning the heavy concentrate into the sea. Once these operations were under weigh *Franklin* backed delicately out of that mouthful of granite teeth and laid two sets of ground tackle, two thousand feet to seaward. By dusk the pumps and clams were operating and the ground tackle was set up.

The preliminary work had been done as expeditiously as any expert salvor could have wished. Now it but remained to clam the remaining cargo out and dry the holds before the attempt to free the *Fort Boise* could be made. Brushett estimated that forty-eight hours of calm weather would see the job completed.

August the twenty-sixth was calm. All day the clams grappled with the thick slime in the wreck's holds. All day the pumps—three four-inchers and two eight-inchers—bellowed and belched under the guiding hand of Bob Cooper. By dusk the water in number one hold was under control and its level was slowly falling; by dusk five hundred tons of concentrate had gone into the sea.

That was the good news the day brought. It brought bad news as well. That morning the *Traverse,* carrying Featherstone and additional pumps, had put out from Sydney to join *Franklin.* At noon Brushett received a message from Featherstone to the effect that a sou'easter had made-up so fast and strong that *Traverse* had been forced to heave-to. Two hours later the news came that the *Traverse* had been driven back to port.

Brushett waited for that wind to reach St. Pierre.

He spent the night on deck while the pumps and derricks on *Fort Boise* worked at a desperate pace. An hour before dawn the fog began to thin, and Brushett felt the wet touch of the easterly upon his cheek.

At 10 A.M. Nolan came up on *Franklin's* bridge.

"Give us just six hours more," he begged, "and you can haul her off on the evening tide."

He knew full well what he was asking. *Franklin* had only a skeleton crew aboard, for all but three or four of her people were needed on the *Fort Boise* if there was to be any hope of saving that vessel. This meant, in turn, that Brushett could not take his tug into safe waters off the shore, but would be forced to remain tied to the wreck, in the middle of a murderous shoal, while a rising sou'east wind beat the sea into a weapon of destruction. The temptation for Brushett to recall his crew and put to sea at once must have been nearly irresistible.

Franklin remained fast to the *Fort Boise.*

Brushett gave them their six hours, and two more for good measure. Then at 6 o'clock he took some of his crew aboard, connected his tow wire to *Fort Boise's* stern, cast off his lines, and began jockeying his way out of that deathtrap against a stiff sou'east wind and a mounting sea that was baring the teeth of a hundred rocks not seen before.

Franklin sailed with only four men on deck and four below. Both Brushett on the tug and Nolan on the wreck were taking a calculated risk—the one that he might lose his men; the other that he might lose his life. Both knew that there was no chance of success unless Nolan and his gang remained upon the wreck to work the pumps and winches. It was a risk to which they had not wished to expose *Fort Boise's* crew, and before he cast-off, Brushett had tried to persuade the wreck's master to send his people on board *Franklin*. That suggestion had been met with a sharp rebuff, perhaps because of the unfounded suspicion that Brushett might be hoping to increase the salvage award by rescuing a ship abandoned by her crew.

High water was due at 9 P.M. At 8 P.M. *Franklin* began to work up power and Nolan's gang began to heave in on the ground tackle. *Fort Boise* was lifting and pounding heavily as the seas rolled in under her. From *Franklin's* bridge Brushett could see her only as a formless bulk picked out with yellow lights and outlined by the faint phosphorescence of the breaking seas that dashed against her stern and broke upon the rocks to either side. Darkness was now almost complete.

Marryat was listening intently for the voice of the operator on *Fort Boise*—waiting for one phrase which would release him and all of *Franklin's* people from the growing tension. But the phrase "She's moving" was never spoken. Instead, at 8:27 *Boise's* operator began to shout into his radio telephone:

"Something's gone wrong . . . she's starting to break up . . . I can hear the plates begin to . . ."

At that instant the voice cut off and every light aboard *Fort Boise* went out.

"One minute I could see her outline plain enough—the next she seemed to vanish," Brushett said. "Marryat came running to the bridge to tell me all he knew—which wasn't much. We had no idea if she had bust in two and sunk, or what. We only knew the tow wire was still fast to something that wouldn't move."

The five minutes of waiting which followed seemed interminable. Although Brushett knew that disaster had struck in the darkness astern of him, he did not know what form it had taken, and until he knew, he could make no move to counter it. Clinging to the bridge rail he waited for some sign, and as he waited the fog crept back from the sounding sea to the eastward and began to turn the darkness into an impenetrable shroud.

Through that as yet imperfect veil, a faint light flickered suddenly. Marryat and Brushett reached out their minds toward it.

"Aldis lamp," Marryat muttered. "Wait . . . "

Letter by letter he read the message from the wreck.

Fort Boise's number two bulkhead had fractured right across. The seas had rushed into her engine room and stokehold. She was holding together by a thread of steel and might break apart any instant. Her master was asking *Franklin* to go down to leeward (which was to say inshore, through the whole depth of the shoals) and stand by to pick up the lifeboats as they were blown through the white foam of the breakers.

Brushett ordered a signal sent to have the tow-line cast off from *Fort Boise's* stern. There was no answer to this message, and Brushett could not wait; he ordered the line cut free aboard the *Franklin,* and then after ringing for half speed he prepared to do a thing that turned the St. Pierre pilot who was with him in the wheelhouse into an old man.

In darkness; in thickening fog; in half a gale of wind, and with a big sea rolling, he turned *Franklin* straight into the heart of the Great Shoal.

Cecil Bellfountain was the mate that trip. He stood by the fathometer, an awkward mechanical device on the after part of the boat-deck, and called out the soundings.

"I called them until we reached four fathoms. After that the machine was no good anyway, so I just stood there and watched him take her in. We had the searchlight on, but the fog muffled it pretty much. I think he must have taken her in by ear alone. I could see a sunker right alongsides us to starboard, then there'd be one to port, then one dead ahead—and all of them breaking white. Once she rubbed her side against one of them. He kept on nosing her in, it seemed like for an hour, and then all of a sudden there was a faint hail. The searchlight swung to port and I could see a boat trying to work out to us, but not making any headway. It was right in a patch of breaking water—*Franklin* sidled over and headed right in there too."

The boat contained Cooper and Nolan and the fourteen men of *Franklin's* crew who had been aboard the wreck. They had stayed with *Fort Boise* some thirty minutes after she had been abandoned by her own crew, who had put out in a big, powered lifeboat which stood a reasonable chance of being able to angle off across the wind and get clear, not only of the shoals, but of the dangerous lee shore of St. Pierre itself. Nolan had lingered in an attempt to persuade *Fort Boise's* captain, radio operator, chief officer and chief engineer to leave their vessel. He had been unsuccessful, and to ensure the safety of his own gang he had finally been forced to leave.

When they came to launch Nolan's boat she dropped full on a head of rock and stove her bottom so that she floated on her buoyancy chambers alone. Up to their waists in water, the eighteen men struggled to fight free of the surrounding reefs. There were four oars in the boat but only three oar-locks. So three men rowed, while the rest paddled with their hands.

They did not try to follow the track of the power lifeboat. That would have been suicidal, for had they escaped the reefs they must have inevitably have been cast up upon the island's shore, where neither men nor boats could have survived the waiting surf. They had only one hope of living—and that was to get to windward and work out to sea.

It was a pitifully slim chance, for the half-submerged boat was as lifeless as a log and their trivial efforts with three oars, and with their hands, could accomplish little more than to prevent her from sweeping backward on the nearby reefs.

Although they were all aware of the imminence of death, yet only one man cracked. Staggering to his feet he began to scream against the whining wind: "Turn round and run for shore! For the love of God turn round and run for shore!" The unrelieved fear in his voice froze sixteen of his companions into the immobility which precedes panic. The seventeenth man was Nolan. He seized an oar and brandished it like a battle-ax.

"Shut up!" he roared. "Shut up or else I'll kill you now!"

It was at this instant that the fog-diffused beam of *Franklin's* searchlight touched the boat.

"Although we could see where *Franklin* was, we hadn't a chance of reaching her," Tom remembers. "The lifeboat was as hard to move as one of the rocks, and it was all we could do to hold her where she was. I was sure that we were done. I never figured Brushett would bring his ship any deeper into that stuff.

"But that's just what he did. He nosed her in until her stem wasn't twenty feet off of us; then someone threw a heaving line and we caught holt of it and made it fast. At the same time Brushett began to back the *Franklin* out.

"I don't know how far it was he pulled us backward, but it must have been close to a thousand yards. He'd come that far into the reefs to pick us up. . . . Well now, there may be other skippers who would have done as much, and other boats that could have done it. But I never met the one nor the other yet, and I don't think I ever will."

Once clear of the reefs the boat was hauled alongside and her crew taken on board the tug. The last of them was hardly over the rail when Brushett spotted the faint flicker of a tiny light—probably a flashlight—in the direction of the wreck. It was accompanied by the prolonged and hideous clangor of tearing steel—*Fort Boise* was breaking up.

Marryat had joined Brushett on the bridge and he was spelling out the fragments of a message from the dim and stuttering light. The four officers were abandoning the wreck on a life-raft, and they were asking for the *Franklin's* aid.

"Tell them to stay put," Brushett said urgently to Marryat. "Tell them to put a line on what's left of the ship and hang on in her lee until we can slack a boat down to them on a line. If they cast-off from her, they're done."

Marryat rapidly tapped the message out on the big signal lamp—but there was no acknowledgment. Again and again he repeated it—but there was no further sign of life from the dead ship.

The severing of communciations put Brushett in a hideous quandary. He could not tell if his message had been received; but he knew that if it had not, the four officers were as good as dead. For a moment he considered whether to try to penetrate the shoals once more; but there could only have been one answer to that. He could no longer accept the risk. Now there were the lives of twenty-six men to think about, and he could not gamble them on the faint possibility that he might be able to save the other four.

Reluctantly he gave the order to swing the *Franklin's* head out to sea, and then he laid a course down into Fortune Bay in pursuit of *Fort Boise's* other boat. It was his intention to return at dawn, and if the life-raft was still attached to the wreckage, to stream a boat down to it.

It was just after dawn when *Franklin* came into St. Pierre with the balance of *Fort Boise's* crew, who had been picked from their drifting boat some twenty miles nor'west of the island. Brushett proposed to land them here, before returning to the wreck.

But there was no need to return to her. The officers aboard *Fort Boise* had either failed to receive Brushett's message, or had ignored it. The life-raft, smashed into flotsam, had come ashore at Columbia, and the *St. Pierraise* had already recovered the broken bodies of its four passengers.

29 ✤ THE WRITING ON THE WALL

GREAT CHANGES HAD BEEN in the making at Foundation Maritime during the concluding months of 1946. The company had learned that the British Admiralty was offering one of its famous Bustler class tugs for long-term charter. The vessels of this class were built during the final years of the war, and they were designed to be the most powerful and efficient salvage tugs afloat. Twelve-hundred-tonners powered by twin diesels that developed thirty-five-hundred horse-power, they could cruise at sixteen knots and stay at sea under full power for thirty days. In the new tradition of our times they were completely mechanized, for all their gear was run by electricity. They were handsome vessels with something of the dash and flair in their appearance which is the hallmark of fast naval craft.

The opportunity to charter one of these new ships, combined with the growing feeling in the executive branch of the company that *Franklin* had outlived her time, proved irresistible.

So Foundation Maritime acquired H.M.S. *Samsonia*. Under the name of *Foundation Josephine* she hoisted the red ensign of the Canadian Mercantile Marine in late December of 1946. She bore that name for the next five years, and during that time she was to build a magnificent reputation. Ranging the Atlantic from the coasts of Britain south to Portugal, west again to the Bahamas, and north to Labrador, she wrote a record that came close to equaling the one which had been written by the vessel she displaced.

For with the arrival of *Foundation Josephine*, the *Franklin's* fate was settled.

It was inevitable that she would have to go. The days of the rough, hard little vessels like the *Franklin* were coming to an end the wide seas over. But what was more tragic was that this also applied to the kind of men who had made *Franklin* great. They were being supplanted by a new breed, able enough, but men who were more and more technicians, and less and less seamen. *Franklin's* people were becoming anachronisms too.

Brushett was one of the first to recognize the truth of this. And he was not prepared to make himself over into the new pattern. Resolutely—brusquely—he turned his back on the sea and on the long years when he had lived as part of it. In January of 1947 Harry Brushett went ashore to stay.

Franklin went into limbo.

While *Josephine* dashed out at sixteen knots and earned the banner headlines, *Franklin* grew dingier and faded farther into obscurity. She was kept in commission—barely—but she was given only the trivial and unwanted jobs to do; the jobs that offered little prospect of success or, if successful, that gave little hope of profit.

In mid-January they sent her to sea for eight bitter days in search of the American vessel *Tecumseh Park,* which had radioed ambiguously for aid, and which had then proceeded at eight knots for Bermuda. *Franklin* was still two hundred miles behind her when the freighter made St. George.

In late February she spent nine days at sea in one of the worst storms she had encountered in all her time, in the financially unrewarding rescue of a four-hundred-ton fishing trawler called the *Princess Pat.* She saved the lives of seven men on that occasion; but there is little material gain in the saving of men's lives.

There was to be little profit in anything that her owners gave her to do in the months ahead.

In June she was dispatched to the assistance of the *Empire Success,* five hundred and fifty miles at sea, when that vessel indicated that she might need a tow. *Franklin* came out to her and was turned away again, for the casualty had effected repairs and no longer needed help.

In July they sent her on another forlorn hope to Sable Island in a useless attempt to salvage the steamer *Manhasset,* who had doomed herself in those insatiable sands.

Later that same month she was dispatched to the *Amberton* ashore at Cape Pine, Newfoundland; only to discover on her arrival there that the *Amberton* was a total loss.

In November she had another failure when she was sent to help the *Empire Wallace,* whose main engines had broken down while that vessel was close off Sable's bar. But again *Franklin* was rebuffed, but the *Wallace* repaired her engines and steamed into Halifax under her own power.

Had there been a deliberate plan to undermine the legend *Franklin* had built about herself, it could hardly have been better executed. At the end of November they said of her:

"Look at her record this last year. She hasn't even earned her keep. Let's scrap her and be done."

They gave the argument point and substance in late November of that year when the company purchased a spanking new diesel tug from the United States. This vessel, the *Foundation Lillian,* had been built in 1944 for the U.S. Navy and she was rated at nineteen-hundred horsepower even though she was smaller than the *Franklin.* She was new. She was very modern. She looked superbly efficient.

In point of fact she turned out to be a liability; but in the meantime she was *Franklin's* nemesis.

The day the *Lillian* steamed into Halifax was the day the fires were allowed to die under *Franklin's* boilers.

"She lay at the wharf, a dead ship, you might say," Captain Powers remembers. "I visited her a couple of times and then I gave it up. It's no good looking at a vessel you used to know so well, when she's been abandoned to wait for the convenience of the ship breakers. That isn't any good at all . . ."

So she lay there as she had lain one winter almost thirty years earlier at the docks in Hamburg. Her paint was streaked with salt, and scaling badly. Rust ran down her stacks, and the brass of her bell grew green with verdigris. She waited —but this time there was no Captain Sutherland to come upon her in her desolation and to save her from it.

Christmas came, and then a January that was memorable in the annals kept by meteorologists, but which was of such a violent nature that the men who had to cope with the weather preferred to put the memory of it out of mind. It was a brutal period in the North Atlantic. Many scheduled sailings were canceled or postponed, and many ships which did essay the passage of the Western Ocean were forced to turn about or heave-to and wait for better times. Day after day new gales struggled to outdo their predecessors. When one had paled into exhaustion another rose to take its place. Conditions grew so bad that almost all the trans-Atlantic traffic turned to the southern great-circle routes in an attempt to escape the worst of it.

Consequently *Foundation Josephine* was dispatched to take up station at Bermuda, where she could be handy to the southern tracks. Her departure left Halifax and the northern reaches devoid of salvage or rescue ships, for the *Lillian* had proved herself a temperamental female and a score of baffled technicians had spent weeks trying to get her complicated machinery to function properly, without result. Yet in order to keep *Josephine* free to remain in Bermuda it was essential that the *Lillian* be put in service. When she balked, and balked again, her owners turned to the forgotten ship.

They brought the *Franklin* back to life.

They did it grudgingly, and as sketchily as possible. No time or money was wasted on any but vitally essential repairs. The rest was "jury-rig" or else was left undone.

Four days after the order to revive her was issued, she went to sea under the command of yet another Newfoundlander, big John Lahey. With a scratch crew, Lahey was ordered to take the old ship to Louisburg and go on station there.

Meanwhile *Josephine* had been busy. On January 7 she had gone to the rescue of the Greek steamer *Themistocles* six hundred miles south-east of Halifax and, after a twenty-four hour delay because of the ferocity of the weather, she managed to connect-up to the cripple and begin towing her to New York. Despite her size and power it took the *Josephine* thirteen days to complete the tow, and the casualty was not anchored safely in port until January 20. And *Josephine* herself sustained such damage from the storm that she was forced to limp back to Halifax and go into dry-dock for repairs.

Thus, on January 24, 1948, there was only one ocean-going salvage ship available to take up arms against the hungry sea.

30 ❦ THE LAST RETURN

EARLY ON MONDAY MORNING of January 19 a vessel stood out of Newport News bound for Sweden with a full cargo of mixed freight. She was the Norwegian motor ship *Arosa*. She was a well-found vessel and a handsome one, for she had been built with the sweeping sheer and the graceful lines which the Scandinavians so often give their ships. She was stanch as the Trondheim men who manned her and neither they nor she were intimidated by the unconscionable fury of the month-long sequence of gales which had worked the North Atlantic into a primordial chaos.

The *Arosa* came out from the shelter of the land and laid her course along the great circle track for full-powered steamers bound for Europe. She had chosen a good moment to begin her passage, for the winter hurricane which had sent *Foundation Josephine* on her eighteen-day voyage to succor the *Themistocles* had now blown itself out and there was a lull in the gales. At fourteen knots *Arosa's* shapely stem thrust into the heaving swells the hurricane had left behind it, and by January 22 she had made good a thousand miles of easting.

It had not been easy. Deep laden as she was, *Arosa* had labored in the great troughs and on the long slopes of the grey-beards. The strain upon her gear had been continuous. Fatigue lay on her men and on the thudding heart of her machinery. At noon on January 22 the sky drew down, opaque and ominous, and the wind returned.

It began to blow out of the worst quarter, the nor'east, and *Arosa's* master knew that he was in for trouble. His ship was already battened down for weather and there was not much more that could be done. He rang for a reduction in speed to ease *Arosa's* motion and then he, his men, and his vessel prepared to endure the mauling which must come.

With a fetch of nearly a thousand miles of open ocean in which to build up strength, the new storm-driven seas began to march down upon the old hurricane-born sea, and the turmoil which ensued flung living water high over *Arosa's* bridge. Her screw came up into the froth astern, then sank into the solid depths. All night she plunged and wallowed while her diesels thundered in protest, and then at dawn

Arosa's screw turned slowly to a stop. The main reduction gears had proved unequal to the strain upon them, and the ship was dead.

Arosa's SOS was received in New York early on the morning of January 23. It came in across a gale that had already risen to force 8, although it was still in its infancy. The weather bureau had reported a new depression coming from the south, and hurricane warnings were being broadcast. In New York there was no salvage vessel able to proceed to the *Arosa's* aid, since the distance alone made it almost certain that no tug could make the journey out and back without herself becoming disabled from lack of fuel.

It took time for this to become apparent to *Arosa's* agents, and it was not until a further twenty hours had elapsed that the telephone in the offices of Foundation Maritime began to ring.

As he listened to the request for a deep-sea tug, Woollcombe gave no hint of the fact that two-thirds of his salvage fleet was out of action. And in his usual optimistic manner he made light of the difficulties which would be encountered in any attempt to rescue the *Arosa*. A Foundation tug would sail at once, he said. He did not specify which tug, and if the *Arosa's* agents assumed he meant the *Josephine*, that was no fault of Woollcombe's.

One hour later *Foundation Franklin* was standing out to sea from Louisburg. The thick black smoke from her twin stacks streamed flat to the south-west as the full strength of the nor'east gale struck on her port quarter. In the pilothouse Captain Lahey laid out his course and scaled it off to the last reported position of the motor ship *Arosa*. The distance from Louisburg was five hundred and eighty miles.

Once clear of the land *Franklin* came down on her course bringing the wind and seas hard on her port beam. The gale was still at force 8, but it was making-up and already it was laden with ice crystals. The temperature, which had stood near the freezing point earlier that morning, had now fallen close to the zero mark. As the old tug drew out from shore and the seas gained in stature, she lay down to them and began to roll as abominably as she had ever done. Lahey gave her no ease. He held her at full revolutions, for he knew that his only hope of salving the *Arosa* was to get to her and take her back before the combination of a new hurricane and mounting seas could exhaust his slender reserve of fuel. *Franklin* drove into it at ten knots—and the anemometer on the bridge changed the quality of its metallic whine with a steady rise in pitch as its cups spun faster still.

At midnight the wind began to shift and by dawn it was almost due west. *Franklin's* motion eased a little, but Lahey felt no relief. The change in wind meant that his quarry was now driving out to sea at about four knots. Each hour that the westerly continued meant an hour added to the time it would require to bring the cripple back to port. And each hour of a tow in such a wind and sea meant three more tons of bunkers burned.

Lahey called the chief on the voice pipe. "Push her, b'y!" he shouted. "Give her steam!"

The shaft-revolution needle crept up slowly until *Franklin* was bulling her way at twelve knots. She came on like some antediluvian sea-beast, half awash. The brief hours of daylight passed; the long winter night came down to the sustained roar of a full gale. Then as dawn approached on January 27 the wind suddenly began to haul into the north and to fall light.

Lahey was grateful for that, but he recognized it as a respite that must be of short duration. The glass had been falling steadily for fifteen hours and it was now so low that a Magdalen Island seaman, coming onto the bridge to stand his trick, glanced at it and crossed himself. It was an involuntary gesture and as he took the wheel the seaman had no conscious thought in mind except to hold the vessel on her course.

Lahey had many other thoughts. Sparks had been in constant contact with the *Arosa* for some time and he reported that the casualty's master believed her to have been drifting east at between four and five knots since noon of January 24. He had no position to offer, for it is impossible to obtain an accurate dead-reckoning on a powerless ship which is moved only by the wind and seas, under a sky that hangs down to the mastheads. Nevertheless Spark's DF bearings indicated that the *Arosa* was at least a hundred miles farther eastward than she was thought to be. Lahey altered course a little.

Three hours before dawn *Arosa's* radio signals were booming into Spark's ears. He passed a message to the skipper. Lahey rang down for half-speed. *Franklin* nosed slowly through the darkness, her bow lifting and falling in a great uneasy arc like the head of a hound that sniffs the trail then lifts again to catch a sight of the quarry through short-sighted eyes. At 6 A.M. the lookout on *Franklin's* bridge bellowed his warning and a faint gleam of lights came hard on the starboard bow.

There was only an uneasy breath of wind, but the tormented seas were so ugly that a master who risked his tug trying to make a connection in that heaving darkness might have been thought insane. Lahey was very sane. He knew with all the certainty of ten generations of sea-dwellers that he had no other choice. He knew that the calm of the moment was the center of a great circular storm—a hurricane—and once the center had spun past there would be little hope of putting a line aboard the merchantman.

So *Franklin* came up in almost utter darkness, with only the pale beam of the little searchlight on Monkey Island to give her sight. The seas were towering straight up, for they were masterless without the wind. The tug rose and descended with an abrupt and frightful motion. Nevertheless she still came in.

On the wing of the bridge *Franklin's* mate stood with his legs entwined around a stanchion, and with the rocket pistol in his hands. Above him the bulk of the *Arosa* towered and inclined like a falling mountainside. He pressed the trigger and in the red glow of the rocket the line snaked from its pegs and vanished into darkness.

By 6:30 A.M. *Arosa* was no longer drifting and alone in mid-Atlantic. The connection had been made.

The position of the two vessels was then eleven hundred and twenty miles east of Boston, six hundred and eighty from Louisburg, six hundred and fifty south of St. John's, Newfoundland, and about eight hundred and forty miles east-south-east of Halifax. *Franklin* had sufficient bunkers left to allow her to steam about nine hundred miles under optimum conditions. Boston was impossible. The choice lay between Louisburg, Halifax and St. John's, but the choice depended almost entirely upon what happened when the eye of the storm had passed and the gales had begun anew. Once more Lahey drew on his intuitive knowledge of the Western Ocean. St. John's was out; for the gales which would soon be upon him would almost certainly be strongest from the north and north-west quarters. Between Louisburg and Halifax there was but little choice except that *Foundation Josephine* was in Halifax and, though still under repair, might yet be able to assist the *Franklin* if need arose.

Lahey gave his orders and the wheel came over. The course was east by east-north-east—for Halifax.

The *Arosa* was a heavy ship and in that gigantic and jumbled sea the strain upon the towing wire was excessive at a towing speed of three knots. Lahey did not dare exceed that speed. Progress was desperately slow, too slow. By 8 P.M. on January 27 the two ships had made good no more than fifty miles towards the west. And by that time the uneasy armistice had long since ended. The storm center had gone by shortly before dawn on the twenty-seventh and by 9 P.M. the vessels were beset by a full hurricane blowing ninety miles an hour out of the north-west. The temperature, which had been steady at ten degrees of frost until noon, dropped down to zero. The old sea giants rose to the new impetus of wind and were cut off like grain in a wheat field, so that their white heads were driven level with the horizon striking *Franklin's* upper works with the savagery of shot, and freezing where they struck.

Nevertheless, and incredibly, *Franklin* was still making a passage west at the rate of half a knot.

She held on to that half knot until midnight. And then the event that every man had known was coming happened. The wire parted. Because of her great bulk *Arosa* began to blow off to the south-east at a speed which *Franklin* hardly dared to match under power, for fear she would be pooped.

All the rest of the night the two vessels drove back out to sea. At 7 A.M. in the false dawn, Lahey came in to reconnect. The wire was made fast at the first attempt—for the Norwegians are great seamen too—and the tow began anew.

The first fury of the gale was spent and now the wind settled down to accomplish by attrition what it had been unable to do by direct assault. Blowing steadily out of the north-west at velocities between sixty and eighty miles an hour it thundered with such incessant violence that the men aboard the *Franklin* could no longer hear it. Only a cessation of sound would have penetrated into their conscious minds; and there was no cessation. The old vessel herself was such a cacophony of complaint as she rolled and pitched and yawed that the men below could not have heard the gale if they had so desired. They clung to whatever handgrips they could find, and time went on.

They towed from 7 A.M. on January 28 until noon on January 30, and in that stretch of time they only succeeded in recovering the distance they had lost in seven hours on the night the wire parted.

The log entries for those days are succinct, but their brevity was not due to a lack of appreciation of conditions or to the indifference that men display in the face of the inevitability of things over which they have no control. The log entries were brief because there was no more that could be said.

January 29. . . . *Towed twenty miles in past twenty hours. Whole gale from NW. Very heavy head seas. Low temperature continues. Ship icing heavily. Continuous snow blizzards.*

January 30. . . . *Weather unchanged. Ship icing badly. At 2100 radio out of action due to loss of aerial from icing. Towed twenty miles in last twenty-four hours. Fuel will not last to Halifax.*

Two days and nights . . . six lines of spidery handwriting on a long, ruled page that looks for all the world like a ledger sheet from a counting house. And that is all. Only in that one phrase, *"Fuel will not last to Halifax,"* is there any hint of an awareness that not only the battle might be lost, but that *Franklin* herself was desperately beset.

And she was so. Her radio was permanently out of action. It had proved impossible to keep the constantly making ice reduced to a safe margin and the little tug was in danger of losing her stability—a matter of deadly concern considering the manner in which the seas were mauling her about. This danger increased hourly as the bunkers became lighter, and as the load of ice on the decks and the superstructure became heavier. Nor was this all. The aged machinery, so superficially repaired a few weeks earlier, was, for the first time in *Franklin's* history, displaying signs of serious fatigue. The engineers were never still. Nursing the auxiliaries and watching the main engine with eyes in which weariness had been banished by the anticipation of disaster, the engine-room crowd were living with an almost momentary expectation that finally the heart of the old ship would falter, and would stop. There was more. The bilge pumps were working harder than they should have needed to. *Franklin* was making water.

During the morning of January 31 the wind rose to force 10 out of the north-west, and since it was then impossible to make a course for Halifax Lahey eased off to the westward.

He had barely swung his vessel off the wind when the gale veered into the north-east.

Arosa now refused to tow. She fell off until she was lying right out abeam of *Franklin*. The consequent strain on the towing gear soon became intolerable and in desperation Lahey attempted to bring *Franklin's* head up into the new gale so that he could at least hold *Arosa* steady, even while both vessels were being blown back out to sea.

For the first time in her life *Franklin* was slow to answer her helm. The loss of trim had brought her down by the head and she came around slugglishly—too slowly—into the teeth of the new enemy. Rolling heavily as the seas struck full on her starboard bow she lurched like a stricken thing—and then fell off. The tow wire rose almost clear of the seas. For an instant it held the strain, and then with a horrifying wrench the towing winch itself tore loose from its bed on *Franklin's* after deck. Ripped deck plates curled like paper in a breeze. The drum tore from its socket and half a mile of wire screamed out into the depths astern.

Completely out of control now, *Franklin* rolled down into a trough and was instantly swept from end to end. The sea poured in through the gaping wound where the winch had stood. The dynamos were inundated and all electric power failed. Water rose above the bed plates and swirled about the auxiliaries. The engine slowed suddenly, and when it again picked up its beat there was a clatter in the main bearings that brought the heart of every man who heard it into his throat.

On the bridge Lahey had seized the wheel himself, and with his great hands and his indomitable will he strove to bring his vessel up out of the trough where she lay drowning.

The officers on *Arosa's* bridge had watched events with agonized emotions. Through a curtain of driven snow they had seen the wire go slack, and seen *Franklin* go over until her stacks were lying almost level with the sea, and had seen her swept so that she vanished from their sight in a towering column of grey spume.

They never saw her again. The wind screamed down to drive the scud into their eyes and when it lifted briefly a few minutes later, the tug had vanished.

Arosa's radio was still operational. Her new SOS was received in Halifax within the hour. It gave no details of what had happened and the Foundation staff assumed that *Franklin* had only suffered minor damage, but needed relief. It was not until several hours later, and until several messages had crossed the grey sea void between *Arosa* and the land, that fear began to grow. Then call after call began going out under *Franklin's* code sign. There was no reply.

All that night the shipwrights and fitters worked on the *Josephine* so that by morning of February 1 she was again ready for sea. As she left Halifax that port was blanketed under a two-foot fall of snow. The north-east gale met her at the harbor entrance and she was taking it green over her foredeck before she cleared the outer automatic buoy. But *Josephine* was being driven. It was no longer entirely a matter of succoring a crippled merchantman; now there was the additional incentive that a sister tug was dying somewhere in that passionless expanse of broken sea.

Captain Cowley, on *Josephine's* high bridge, doubled the lookouts. His course was out along the track that *Franklin* might be following if she was still afloat. In the radio shack *Josephine's* operator never left his set, and at ten-minute intervals he tapped out *Franklin's* call-sign. There was no response. At noon on February 2 the master of *Arosa,* queried by Cowley, gave it as his opinion that the *Franklin* had gone down. Neither he nor his officers believed that she had been able to survive the blow that they had seen her take.

In Halifax the tension mounted. Nothing was known. Everything was feared.

Josephine came on with a disregard for the pounding she was taking that gave a lasting greatness to her, and to her master too. At 6 P.M. on February 3 she raised the grey hulk of the *Arosa* about one hundred miles east of the point where she had parted from the *Franklin*. During a lull in the gale Cowley connected his towing wire, and with an inner reluctance that he did not show, he turned westward, Boston bound. The merchantman came first. Somewhere to the east the *Franklin* might have been still alive, disabled, dying slowly—but he could not search for her. The merchantman came first.

Josephine's battle to bring the *Arosa* into Boston is an epic in itself. Some measure of the trials of that voyage can be taken from the fact that even *Foundation Josephine* could not hold fast to the Norwegian and on one occasion was parted from her for twenty-nine hours. It was not until February 11 that she was able to ease her battered charge into safe anchorage.

It was an end to the twenty-one-day ordeal of the *Arosa*. But it was not quite the end of the story of *Foundation Franklin*.

That tale ended in the wind-swept dawn of February 5. It ended when there came a message from the signal station at Chebucto Head—a message that brought Featherstone out of his bed, and sent him racing through icy streets toward the company wharf.

In the first bleak light of day he stood with a dozen others on the Foundation dock and watched with unbelieving eyes the slow, infinitely painful progress of as strange a phantom as ever fumbled its way into Halifax harbor.

She came in under quarter power, which was all that she had left within her. She was so heavily encased in ice that she would not have been recognizable to any man who had not known her well. She was listing twelve degrees to port, and she was so far down by the head that those who watched her held their breaths for fear that she would plunge back into the hungry seas from which she appeared to have risen, wraithlike, in the winter dawn.

The watchers on the dock need have had no fear that she would fail to reach her old familiar berth. It was the grey seas under and the white winds above who had failed, in this their last attempt to take her to themselves.

The *Franklin* had come home from her last voyage.

Franklin *never sailed again.*
She had come to the last of her days, and there remained

only the inevitable dissolution under the hands of the ship-breakers. Yet she did not pass entirely into oblivion, for they took her bell and hung it in a room overlooking the harbor and the berth which she once occupied.

It hangs there now. And on clear and sunny days the light streams in through the windows and kindles a yellow fire in the polished brass so that the black inscription, incised deep into the metal, stands out with a bold clarity:

H.M.S. FRISKY
Dundee—1918

The bell sleeps silent in the warm sun, nor does it still ring the changes in the watches as it did through four decades. It is somnolent on those fine days.

But there are other days—days when the Western Ocean takes up its ancient feud against all ships; when the storm-scud drives low over a foam-flecked harbor; when the international distress frequency quickens to sudden life. And in those times the bell, and the spirit of the gallant little ship whose voice it is, awaken from their sleep.

The old bell sounds. Its voice rings sharp and urgent over the docks, and men pause in their occupations and turn toward the berth—once Franklin's—where the latest of her inheritors lies ever ready. The bell sounds. Foundation Vigilant's lines are slipped. She backs into the stream and swings her head toward the open sea, toward the storm-shrouded distances where a crippled vessel lies beset by the hungry ocean.

The eternal battle between the rescue ships and the grey seas begins anew—and it is Franklin's voice that sounds the call to arms.

Look for

THE
SERPENT'S
COIL

Farley Mowat

A factual story
about the sea,
about the savage
and implacable fury,
of the hurricane,
about the men and ships
that do battle with them.

$1.25